D0627882

Apartheid is a heresy

EDITED BY JOHN W DE GRUCHY &
CHARLES VILLA-VICENCIO

Grand Rapids, Michigan
WILLIAM B. EERDMANS PUBLISHING COMPANY

© 1983 David Philip, Publisher (Pty) Ltd, Cape Town

First published 1983 in Southern Africa by David Philip, Publisher,
South Africa and in the United Kingdom by Lutterworth Press, England

This American edition published 1983 through special arrangement
with David Philip, Publisher by Wm. B. Eerdmans Publishing Co.,
255 Jefferson Ave., S.E., Grand Rapids, MI 49503

Library of Congress Cataloging in Publication Data

Main entry under title:

Apartheid is a heresy.

    1. South Africa — Race relations — Addresses, essays,
lectures.   2. Church and state — South Africa — Addresses,
essays, lectures.   3. Church and race relations — South Africa — Addresses, essays, lectures. I. De Gruchy, John W.   II. Villa-Vicencio, Charles.
DT763.A717   1983   305.8'00968   83-8935
ISBN 0-8028-1972-9

Contents

Dedication

One of the most prophetic Dutch Reformed Church leaders at the Cottesloe Consultation in Johannesburg in 1961 was Beyers Naudé, at the time acting-moderator of the Transvaal synod of that Church. Unlike his Church, Dr Naudé was willing to stand by the decisions made at Cottesloe and to follow them through to their logical conclusion. In the process, he and his wife, Ilse, have suffered a great deal, not least because they deeply longed for genuine change within both their Church and South Africa. On Friday 29 October 1982, after five years as a banned person, Beyers Naudé was rebanned for a further three years.

Beyers Naudé's prophetic insight during the past twenty years has been vindicated by the decision taken by the World Alliance of Reformed Churches in Ottawa in 1982. We therefore wish to honour him and to dedicate this volume of essays to him and Ilse with respect, admiration and gratitude.

In academic circles it is customary to honour a distinguished scholar by publishing a *Festschrift* on an important occasion in his life. The WARC decision on apartheid provides us with such an opportunity in the case of Beyers Naudé.

Abbreviations

ABRECSA   Alliance of Black Reformed Christians in Southern Africa
NGK   Nederduitse Gereformeerde Kerk (Dutch Reformed Church)
NHK   Nederduitsch Hervormde Kerk
SACC   South African Council of Churches
WARC   World Alliance of Reformed Churches
WCC   World Council of Churches

The *Afrikaans Reformed Churches* are the three white so-called sister Churches, the NGK, NHK and the Gereformeerde Kerk.

The *Dutch Reformed family of Churches* in South Africa includes the NGK, the NG Sendingkerk (Dutch Reformed Mission Church), the NG Kerk in Afrika, and the Reformed Church in Africa (Indian).

The *English-speaking Churches* normally include the Church of the Province (Anglican), the United Congregational Church, the Methodist Church and the Presbyterian Church of Southern Africa.

The *South African member Churches of the WARC* are the NGK (suspended), NG Sendingkerk, NG Kerk in Afrika, the Reformed Church in Africa, the Evangelical Presbyterian Church, the Reformed Presbyterian Church, the Presbyterian Church of Southern Africa and the United Congregational Church of Southern Africa.

Contributors

Douglas Bax, a minister of the Presbyterian Church of Southern Africa, is presently minister of the Rondebosch Congregational Church, Cape Town.

Allan Boesak, student chaplain at the University of the Western Cape and Assessor of the NG Sendingkerk, is also President of the WARC.

David Bosch, a minister of the NGK, is Professor of Missiology at the University of South Africa and Dean of the Faculty of Theology.

John de Gruchy, a minister of the United Congregational Church of Southern Africa, is Associate Professor of Religious Studies at the University of Cape Town.

Chris Loff, a minister of the NG Sendingkerk, is currently doing research and teaching in the Faculty of Theology at the University of the Western Cape.

Simon Maimela, a minister of the Evangelical Lutheran Church, is Senior Lecturer in Systematic Theology at the University of South Africa.

Desmond Tutu, a bishop of the Church of the Province of South Africa (Anglican), is presently General Secretary of the SACC.

Charles Villa-Vicencio, a minister of the Methodist Church of Southern Africa, is a Senior Lecturer in the Department of Religious Studies at the University of Cape Town.

Willem Vorster, a minister of the NGK, is Director of the Institute for Theological Research at the University of South Africa.

Acknowledgements

David Bosch's contribution was first published in *Missionalia* vol. 10, no. 1, April 1982. The articles by Simon Maimela, Douglas Bax and Willem Vorster have been thoroughly revised and rewritten for this volume. They originally appeared in the *Journal of Theology for Southern Africa*, no. 36, September 1981, in *A Different Gospel: A Critique of the Theology behind Apartheid* (published by the Presbyterian Church of Southern Africa, 1979), and in *Ekumene Onder die Suiderkruis* (ed. A. C. Viljoen, published by the University of South Africa, 1979), respectively.

ALLAN BOESAK
Foreword

The decision by the World Alliance of Reformed Churches to declare apartheid sinful and the theological and moral justification of it a heresy, and to suspend the NGK and NHK from their privileges of membership of the world body, is now history. Yet, for our South African Churches, it is only a beginning. In one sense the decision is the logical outcome of many years of struggle against the ideology of apartheid. In quite another sense, at least for the Dutch Reformed family of Churches, the decision places this struggle on a completely different level. Political condemnations of apartheid have for a long time been part of the struggle, but such an uncompromising theological decision followed by such decisive action is rare not only within this family of Churches by within the history of the ecumenical movement as a whole.

The Church has dared to call apartheid a heresy. This means that apartheid is taken from its political framework and placed in the centre of the life of the Church. Dealing with apartheid means dealing with the very heart of the Gospel: the Table of the Lord.

It was, therefore, of singular importance that at the Ottawa Conference itself the whole issue of apartheid was first raised, not on the conference floor with all its political dynamics, but at the first church service where the Lord's Supper was to be celebrated. Apartheid began its life in the Church around the Table of the Lord when white Christians of the Dutch Reformed Church refused to take Communion with those Christians who were not white. This sinful attitude was not only tolerated in the Church of the nineteenth century, but in 1857 became a law for the life of the Church, even while the Church knew (and confessed) that this decision was contrary to the Gospel. And this really is the heart of the matter. Dealing with apartheid means dealing with the integrity of the Gospel, the credibility of the witness of the Church in the world, the essence of the common confession of the Christian Church that Jesus Christ is Lord.

In a significant paper presented to the WARC Assembly in Ottawa, Edward Huenemann reminded us that John Calvin himself designated heresy and schism as the key threats to the life of the Church. Heresy is not merely the expression of a false idea, but the use of the Word of God in such a way that it becomes divisive and separates human beings from God and each other. It threatens the community of love. Heresy is an expression of the Word in service of some other interest than the love of and communion with Jesus Christ. It is a proclamation that creates distrust rather than trust, confusion rather than understanding, isolation rather than community. Heresy is a use of the Word that violates its intent and purpose. It ceases to be the proclamation of Christ or witness to his will and instead cloaks self-interest in religious terminology. It therefore becomes ideological self-deception. It does not mean what it says and is therefore false.

Schism is the division of the body of Christ. It means separation at the Lord's Table. It means that the common elements of bread and wine are used not to signify the unity of the common life of the Lord and all the members of his body, but rather the separation of members from one another and the denial of both communion and community. Whether or not one can eat and drink worthily is determined by criteria other than Christ's sacrificial giving of his body. Not *giving*, but *possession* becomes the criterion of worthiness, and schism voids the Sacrament.

All of this raises some serious questions for the life of all the Churches in South Africa. We are challenged on our commitment and ability to speak the truth *theologically* about our faith and our commitment. Therefore it is not so that the 'trial' of the NGK and the NHK is over and that they have been judged. *Our* trial has just begun and we shall be judged by our reactions to the truth that has been revealed about our situation and therefore about all of us in this country. For if the WARC is right, and apartheid is a heresy, and if we have known this to be true, why have we not said so earlier? And why the agonizing reluctance of so many when the South African Council of Churches finally did say it in June 1982?

In a strange fashion, God has chosen the Church in South Africa to be in the forefront of a worldwide battle for justice, peace, human liberation and genuine reconciliation. After all, apartheid is but a microcosm of a worldwide situation.

Also, we are being challenged by a move towards the emergence of a Confessing Church whose shibboleth will be the very issue that symbolizes so much in our society and in the life of the

Church: apartheid and the struggle against it. The question is, will we have the courage to grasp this opportunity and witness to the power of the Gospel in a new way in South Africa, thereby giving new hope to the whole Church of Christ in the world? Will we be able to restore the real meaning of the Sacrament in the life of the Church in South Africa, and by so doing make clear that the Sacrament was not intended by our Lord to become a sign of status or position, but of self-giving and self-sacrifice in which the elemental needs of the body (bread and wine) and the body itself are offered in the service of the other.

We are facing great challenges—we are chosen for great things. It is true that many are called, but few are chosen. And that the chosen shall be known by their choices. But how shall we choose?

The editors of this collection of essays have grasped the urgency of this question, and through its timely publication have clarified the issues and challenged the Churches and their members to decide for or against the Gospel of Christ's reconciliation. We are indebted to them for this.

Allan Boesak
Cape Town
November 1982

THE EDITORS
Introduction

The decision by the World Alliance of Reformed Churches to declare apartheid a heresy is probably the most significant ecclesiastical event affecting the Churches in South Africa since the Cottesloe Consulation held in Johannesburg in 1961. This observation is confirmed by the widespread coverage which the decision received in the media as well as by the intense debate it provoked in church and political circles.

Cottesloe brought together the South African member Churches of the World Council of Churches in order to consult on the role of the Church in South Africa following the tragedy of Sharpeville. At that time the NGK Synods of the Cape and the Transvaal, as well as the NHK, were members of the WCC. The Consultation Statement issued by the delegates at the conclusion of their deliberations was far-reaching in its implications for the Church and society in South Africa. Nevertheless, it cannot be regarded, especially by today's standards, as in any way radical. It was a compromise document which went further than the Afrikaans Reformed Churches had hitherto gone in questioning elements within the accepted apartheid policy of the National Party government, but not as far as the English-speaking Churches would have liked. Much of it was based on a preparatory document drafted by NGK theologians, indicating important changes within the thinking of some NGK circles.

Perhaps the most radical political recommendation emanating from Cottesloe was that which stated that there could be 'no objection in principle to the direct representation of coloured people in parliament'. The prohibition of racially mixed marriages was seen to be without Scriptural warrant, but such marriages were regarded as inadvisable in practice. Some labour laws, such as job reservation and those affecting migratory labour, were also found to be undesirable. Indeed, the political thinking reflected in the Consultation Statement is not very different from some Nationalist opinion today.

With regard to apartheid and the Church, Cottesloe resolved that 'no one who believes in Jesus Christ may be excluded from any Church on the grounds of his colour or race' and that 'the spiritual unity among all men who are in Christ must find visible expression in acts of common worship and witness, and in fellowship and consultation on matters of common concern.' Virtually all Churches throughout the world would take such a statement as self-evident, but not necessarily so in South Africa. The NHK's own constitution included a clause that excluded blacks from membership; the NGK had a policy of segregated Churches; racial discrimination was prevalent in the English-speaking Churches. So it was of vital importance that Cottesloe should affirm the non-racial character of the Church.

The NHK delegates to Cottesloe rejected the Consultation Statement out of hand, and their Church subsequently withdrew from the WCC. The majority of the NGK participants accepted the Statement. However, the position they adopted aroused the anger of Dr Verwoerd, then Prime Minister, and his powerful influence ensured the continuing support of the NGK for his grand apartheid plan. Thus the NGK rejected Cottesloe and continued to provide theological justification for government policy. Later that year the NGK also resigned its membership of the WCC. Its drift towards ecumenical isolation had begun, and by its own decision.

During the twenty years that separate Cottesloe from Ottawa ecumenical opinion has increasingly recognized the need to combat racism. In the process the Afrikaans Reformed Churches have come under increasing pressure to change their ways. Reformed Churches in several countries, notably Germany, the Netherlands, Switzerland, and the United States, have recently decided to terminate all dialogue with the NGK until it has rejected apartheid. Similar developments have taken place in South Africa itself. Whereas in the past the English-speaking Churches have almost fallen over backwards to engage the NGK in dialogue, several Churches have recently refused any further conversation until the NGK indicates that it is willing to move away from supporting apartheid. The SACC, which also has a long tradition of encouraging relations with the NGK ever since the latter withdrew its membership in 1941, decided in 1982 that this could continue only when the NGK agreed with the SACC that apartheid is a heresy.

And so we come to the decision made at Ottawa. The WARC took Cottesloe to its logical conclusion and declared apartheid a heresy, thereby calling into serious question the right of the NHK and the NGK to remain within the fellowship of Reformed Churches. Thus, the situation has reversed itself. Following Cottesloe, it was their own decision that led the NHK and NGK out of the WCC; now, it is the WARC that has taken the initiative by suspending the privileges of their membership until they change. This has led the NHK to withdraw and to enter into almost total isolation. The same could happen to the NGK, in which case, with the exception of its membership in the small Reformed Ecumenical Synod, it too would be ecumenically isolated.

This volume is not intended as a diatribe against the Afrikaans Reformed Churches. After a long and sometimes tedious period of dialogue, it must now be obvious to the NGK that most Churches within South Africa and elsewhere reject any attempt to justify apartheid theologically. Our intention is to record the reasons for this, so that no one may be in any doubt that Christianity, whether it be of the Reformed variety or any other, may not be used to legitimate a policy which contradicts the Gospel.

It is inevitable, however, that the focus of attention is on the NGK, and the debate within the NG family of Churches. This is one of the irksome penalties the NGK cannot avoid simply because it is such a large institution and a powerful influence in South African society. Such responsibility as the NGK inevitably has to shoulder implies that it cannot escape being under scrutiny, even from outsiders, especially when the destiny of outsiders is bound up with the decisions the NGK may or may not make. Moreover, the NGK has the potential to help bring about those changes within South Africa that are desperately needed today. Some would argue that the NGK will not change until it is forced by political events to change—we hope they will be proved wrong.

But what of the English-speaking Churches? There is a danger that these Churches, of which the editors are members and ministers, will regard the debate about apartheid being a heresy as something that does not really concern them any longer because they have more or less agreed that this is so. However, they cannot stand aloof and pass moral judgment on the NGK or any other Church, for they too are deeply implicated in the racism that pervades our society. It is true, of course, that they have consistently rejected all attempts to justify apartheid theologically, and that they have regularly protested against apartheid legislation and practice, but they have by no means escaped the all-pervasiveness of racism. Their sin is that of practice, for their life reflects racial division and discrimination which is sometimes as consistent and intense as that which is to be found in the Afrikaans Reformed Churches. We are all guilty and need to recognize the fact.

Our intention, then, in publishing this volume of essays, is to enable all Christians of whatever Church they may be, in South Africa or abroad, to look critically at themselves in the light of the judgement that apartheid is a heresy. In order to enable this critique we have deliberately included essays written by thologians belonging to different denominational traditions and coming from different cultural backrounds. Without any equivocation they all reject apartheid as a heresy, but their existential experience and differing academic disciplines enable each to focus on complementary dimensions of the issues at stake.

The first essay is, of course, the address that Allan Boesak delivered at the Ottawa conference of the WARC. This provides the focus for what follows. Chris Loff, a minister of the NG Sendingkerk then gives us an historical analysis of the events that led to the introduction of apartheid into the life of the NGK during the first half of the nineteeenth century, thus creating segregated Churches. David Bosch sets this historical discussion in the wider framework of theological and especially missiological debate that has developed during the past century. His paper was first delivered at a theological conference early in 1982 in Pretoria, when he publicly dismissed the NGK's rationalization of separate churches as 'nothing but a heresy'. Desmond Tutu has focused on the way in which apartheid fundamentally contradicts the Gospel of Jesus Christ and attempts to accept as normal and God-given that which is the result of sin and contrary to God's reconciling purposes. At the heart of the ideology of apartheid is a false view of man. Simon Maimela has identified this and in his article reflects on the anthropological heresy which is to be found in 'white' theology, whether Afrikaans or English. The way in which racism has pervaded the life and practice of the English-speaking Churches, as compared to that of the NGK, and the implications of radical obedience to God are addressed by Charles Villa-Vicencio. John de Gruchy examines the meaning of heresy in relation to some of the objections which have been made to labelling apartheid a heresy, indicating the significance of a *status confessionis* in South Africa.

Those who have defended apartheid in South Africa have often claimed the support of the Bible in doing so. We have therefore included two critiques of this claim, focusing on the way in which the Bible is used in the important NGK publication *Human Relations and the South African Scene in the Light of Scripture*. This Report, approved by the General Synod of the NGK in 1974, claims that Scripture allows the Church to support 'separate development' and much of that which is part and parcel of traditional apartheid policy. Douglas Bax writes an exegetical critique of this Report, and Willem Vorster shows up its interpretational weaknesses. Scripture cannot be used to support apartheid, indeed the reverse is only too patently obvious. We have included in an Appendix several documents related to the discussion and referred to at various points by the authors of the essays.

It is our conviction, grounded in the theological debate which justifies the decision of the WARC, that the basis of both theological and political renewal in our country is a mutual confession of our sins for that all-pervasive racism which constitutes South African society. There is a broad and firm base for ecumenical debate in South Africa which is the fundamental confession that apartheid is heretical. If it is not recognized that apartheid is morally and politically indefensible, the future for all people living in this subcontinent is bleak. It took a great NGK theologian, Professor B. B. Keet, to remind white South Africans more than two decades ago that 'the bell has already tolled'. We can no longer waste time debating whether apartheid can be defended as Christian, investing our energies in the irrelevant exercise of defending past decisions which time has rendered uncouth. We need to reject apartheid as heretical, confess our sinful participation in it and commit ourselves in obedience to God to create a just and peaceful country.

There is a spirited debate in South Africa at present as to whether apartheid is the real problem facing South Africa, the suggestion being that if apartheid were dismantled social and economic discrimination and oppression would probably remain. We would agree that racism is but one dimension of a more complex sociopolitical and economic programme of discrimination in South Africa. Apartheid is, however, the 'sacred canopy' which has systematically been created and theologically undergirded in order to promote and justify a system of oppression in South Africa. The WARC has correctly recognized this and struck at the religious identity of the South African problem. In calling for the rejection of this policy we fully recognize that any programme of social change in our country must address far more than the 'race' issue.

We are grateful to the contributors to this volume, most of whom worked extremely hard to produce essays promptly in response to our urgent request. Several of our colleagues have helped us in making this publication possible at a very busy time in the academic programme of a university department. We are grateful to them. We are also grateful to our departmental secretaries, Shaan Ellinghouse and Kathy Bakker, as well as to Glenda Kruss and Gabrielle Meyer, without whose help this book could not have been published so speedily.

John de Gruchy
Charles Villa-Vicencio
Cape Town
November 1982

Apartheid is a heresy

1 ALLAN BOESAK
He made us all, but . . .

Since the Nairobi meeting of 1970, the World Alliance of Reformed Churches has not really given much attention to the issue of racism. Granted, it may have held a deliberately low profile on this matter because of its desire to support the World Council of Churches in its efforts to combat racism. Or it may have wanted to give its member Churches ample opportunity to give such support. It may have argued that duplication of such efforts is not necessary. Be this as it may, I am convinced that the time has come for the World Alliance to take a firm stand on the issue of racism, a stand which will be its own, based on its concern for and solidarity with those Churches within its fellowship who suffer under racism, and based on its own understanding of the Gospel and the Reformed tradition.

There are a number of reasons why I believe that the WARC should assume a more active role in the struggle against racism.

(a) The black thinker and activist W. E. B. Dubois has been proved absolutely correct in his assertion that one of the central problems of the twentieth century is the race problem.

(b) The admirable work of the WCC in this regard for the last ten years or more has shown beyond doubt the insidious and extremely dangerous nature of racism.

(c) Instead of abating, racism has grown. Christians in western Europe have become increasingly aware of the problem there, and in the United States racism in numerous ways has once more taken on a cloak of respectability.

(d) Racism has taken on new, more subtle forms, and has found powerful allies in such ideologies as militarism, nationalism and national security.

(e) In the political field, it seems as if 'liberal politics' has come to the end of its solutions and its energy. The responsibility of the Church in such a situation is now greater than ever before, not only to challenge the myopic theologized patriotism of yet another brand of 'evangelicalism', but to proclaim the vision of the Kingdom of God, transcending the narrow boundaries of race and nationalism and bringing justice to the poor and oppressed.

(f) The last reason lies in the reality of the situation of the Republic of South Africa itself. Not only is South Africa the most blatantly racist country in the world, it is also the country where the Church is most openly identified with the racism and oppression that exists in that society.

In 1980, black Christians made a statement in which this painful realization was put on record:

... the Churches to which we belong have conformed to the patterns of a racist society. The persistent cries of the black people that the Church is not consistent with the demands of the Gospel of Jesus Christ have fallen on deaf ears.(1)

Whilst this was said of *all* Churches in South Africa, it remains true that the white Dutch Reformed Churches must assume special responsibility for the situation. And since the work of the WCC has clearly not directly influenced these Churches, the only truly ecumenical family that remains to utter the direct prophetic word is the WARC.

It must be said, however, that while black Christians in South Africa are almost unanimous in their acclaim and support for the actions of the WCC and to a lesser extent that of the Lutheran World Federation, the three million blacks in the member Churches of the WARC remain painfully uncertain about the stand of their own confessional family. This is felt all the more acutely since it is the Reformed tradition which has been so effectively and ruthlessly used to justify white racism and white oppression in South Africa.

The struggle in South Africa is not merely against an evil ideology; it is against a pseudo-religious ideology which was born in and is still being justified out of the bosom of the Reformed Churches. The importance of this for the future of the Christian Church in South Africa is enormous, for ultimately, beyond denomination and tradition, the credibility of the Gospel of Jesus Christ is at stake.

RACISM IS SIN

It is not my intention here to join the current debate about the 'right' definition of racism. Even while this debate is going on, the oppression of people on the basis of colour, the dehumanization and suffering, the exploitation and rejection continue. The cries of anguish of the rejected children of God are far more articulate, and the suffering and pain far more real, than mere definitions will allow. Yet we need to have a precise idea of what we are talking about.

First of all, racism is an ideology of racial domination that incorporates beliefs in a particular race's cultural and/or inherent biological inferiority. It uses such beliefs to justify and prescribe unequal treatment of that group. In other words, racism is not merely attitudinal, it is structural. It is not merely a vague feeling of racial superiority, it is a system of *domination*, with structures of domination—social, political and economic. To put it another way: racism excludes groups on the basis of race or colour. But it is not only exclusion on the basis of race, but exclusion for the purpose of subjugating or maintaining subjugation. It is in this light that the current 'changes' in South Africa's racial policies must be understood. The government, instead of bringing about fundamental changes that will secure meaningful participation, peace and well-being for all, is making certain concessions, which will do no more than allow a selected group of blacks to have limited economic benefits and limited political participation under white control. The overall effect will be not to bring justice to all, but to strengthen white supremacy. In all these matters the Church is called on to be particularly watchful and sensitive, so that we acquire the ability to ask questions of a fundamental nature. Racism is an ideology which justifies white supremacy.

Secondly, racism has not always been with us. It is a fairly recent phenomenon that has become an essential part of an historical process of cultural, economic, political and psychological domination. It manifests itself in all these areas. It is important to note that racism became essential to what Helmut Gollwitzer has called the 'capitalistic revolution': 'The revolution of the white, Christian, Protestant peoples that spread all over the world to open the era of slavery, which even today (albeit not in the same form) is not yet ended.'(2) I note this to make the point that racism cannot be understood in individual, personal terms only. It must be understood in its historical perspective and in its structural manifestations.

But, thirdly, however important these observations may be, the Christian must say more. Racism is sin. It denies the creatureliness of others. It denies the truth that all human beings are made in the image of the Father of Jesus Christ. As a result, it not only denies the unity of all humankind, it also refuses to acknowledge that being in the image of God means having 'dominion over the earth'. Human beings were created in the image and likeness of God. In the Bible, 'image' and 'likeness' do not of course allude to any kind of *physical* likeness, but rather describe our unique relation to God. The likeness is not morphological but functional, dynamic.

The whole story of Genesis I and II is an attempt to give expression to this creaturely relatedness to God. The responsibility that flows from this relationship is 'dominion over creation'. This has not only to do with the source of this power—God—but also with those with whom we are to share this unique gift: our fellow human beings. At the same time, we are reminded in Genesis II that this 'dominion' is *service*, that there is an interdependence between human beings and between human beings and creation. To have this dominion is to share this dominion—it is to be truly human. It means to be able to be, to live, in accordance with one's God-given humanity. It means to be able to realize this essential humanity in the social-historical world in which we all have responsibility.

To share in this dominion as a free person created by God enables human beings to become the subject of their humanity, to assume responsibility, to act responsibly and in acting to realize their own being and that of others. All this racism denies. It usurps this power to be truly human for one group only, and it justifies this action by placing the other on a sub-human level, not truly human, or not 'equal', or 'equal, but. . .'.

Racism is a form of idolatry in which the dominant group assumes for itself a status higher than the other, and through its political, military, and economic power seeks to play God in the lives of others. The history of white racism is full of examples of this.

Racism has brought dehumanization, has undermined black personhood, destroyed the human-beingness of those who are called to be the children of God. It has caused those who are the image of the living God to despise themselves, for they cannot understand why it should be their very blackness that calls forth such hatred, such contempt, such wanton, terrible violence.

Most of all, racism denies the liberating, humanizing, reconciling work of Christ, the Promised One who has taken on human form, thereby reaffirming human worth in the sight of God. Through his life as a human being he has given flesh and blood to the words of the psalmist concerning the life of God's weak and needy people:

From oppression and violence he redeems their life; and precious is their blood in his sight. (Ps. 72:14)

Through his life, death and resurrection he has reconciled people to God and to themselves, he has broken down the wall of partition and enmity, and so has become our peace (Eph. 2:14). He has brought us together in the one Lord, one faith, one baptism, one God who is the Father of us all (Eph. 4: 5,6).

Racism has not only contaminated human society, it has also defiled the body of Christ. And Christians and the Church have provided the moral and theological justification for racism and human degradation.

APARTHEID AS PSEUDO-GOSPEL

South African society is based on white racism, maintained by violence and oppression. Legalized discrimination in all areas is a way of life. Apartheid means that in 1970 whites, only 17,8% of the population, received 71,9% of the national income, while blacks received 19,3%. It means that whites claim 87% of the land whilst 13% is 'allotted' to black people. It means that blacks are denied any meaningful participation in the political decision-making process so that the process of 'democracy' here has become a farce. It means a capitalist economic structure for which atrocities like the migrant labour system apparently are necessary, a system that, as South African economist Dr Francis Wilson has pointed out:

... can and does compel old people living amongst their friends and relatives in familiar surroundings, where they have spent their entire working lives, to endure resettlement in some distant place where they feel they have been cast off to die. This system can and does force a man who wants to build a house with his wife and children to live instead for all his working life in 'bachelor' barracks, so far away from his loved ones that he sees them only briefly once a year, and his children grow up without his influence, regarding him as a stranger. One may close one's mind to these facts; one may dismiss them as being isolated casualties for the sake of a greater goal; but the harsh reality is that there are hundreds of thousands of people in South Africa who are cruelly affected in this way.(3)

Apartheid means that the most important thing about a person is not that he or she is a human being created in the image of God with inalienable rights, but his or her racial identity. It means that racial identity determines, with an overwhelming intensity, everything in a person's life. It means that hundreds of children must die—not only from hunger and malnutrition amidst South Africa's plenty, but shot down by riot police on the streets of our townships. But why go on? One should not pretend that the human suffering caused by this system can be described in words.

All of this is not unique. South Africa is not the only place in the world where oppression and exploitation are the daily bread of the poor and the defenceless. What *is* unique, however, is the role of the Churches, more specifically, the Reformed Churches. In a very important address given in 1980, Ds D. P. Botha showed conclusively that the present policy of apartheid is essentially the missionary policy of the white Dutch Reformed Churches, that these Churches not only provided a theological justification for this policy, but also worked out, in considerable detail, the policy itself. It is these Churches that from 1932 on sent delegation upon delegation to the government to get proposals for racial legislation accepted. It is these Churches that worked hard to devise practical policies of apartheid that could be implemented by the government, while at the same time formulating a theological construction to justify the policy plans. It was these plans that the Churches finally presented to the National Party in 1947—which accepted them as a programme that became a winner at the polls in 1948.(4)

It is no wonder therefore to find in a 1948 issue of the *Kerkbode*, the official mouthpiece of the DRC, the proud assertion:

As a Church, we have always worked purposefully for the separation of the races. In this regard apartheid can rightfully be called a Church policy.(5)

In fact, as Botha says,

The role of organizations like the FAK and the Broederbond fade into insignificance compared with the overwhelming role of the Church [the white DRC] in preparing the Afrikaner to accept and vote for a socio-political programme that would revolutionize South African life.(6)

And this policy is 'all-embracing, soteriologically loaded', complete with a theology to rationalize it. As such it has become a pseudo-gospel, challenging the very authority of the Gospel in the lives of all in South Africa. The white Reformed Churches in South Africa have not yet been able to repent, to correct their stand on the basis of a new understanding of the Gospel. In spite of all the open human suffering, the violence necessary to maintain the system, the damage done to the Church of Jesus Christ, apartheid still has their support. Our Reformed Churches are divided on the basis of race and colour, a situation that is defended as a truthful expression of the will of God and a true interpretation of the Reformed understanding of the Church.

Within the Reformed family, racism has made it virtually impossible to share with one another that most significant act within the community of the faithful, that natural expression of the unity of the body of Christ, the Lord's Supper. And so white and black Reformed Christians miss the meaning of the sacrament which Calvin so much wanted to impress upon our minds:

Now since he has only one body, of which he makes us all partakers, it is necessary that all of us also be made one body by such participation. . . . We shall benefit very much from the Sacrament if this thought is impressed and engraved upon our minds: that none of the brethren can be injured, despised, rejected, abused, or in any way offended by us, without at the same time injuring, despising, and abusing Christ by the wrongs we do; that we cannot disagree with our brethren without at the same time disagreeing with Christ; that we cannot love Christ without loving him in the brethren.(7)

THE RESPONSIBILITY OF THE WARC

The World Alliance of Reformed Churches is a confessional family. The rationale for its existence, the *strength* of its existence, is the uniqueness and significance of the Reformed tradition and its contribution to the witness of the Church of Jesus Christ in the world. It is clear that it has a special responsibility in this particular situation. Since 1976 the crisis in South Africa has taken on frightening proportions. The events of 1980 have underscored this and the blood of hundreds of children on the ground is a chilling reminder of the sacrifices needed to still the cravings of the Moloch that apartheid has become. Thus black Christians have said:

We realize that the racial situation in this country has reached a critical stage and that God is calling the Church as a liberating and reconciling community to identify itself with the oppressed and the poor in their struggle for the dignity which is theirs as human persons created in the image of the Triune God.(8)

The WARC has no less than ten member Churches in South Africa. The great majority of them form the 'poor and oppressed' the statement talks about. They have a right to know what the Reformed tradition has to say about a situation like theirs. As far as the white member Churches are concerned, they have direct responsibility and the power to change the situation fundamentally if they want to. They should be addressed in terms of that responsibility and in terms of the historical development of apartheid as it has been directed by the Churches. The WARC should accept the challenge to address the meaning of an apartheid that has been undergirded by the Gospel and presented as commensurate with the Reformed tradition.

The WARC should reaffirm that racism is a sin; reaffirm its support for the WCC and encourage those member Churches who are also members of the WCC to continue its prayerful support of the WCC programme to combat racism.

With regard to the South African situation, the WARC should accept it has a special responsibility. It should declare that apartheid, in the words of the 1978 Synod of the (black) Dutch Reformed Mission Church, is 'irreconciliable with the Gospel of Jesus Christ'. And, if this is true, and if apartheid is also a denial of the Reformed tradition, then it should be declared a heresy that is to the everlasing shame of the Church of Jesus Christ. To accept the Reformed confession is more than a formal acknowledgement of doctrine. Churches who accept the confession thereby commit themselves to show through their daily witness and service that the Gospel has empowered them to live as the people of God. They also commit themselves to accept in their worship and at the table of the Lord the brothers and the sisters who accept the same confession. Confessional subscription should lead to concrete manifestation in unity in worship and in working together at the common tasks of the Church.

It is one thing when the rules and laws of unjust and oppressive governments make this difficult or impossible for the Church. But it is quite another thing when Churches willingly and purposely reject this unity for reasons of racial prejudice—as the white Reformed Churches of South Africa have consistently done.

In South Africa, as I have noted, apartheid is not just a political ideology. Its very existence as a political policy has depended and still depends on the theological justification of certain member Churches of the WARC. For Reformed Churches, this situation should constitute a *status confessionis*. This means that Churches should recognize that apartheid is a heresy, contrary to the Gospel and inconsistent with the Reformed tradition, and consequently reject it as such.

I am not unaware that for the WARC this may become a difficult issue. But this is an issue too long deferred. It would be well to remember the words that Dietrich Bonhoeffer, a fearless partisan in the service of Jesus Christ, spoke to the ecumenical movement in a time not unlike that in South Africa today:

Not to act and not to take a stand, simply for fear of making a mistake, when others have to make infinitely more difficult decisions every day, seems to me to be almost a contradiction of love. . . . Too late (in our situation) means 'never'. If the ecumenical movement does not see this now and if there are none who are 'violent to take heaven by force' (Mt. 11:12) then the ecumenical movement is no longer the Church, but a useless association for making fine speeches. . . .'(9)

Calvin's comment on I Cor. 7:23 takes us to the heart of the matter:

We have been redeemed by Christ at so great a price as our redemption cost him, so that we should not enslave ourselves to the wicked desires of men—much less be subject to their impiety.(10)

Notes

1 Statement by the black participants at the SACC *Consultation on Racism*, Feb. 1980 (published in a booklet under the same title, Johannesburg, 1980).

2 H. Gollwitzer, 'Zür Schwarzen Theologie', in *Evangelische Theologie*, Jan 1974, Vol. 34, No. 1, pp. 43–69.

3 Francis Wilson, *Migrant Labour in South Africa* (Johannesburg, 1972) p. 189.

4 D. P. Botha, *Church and Kingdom in South Africa* (address to the SACC, May 1980).

5 *Die Kerkbode*, 22 Sept. 1948, pp. 664, 665.

6 D. P. Botha, op. cit.

7 John Calvin, *Institutes of the Christian Religion*, ed. John T. McNeill (Philadelphia, 1960), book IV, chap. XVII, par. 37.

8 Statement, op. cit.

9 D. Bonhoeffer to Henriod of *Life and Work* in Geneva, 1930s, *Gesammelte Schriften, VI* (Munich, 1974), p. 350ff.

10 John Calvin, op. cit., book IV, chap. XX, par. 32.

2 CHRIS LOFF
The history of a heresy

During the recent meeting of the World Alliance of Reformed Churches in Ottawa, a group of eleven South Africans decided not to participate in the celebration of Holy Communion. This was not meant merely as a protest or as a boycott but as a confession of faith. The Lord's Supper is a community meal, and as such it ought to give expression to the unity that Christians have with one another. The three Afrikaner Churches have, however, consistently practised racial separation at Church services in general and during Holy Communion in particular, and the eleven who refused to participate in the celebration of Holy Communion in Ottawa were giving expression to their protest against this separatism. They refused to share Holy Communion in a foreign country with members of the NGK and NHK for the sake of appearances, knowing from experience that such an event would not normally happen in South Africa.

This decision has caused a stir. The NGK has emphatically denied that there is a rule that forbids black people from sharing in Holy Communion with white people. On the contrary, it is said, as far back as 1829 it was decided that there should be no segregation during Holy Communion. We are told that this decision of 1829 is even quoted in the Church Order. How then can such a statement be reconciled with the exposition given by Dr Dirk Fourie in connection with the question whether the NGK is an 'open Church'? In *Die Kerkbode* of 23 June 1982, Dr Fourie, an authority on church law, explained that his Church is not 'open'–neither in principle nor in practice. In other words, black people would have to get special permission to attend services in white NG Churches, let alone become members of such Churches. Dr Fourie's argument in June vindicates the standpoint of the eleven in Ottawa. On the other hand, Ds G. S. J. Moller, editor of *Die Kerkbode*, treating the decision of 1829 in isolation, and disregarding Church practice, contends that there is an open Communion Service in the NGK. This confusion warrants a closer investigation of the problem.

THE BACKGROUND TO THE 1829 MEETINGS

The minutes of the Synod of 1829(1) reveal that a certain Ds J. Spijker put forward a proposal to the meeting in connection with segregation. Why did he do this?

From 1823 to 1849 Ds Spijker was the minister of the Somerset West congregation (then called Somerset-Hottentots Holland). Originally from the Netherlands, Spijker began his ministry in 1817 in Swellendam, where he remained until he was transferred to Somerset West.(2) During 1828 the Church Council of Somerset West considered the question of members of colour in the congregation, especially regarding attendance at Holy Communion services.(3)

For the first time since its establishment in 1819, the Church Council's minutes of 27 March 1828 mention a 'bastaard' who wanted to become a member of the congregation. On this occasion, elder H. K. de Vos refers to an employee who wished 'to be confirmed and baptised as a member'. Because De Vos gave a very good testimony about this person, the Church Council saw no difficulty in granting the request. The minister was asked to give him the 'necessary guidance' in order to prepare him for his declaration of faith.

Yet before the case was closed it was asked if 'such persons' would be allowed to partake of the Lord's Supper with 'born Christians'. The minister was of the opinion that there should be no discrimination, especially at Holy Communion, and suggested that the congregation ought to be pleased that 'such as him' could be permitted to share this Christian privilege with them. However, it was not going to be so easy. The Church Council made clear to their minister that they were not going to introduce a new practice in their congregation. A very explicit example was set by their neighbouring congregations, Stellenbosch and Caledon. In those congregations, so they explained to Ds Spijker, the white members were administered to first (men before women) and thereafter the black members. Although Ds Spijker was not convinced that this practice was correct, he nevertheless felt obliged to abide by the wishes of the Church Council and follow the example of Stellenbosch because 'the reasoning was generally considered to carry some weight'.

From the Baptismal Register we know that the person thus far

only referred to as a 'bastaard' was born on 20 October 1790 and
baptised on 26 October 1828. Originally he was known as Bentura
Visser, but at some point after his baptism he became Bentura
Johannes. Judging from the handwriting and the colour of the ink,
the 'Visser' was added later. The Church Council minutes of 1 November 1828 refer to him only as Bentura. It remains a tantalizing
question as to why the 'Visser' was changed to 'Johannes'. In any
event, on the occasion of his baptism, Communion was also administered. On this first occasion of partaking of the Lord's Supper,
brother Bentura did so together with the white members. Deacon
J. Theunissen told the Church Council meeting of 1 November
1828 that the people were very unhappy that Bentura had dared
to partake of the Lord's Supper together with the 'born Christians'. The malcontents let it be known that, should such a thing
happen again, they would rather stay away from Holy Communion. Most of the members agreed with Theunissen, and insisted
that the Council decision that strict separation be maintained be
adhered to. The minister explained that such an attitude was not
Christian, and that he did not want to convey this decision, which
was in contradiction to his own convictions, to Bentura. He therefore referred him to the elders.

On the day on which Communion was to be administered Bentura made enquiries via the verger to Spijker concerning the matter. His own clear standpoint was that if he had to take the Lord's
Supper on his own, then he would rather not partake at all.
Spijker asked H. K. de Vos, the elder who was present, and the
employer of Bentura, for his opinion, and it was agreed that he
should take the Lord's Supper at the same time as the whites. It
was hoped that the fact that he had been baptised in front of the
congregation would change attitudes, but it did not. The insis-
tance on separate Communion for Bentura remained.

At the Church Council meeting of 22 December 1828 Ds
Spijker had to face fresh criticism for his stance. Then a new
objection was advanced. Elder Wouter de Vos stated that Bentura
was guilty of 'prostitution': he was not married to the slave with
whom he lived and who had borne him children. The minister's
answer to this was that if he were indeed a 'whore' he should not
be permitted to partake of the Lord's Supper at all. Furthermore,
this objection should have been raised before, when application
had been made for him to be confirmed and baptised, but there
had been no such objection—on the contrary, he had been given a
good testimonial. It was generally known that his 'wife' and he

shared a good life, although they were not legally married, essentially because his wife was a slave, and as such she was forbidden by law to marry. The minister was convinced that, if there were no legal objections, the two of them would have been married long ago. The objectors could not say anything against this. Furthermore, it was noted that, should Bentura leave this woman because she did not belong to the Christian faith, he would not only leave her and his own children in the lurch but he would also be acting contrary 'to the lesson of Paul, I Cor. 7:13'.

However, this was not the end of the objection. Elder Wouter de Vos then used the Bible to support his argument. He referred to Luke 17:7–8, from which he deduced that, because of Bentura's heritage and 'subservient status' (whether that meant that he was a slave is not clear because only his wife was referred to as a 'slave'), a distinction could be made. He was of the opinion that 'discrimination' could not 'do any harm', 'because the Redeemer himself spoke about it'. The minister's answer to this was that if one 'had very little insight and judged very superficially' then it was understandable that one would confuse an ordinary supper as referred to in Luke 17:7 with the parable of the 'Last Supper'. What was being said about the supper in the parable could not be applied to the Last Supper because that was a 'spiritual meal'.

Further, he said that Christianity allowed such a distinction in civil life, but that it was never permissible as far as religion was concerned. With reference to I Cor. 10:16 the Lord's Supper was precisely an occasion where mutual love among all Christians was promoted without discrimination. Elder De Vos, however, had another text: I Cor. 8:13, where St Paul says that if the eating of meat should cause his brother to stumble, then he would never eat it again. If Bentura's presence at Holy Communion caused so much annoyance that people threatened to stay away or get up from the table if he were present, then he should refrain from taking part. He should not be a hindrance. He should, therefore, be ordered by the Church Council either to stay away completely from the Lord's Supper or to take it separately.

Ds Spijker was of the opinion that the congregation should have tried harder to discuss the question in a calm manner, and that they should have been more concerned about the truth and guarded against the harmful consequences of their actions. He also pointed out the folly of applying what St Paul said about the eating of meat to the case under discussion, and hoped that the next Holy Communion service, which would be at Christmas time, would take place without such discrimination.

From the minutes of 3 February 1829 we learn, however, that
Holy Communion on Christmas Day of 1828 was a sad occasion.
On 27 December 1828 Ds Spijker referred specifically to the events
of the day, and admonished his congregation accordingly. At the
meeting of 3 February the events of Christmas Day and 27 December were discussed at length. We have a reasonably complete picture
of what happened. Many people were absent from the Holy Communion service on Christmas Day, with some taking the Lord's
Supper in other congregations. Before the service, the people spoke
in such a way that Ds Spijker considered them to be unworthy to
attend the Table of the Lord. When Ds Spijker pointed this out on
27 December, elder Wouter de Vos left the church building. During
the singing of the hymn, after the sermon, deacon Tielman Roos
also left the church and his example was followed by deacon G. M.
de Villiers. After the close of the service, Wouter de Vos and Tielman Roos went to the vestry to explain their dissatisfaction to the
minister. De Vos was not at all satisfied with the minister's initial
reaction and requested that the matter be discussed at the next
meeting. Finally, Ds Spijker was obliged to leave the vestry suggesting that, if they so wished, they should refer the case either to the
government or to one or another church meeting where Bentura
would be able to defend himself.

At the meeting of 3 February 1828 De Vos explained that the
minister had insulted him in two ways: first, because his proposal
that Bentura should be prevented from sharing Holy Communion
with white people was rejected out of hand. Secondly, because the
minister made a remark from the pulpit about the people going to
another congregation to take the Lord's Supper. De Vos further
demanded that his earlier proposal be accepted, but the minister
refused to comply with this request. Whereupon De Vos announ-
ced that he would in future attend the church services and pay the
chair and bench money, but that he would not make any further
contributions. If necessary, he would write a letter to the government explaining why he refused to make any further contributions
to the Church.(4)

Ds Spijker had hoped that the case was now closed, but Tielman
Roos came up with a new argument. He referred to Deuteronomy
23:2 where it is said that 'A bastard shall not enter into the congregation of the Lord, even to the tenth generation.' Bentura was a
'bastaard' and therefore it would be against the law of God if he
were allowed to partake of the Lord's Supper with 'born Chris-

tians'. Spijker also refuted this argument as a wrong interpretation and application of the text. Roos was still not satisfied, because, he said, Jesus himself had said that he had not come to disrupt the Law and the Prophets. What was prescribed for the Jews, was to be maintained by the Christians. Roos was of the opinon that arguments such as those of Ds Spijker were 'idle evasions' and that he (Roos) could not consider people who held such views as Christians.

Spijker responded by asking the meeting to consider certain factors. First of all, he wanted to know if there was any criticism about the moral behaviour of Bentura. The answer to this question was negative. Then elder De Vos pointed out that Bentura had not attended the thanksgiving service after the Communion. Spijker responded to this accusation by pointing out that the insulting behaviour towards Bentura had made it impossible for him to attend. He also pointed out the responsibility of De Vos and others in this regard, especially as it was well known that Bentura had previously attended church on a regular basis, even before he became a member. Secondly, Spijker wanted to investigate whether it would be possible for Bentura to get married. He posed certain questions to Bentura's employer, and to the owner of the slave woman with whom Bentura lived, reminding them that no one had any objection concerning Bentura's behaviour in general, and that there was no reason to believe that the woman with whom he lived would not wish to become a member of the Church also. The slave's owner agreed that she should be permitted to marry if she so desired. Ds Spijker then referred the case to the next *Ringsvergadering* (meeting of the presbytery).

THE PRESBYTERY AND SYNOD OF 1829

The Presbytery of Cape Town, to which Somerset West belonged, met in Zwartland (Malmesbury) on 29 April 1829, and the enquiries of Somerset West in connection with the administering of Communion to 'persons of colour' were dealt with.(5)

The question was asked whether 'persons of colour', who were confirmed and baptized, should be allowed, together with 'born Christians', to take the Lord's Supper. It was alternatively asked whether for such people (i.e. 'Hottentotte', 'Bastaards', 'Vryswartes' and slaves) it should be obligatory to take Holy Communion separately. The minutes do not tell us if this question was in any way discussed. What we do know is that it was 'advised' that, according to the teaching of the Bible and the spirit of Christianity, the Church was forced to make no exception in this case; people should take Holy Communion together. The minister of Somerset West, however, wanted to make doubly sure. He therefore asked how one should deal with members, and in particular Church Council members, who opposed this rule. The answer was: 'according to the law'. What is not very clear was what was meant by 'the law'. It is known that the Church Order of De Mist was at that time still in force. There are not, however, any obvious sections in this Church Order to which such an expression could have referred. Let us, however, first take a look at the Synod that also took place in 1829 and then return to this question.

Before the Synod meeting Ds Spijker had been transferred from Somerset West to the congregation of Zwartland, where other serious cases of colour prejudice had also occurred. These cases probably contributed to the nature of the proposal that Spijker made to the Synod. He submitted his proposal, as was required, to the civil department for church business, and there it was badly edited, with the consequence that it seemed to state that Spijker was *against* 'open' Communion services—and for this he accordingly received a serious reprimand from the Kommissaris Politiek. Whether the question of 'open' Communion was actually discussed at the Synod is a matter about which there exists a difference of opinon. The minutes of the Synod show that 'the members mutually exchanged ideas'. What should be understood by this is not clear because the Kommissaris Politiek declared that 'people ought not to make this proposal an object of deliberation at the Synod'. Yet because this question was so important it is unthinkable that a debate would not have taken place. The role of the Kommissaris Politiek in this case was clearly that of a civil servant who used his authority to prevent a question which was humiliating for the Church from being discussed. He believed that it ought to be an accepted and irrefutable principle that there could be no discrimination at Communion. Such a principle, he contended, was based on the Bible and on congregational practice, and individual Christians were obliged to 'think and behave' accordingly.

At this point it is necessary to say something about the office of Kommissaris Politiek. The government reserved for itself the right to involve itself in church affairs in such a way that all church decisions were first to be approved by the civil authority before they could be enforced. The government was therefore to be represented at all church meetings, i.e. Church Councils, Presbytery meetings and Synods, by a Kommissaris Politiek. (Whether this representative in fact attended all meetings is another question.) His task was to ensure that such meetings kept themselves occupied only with church business, and he had the power to veto decisions and, as in the above case, prevent a point on the agenda from being discussed at all.

For our purposes it is necessary to note that the Synod did not declare itself in favour of integrated Communion services. It was simply prevented from expressing its mind by the Kommissaris Politiek, who pre-empted all debate. Representatives from congregations like Caledon and Stellenbosch, which held segregated Communion services (and Somerset West, which began to follow their example by holding a separate service for Bentura), were not permitted to express their views because the Kommissaris Politiek ruled that racial discrimination had no place in such services.

One might ask what role Ordinance 50 of 1828 played in the deliberations of the Presbytery already referred to. This question is important especially if one thinks of the phrase 'according to the law', used in answer to Ds Spijker's question. Ordinance 50 became law in July 1828. According to it all free people were considered equal before the law. Should the Church have differentiated on grounds of colour at Holy Communion, it could therefore have been in contradiction to this Ordinance. However, in neither the Presbytery nor the Synod meetings was there any direct reference to Ordinance 50.

It is also important to remember that the Synod did not actually make a decision. At best there was a tacit agreement with the standpoint of the Kommissaris Politiek. That this question would for many years to come loom large is shown in the minute books of many a Church Council. That the Presbytery and the Synod of 1829 did not succeed in dispelling prejudice is clearly shown in the fact that it was necessary in 1843 for Ds Edgar to encourage his Church Council to declare that they did not have any objection to allow 'coloured people' at the same Communion Table. Incidentally, 1843 is the year in which Ordinance 7, according to which the Church became free of interference from the authorities, became law. But the next major phase in the development of this question is the Synod of 1857.

THE SYNOD OF 1857

In 1831 a community of Khoikhoi, the socially and politically oppressed original inhabitants of the country, was established on the banks of the Kat River, in the vicinity of Grahamstown.(6)

The religious needs of the new inhabitants were originally ministered to by the London Missionary Society, but in 1831 it joined the NGK, as the first black congregation.(7) However, during the next two decades white people moved to this area and those who were members of the NGK joined the Stockenström congregation. Soon the spirit of prejudice began to be noticeable here. In 1855 it came into the open when forty-five members submitted a petition to their Church Council.(8)

An examination of this petition shows that these members actually wanted a separate congregation within the existing congregation. Although they began with a request for separate administering of Holy Communion, they went further and asked that they be allowed to choose Church Council members from their own ranks to deal with such matters as Baptism, Confirmation and Holy Communion, in order that 'God's name may not be blasphemed but honoured and praised'. The Church Council did not grant this request, and the group wrote a second letter.(9) In this letter an appeal was made to Romans 14:1 and I Cor. 11:33–4, and the Church Council was asked not to be too harsh 'with our weakness' but rather to work in the interest of the building up of the congregation. The petitioners also found it strange that the Church Council was of the opinion that the requested separation at Holy Communion could have a harmful effect on the congregation. They understood that Communion could not be administered to the two groups on different days. They were, however, of the opinion that to celebrate Communion at two different times of the day would not be contrary to I Cor. 11:33–4, and that by separate celebrations of Communion in the congregation 'both classes of people would be more and more bound to each other with ties of brotherly love'.

The Presbytery of Albany that met at Uitenhage on 19 October 1855 was asked for advice regarding the problem of Stockenström. It was decided

... that to the Honourable Church Council of Stockenstöm it be recommended, in order to meet prejudice and weakness halfway, that after the Holy Communion had been administered to the older members of the congregation, one or more tables be administered for the new white members.

But from the minutes of the Presbytery meeting of the following year it is obvious that the problem had not yet been resolved, and by 1862 the whites had established their own congregation, the so-called Grey Kerk.(10)

There were essentially two reasons why the Synod of 1857 had to deal with the problem of integrated Holy Communion services. There was the question of the Church Council of Ceres and the question of Ds Shand, minister of Tulbagh. At that time Shand was also relieving minister of Ceres. At Ceres a proposal was put to the Church Council meeting that consideration should be given to building a separate church were 'coloureds' could be spiritually ministered to. The congregation at Ceres was established only in 1855, which means that it favoured segregation from its inception. Ds Shand turned down this proposal, and the Church Council challenged his right to do so. An elder from Zwartland drew attention to the decision of the Presbytery of Albany in connection with the wishes of the whites in the congregation of Stockenström for Holy Communion to be administered to them separately. At the same time Ds Shand's question as to whether it was permissible to make a distinction of persons at Holy Communion was attended to. It needs to be recalled that since 1829 it had been said that any discrimination at Holy Communion was not allowed, while in practice such discrimination continued. The Synod of 1834 had talked about congregations for 'natives' (meaning people of other than European origin), while the Synod of 1837 had pleaded for the provision of special seating for 'coloureds'. All this points to practices that developed early on: separate congregations where possible, otherwise a separate section of the church for black people, usually at the back of the church, sometimes under the balcony and sometimes on the balcony. The problem was thus not only that of 'colour difference' (Kriel) but colour prejudice, in other words *racism*.

The Synod of 1857 tried to resolve the problem in a strange way. If we read the decision in its entirety it seems that it consists of two conflicting sections.

The Synod considers it desirable and according to the Holy Scripture that our heathen members be accepted and initiated into our congregations wherever it is possible; but where this measure, as a result of the weakness of some, would stand in the way of promoting the work of Christ among the heathen people, then congregations set up among the heathen, or still to be set up, should enjoy their Christian privileges in a separate building or institution.

What happened here was that the Synod declared that according to the Bible it was clear that difference of race and colour should not cause any difference to be made in the preaching of the Gospel, but that it was also accepted that there was such a strong colour prejudice among the whites that they refused to tolerate the black people in their midst, especially when it came to 'Christian privileges' or to Holy Communion. This sinful predisposition of a section of the Church, which came to be called a 'weakness', was accepted and encouraged by people who were in a position of power, in the name of 'the question of Christ among the heathen'.

The standpoint of 1829 was actually the opposite to that of 1857. The decision of 1829 was forced upon the Synod by the Kommissaris Politiek and it ought, therefore, to be viewed as a qualified decision, although the *impression* did at least exist that the Church was against colour discrimination. By 1857 even this impression had disappeared. The decision that finally paved the way for separate Churches was in fact a true indication of the spirit and the practice that prevailed from early on in the NGK. Somerset West of 1828 and Stockenström of 1855 were not just isolated examples of racial intolerance that was nurtured by a deluded theology and went under the name of 'mission'. Therefore it would perhaps be helpful in closing to take a brief look at a few congregations that illustrate the colour or racial segregation practised among white sections of the NGK at the time.

CHURCH RACISM IN PRACTICE

The Presbytery of Cape Town said in 1828 that members who objected to the policy of allowing all members to take Holy Communion at the same time had to be called to order. It was declared that such members would have to be dealt with 'according to the law'. As we have seen, it is not clear what was meant by this expression. What is clear is that this policy was enforcable. Members would not have a choice in the matter. But what actually happened is a question that can be answered relatively easily by history.

Already, before 1829, even before 1824, when the first NGK Synod was held at the Cape, the practice of racial discrimination among some whites was not repudiated by the Church. Thus we read that slaves who transported their owners to Cape Town's *Groote Kerk* had to wait outside in the cemetery while the 'born Christians' worshipped.(11) At an early stage the civil authorities passed a law that controlled the behaviour of black churchgoers. For example, in 1754 the civic leader Ryk Tulbagh, who was an elder of the Church, issued a pamphlet that stated that black Christians were forbidden to remain in the foyer of the church after the church service. In 1794 this rule was once again emphasized by the authorities.(12)

The congregations of both Swellendam and Zwartland initially exemplified the prevailing habit in those days of letting black people sit at the back of the church, but eventually separate churches were built for the 'coloured' people.(13) In 1865 the 'Small Church' meant for black people was built in Zwartland. When these members objected because they were forced to make use of the *Klein Kerkie* both for taking Holy Communion and for the confirmation of members, the Church Council decided 'for the sake of peace and quiet in the congregation' to enforce this segregation.(14)

It is on record that a growing number of black people joined the Church at Beaufort West during the middle of the nineteenth century, but that objections came from many people because 'persons of colour' were taken into the bosom of the white congregation after baptism and the declaration of faith.(15) During the ministry of Ds N. J. Hofmeyr at Calvinia, objections to the practice of black people in the same building and especially to the practice of administering to them 'at the same Communion Table', were strongly heard. There were even objections made to separate services for them in the church. The fact that the minister did not use the pulpit on these occasions and that the black people were not allowed to sit on the usual chairs in the church did not lessen the resistance. Hofmeyr thus decided to hold the service in the vestry for this section of the congregation.(16) On one occasion in Riversdale there were even objections to the use of the vestry, so that the service had to take place under a tree in front of the vestry door.(17)

In Oudtshoorn it was noted that 'a bitter battle was waged before the coloureds were excluded from the white community', while at Riebeeck West they 'had the privilege of attending the religious practices of the white congregations sitting on the back benches of the church'.(18) In Dordrecht(19) the Church Council was prepared 'to grant church privileges to coloureds, but in a separate building', while in Philadelphia(20) separate 'records' were early on 'being drawn up for the non-whites'. In Wellington, by 1835, racial feelings were running high. During that year, Holy Communion was for the first time administered to black people. There was dissatisfaction among the whites: not because it happened in the white church or together with the white people, as there was already a separate church—called 'the practice house'— where it was administered. According to J. A. S. Oberholster(21) the people wanted 'Christian doctrine to be taught to their slaves, but they felt that it went too far to administer the sacraments to them'. That is, the objection was to their receiving Holy Communion at all.

Further examples from Mossel Bay, East London, Murraysburg, Robertson, Darling and many other congregations make it clear that the 'decision' of 1829 was never translated into practice: to be obliged to act 'according to the law' was no real obligation at all. There were simply attempts to bring the 'weak ones', by way of argument, to a different understanding. Not even ministers like N. J. Hofmeyr and W. Robertson, who otherwise had such a great influence in the Church, especially at Synods, could not overcome this prejudice, even in the congregations where they themselves ministered. The black church members were expected to accept the growing number of racist practices with the Christian virtue of 'humility'.

The 'final solution' to the 'problem' was the establishing in 1881 of the racially separate NG Sendingkerk. Instead of the Church committing itself to overcome the sin of racial pride, black people were asked to be the least and to leave the Church. In Mossel Bay there was an extreme case where it was insisted that black members should rather join the Lutheran Church or the Anglican Church. The arrogance of these white people seemed to know no bounds.

In the light of the events outlined above, the objection by the white NGK to the witness of the eleven ministers in Ottawa is hypocritical, and the justification by some white NGK spokesmen who refer to the Synod of 1829 is unfounded.

Notes

1 Acta Synodi, III (1829), pp. 71 and 72.

2 W. A. Alheit, *Gedenkboek van die N. G. Gemeente Swellendam* (Cape Town, 1948), pp. 48–52.

3 Minutes of the Church Council. Also see H. C. Hopkins, *N. G. Gemeente Somerset-Wes 1819–1969* (Paarl, 1969), pp. 61–3.

4 According to the Church Order of De Mist, art. 45, it was not only prescribed what kind of contributions should be made by members, but also how much they should give.

5 Minutes of the Presbytery of Cape Town, 1829, p. 11.

6 For the Kat River settlement, see e.g. J. S. Marais, *The Cape Coloured People* (Johannesburg, 1962), pp. 216–46.

7 C. J. Kriel, *Die Geskiedenis van die NG Sendingkerk in S. A.* (Paarl, 1963), p. 58.

8 Minutes of the Presbytery of Albany, 1855, app. F1.

9 Ibid., app. F3.

10 Compare the article 'Greykerk' in P. L. Olivier (ed.), *Ons Gemeentlike Feesalbum* (Cape Town, 1952).

11 H. C. Hopkins, *Die Moeder van Ons Almal. Geskiedenis van die Gemeente Kaapstad*, 1665–1965 (Cape Town, 1965).

12 N. J. Smith, *Die Planting van Afsonderlike Kerke vir Nie-blanke Bevolkingsgroepe deur die N.G.K. in S. A.* (Annale Universiteit van Stellenbosch, 1973, published in Cape Town in 1980 as *Elkeen in sy eie taal*).

13 For Swellendam see W. A. Alheit, op. cit., and for Malmesbury see A. P. Smit, *Na Tweehonderd Jaar, N. G. Gemeente Swartland* (Cape Town, 1945).

14 A. P. Smit, op. cit., p. 304.

15 W. G. H. and S. Vivier, *Hart van die Groot Karoo* (Cape Town, 1975), p. 90.

16 For Calvinia see A. P. Smit, *Na Honderd Jaar Eeufees, N. G. Gemeente Calvinia 1847–1947* (Cape Town, 1966).

17 A. P. Smit, *Riversdale Eeufeesalbum 1839–1939* (Cape Town, 1939), p. 95.

18 H. C. Hopkins, *Die N. G. Gemeente Oudtshoorn 1853–1953* (Cape Town, 1953), p. 13.

19 J. A. S. Oberholster, *Dordrecht: 'n Eeu van Gods Genade* (Paarl, 1956), p. 113.

20 A. P. Smit, *Philadelphia 1863–1938: Gedenkboek* (Cape Town, 1938), p. 58.

21 J. A. S. Oberholster, *Wellington Eeufees* (Paarl, 1940), p. 89.

3 DAVID BOSCH
Nothing but a heresy

CHURCH UNITY AMIDST CULTURAL DIVERSITY:
A PROTESTANT PROBLEM

In the Roman Catholic Church cultural and ethnic diversity has never really threatened the unity of the Church. The pope as the visible symbol of the unity of the Church, together with the universal use of Latin as the language of the Mass, helped to safeguard global ecclesiastical unity. In recent years, however, this has come under increasing pressure. Latin has ceased to be the universal language of the Mass, and Roman Catholic theologians have increasingly been emphasizing the need for the inculturation of the faith in each local situation.(1) Tension is beginning to develop between what Rome calls 'local Churches' (dioceses or church provinces) and the 'universal Church'. Whereas some seem to argue that a wane of romanity may spell the decay of Catholicity, others plead eloquently for the autonomy and cultural distinctiveness of 'local Churches'.

Whereas the tension between ecclesiastical unity and ethnic diversity is therefore a late comer on the Roman Catholic scene, it has always been at least latently present in Protestantism. Let me mention only two reasons for this.

1 At least the German Reformation was in some sense also a people's movement. Sociologically speaking (I am, for the sake of this argument, putting aside the theological reasons), the success of Luther's Reformation can be partly attributed to the fact that for many people it was a symbol of Germanic resistance to Latin domination. The word *Deutsch* gradually acquired a significance of meaning it had never had before. This anchoring of the Church in the people undoubtedly had merit, yet—as I hope to argue later on—at the same time it contained the seeds of potential danger.

2 Another reason for the higher rating of ethnic distinctiveness in Protestant Churches is to be found in the fact that the Churches of the Reformation were and still are pre-eminently Churches of the *word*. This is already evident in the fact that the pulpit, and

not the altar, dominates the liturgical centre. In what we may call 'liturgical' Churches, such as the Roman Catholic, Eastern Orthodox and Anglican communities, the liturgy, rather than the proclaimed word, receives the main emphasis. And liturgy can communicate without its relying exclusively on the intelligibility of the spoken word. Not so, however, where preaching predominates. It has to be understood, which means that it has to be preached in a language in which the worshipper is thoroughly at home.

The problem remained latent, however, for at least two centuries after the Reformation. The reason for this was simple. The Churches of the Reformation did not get seriously involved in mission work among peoples outside Europe until the eighteenth century. In Europe itself, admittedly, the Reformation message was carried from country to country, but it is important to point out that no truly trans-national denomination developed in those days. What happened, in essence, was that 'national' Churches developed, a different Church for each country. It is true, of course, that the famous Synod of Dort (1618–19) invited Reformed delegates from Britain, Switzerland and Germany to deliberate with them, but in essence it was a meeting of the Dutch Church. As a matter of fact, a much earlier synod at Dort (1578) had already discussed the problem of church unity and cultural diversity, and had decided on separate synods and circuits for Dutch- and French-speaking Christians.(2)

A few small-scale overseas missionary endeavours were launched during the seventeenth century, mainly by the Dutch and the English. But the real history of Protestant missions outside Europe only began in the eighteenth century, under the auspices of the Halle Pietists and Zinzendorf's Moravians. Their emphasis throughout was on the salvation of individuals, or, as Zinzendorf liked to put it, on *'Seelen für das Lamm'* ('Souls for the Lamb'). Pietism moreover tended to have a rather onesided vertical dimension, with little understanding of man's cultural relationships and Christ's universal kingship.

Gradually, however, uneasiness developed over this narrow missionary aim. This manifested itself particularly in German missionary circles, where, during the course of practically the entire nineteenth century, a debate was conducted on the question whether the aim of mission should be *'Einzelbekehrung'* (the Pietistic 'conversion of an individual') or *'Volkschristianisierung'* ('the christianization of a people as an ethnic unit'). The emphasis gradually shifted towards the latter. 'People' (*'Volk'*) increasingly became a normative factor in the establishment of younger Churches.

In Anglo-Saxon missionary circles this was the time of the 'three selves' of Venn and Anderson: the aim of the mission was the founding of self-governing, self-propagating and self-supporting Churches. Thus Venn and Anderson also moved away from the earlier Pietistic understanding of mission. They shared the Germans' misgivings in this respect. Yet unlike the Germans they did not emphasize culture and ethnicity as constituent factors in the founding of younger Churches.

'ALL THE NATIONS'

Of special interest, in this respect, is the 'Great Commission' in Mt. 28:19–29. This so-called missionary mandate has always played a key role in Protestant missions. In the German debate about the choice between *'Einzelbekehrung'* and *'Volkschristianisierung'* more and more protagonists of the latter policy began to appeal to to the Great Commission. Here Jesus commands his followers to make disciples of *'panta ta ethne'*, 'all the nations', which, according to those favouring *'Volkschristianisierung'*, must surely be interpreted as a charge to found separate ethnic Churches.

The best example of this exegesis of *'panta ta ethne'* is to be found in the writings of the father of academic missiology, Gustav Warneck. In his monumental *Evangelische Missionslehre* he admits that *'panta ta ethne'* in the Great Commission has primarily a *religious* connotation: it refers to Gentiles, that is, to those nations outside the divine Covenant. He thus concedes that the entire issue regarding *'Einzelbekehrung'* and *'Volkschristianisierung'* lies outside the scope of the Great Commission.(3) Yet he proceeds to argue in favour of the translation of *ethne* as *'Völker'* ('peoples as ethnic units'), 'even if scientific exegesis has raised some not unfounded objections to this translation'.(4) After all, says Warneck, in the practical execution of the missionary commission the religious antithesis in which the *ethne* stood to Israel became an ethnographic one.(5) History thus proves the correctness of the suggested translation; moreover, it should be remembered that 'the acts of history are also an exegesis of the Bible, and in the final analysis they speak the decisive word when the theological interpretation remains in dispute.'(6)

It is clear that Warneck's exegesis of *'panta ta ethne'* dominated the German missiological scene for almost half a century.(7) German missiology showed a remarkable parallel development with

German political thinking in general. The concept *'Volk'*, deeply influenced by Romanticism, was increasingly given a theological weight. For Bruno Gutmann, who worked as a missionary among the Chagga in East Africa, it was difficult to distinguish between a fellow-Christian and a compatriot; through his sharing in the *'ur-tümliche Bindungen'* ('primordial ties') of blood, neighbourhood and age-group the Chagga Christian was sociologically circumscribed. There was therefore an abiding connection between Church and *'Volk'*.(8) Warneck also influenced Afrikaans Reformed missionary thinking, particularly through J. du Plessis' popularisation of Warneck's views in his *Wie sal gaan?*, published in 1932.

I shall return to South Africa later. For the moment I want to draw attention to the fact that Warneck's exegesis of *'panta ta ethne'* has recently been revived by the American Church Growth movement led by Donald McGavran of the School of World Mission at the Fuller Theological Seminary in Pasadena, California. McGavran, who frequently quotes *'panta ta ethne'* untranslated, interprets it as referring to 'the classes, tribes, lineages and peoples of the earth'.(9) Thus *'ethne'* is interpreted purely in an ethnological and sociological sense: Jesus had homogeneous ethnic units of people in mind, 'families of mankind—tongues, tribes, castes and lineages of man', when he used this expression.(10) Several of McGavran's co-workers, in particular Peter Wagner, concur with his interpretation. As a matter of fact, Wagner finds the homogeneous unit principle not only in Mt. 18:19, but in all the New Testament. He even believes that there were culturally separate homogeneous Churches in Jerusalem, Antioch, Rome and Thessalonica.(11)

I am not suggesting that the Church Growth exponents agree in every detail with Warneck, Gutmann and other German missionary thinkers. At a very early stage in the development of the Church Growth philosophy the American missiologist, Harry Boer, cautioned that by 'peoples' McGavran 'did not have in mind an anglicized version of the German conception of *'Volk'*, with its idea of the socially unifying and integrating power that arises from the bonds of common blood and common soil.(12) We ought to take this caution to heart. McGavran and his colleagues are far more pragmatic than the Germans. Their concern is church growth, and they firmly believe that Churches grow more quickly when they are culturally homogeneous. McGavran repeatedly says, 'Men like to become Christians without crossing racial, linguistic, or class barriers.'(13) Wagner even finds scriptural proof to support this. The disagreement between Greek- and Aramaic-speaking Chris-

tians in Jerusalem, reported in Acts 6, led, according to him, to
the establishment of completely separate homogeneous Churches
in Jerusalem, a decision which, he adds, immediately led to un-
precedented church growth, for we read in vs. 7, 'The word of
God now spread more and more widely; the number of disciples
in Jerusalem went on increasing rapidly, and very many of the
priests adhered to the Faith.' (NEB) (14)

The pragmatism of the Church Growth movement is therefore
quite different from the ideologically loaded thinking of earlier
German missiology. Nevertheless, some uneasiness remains. The
Church Growth exponents have now discovered the German mis-
siologists I referred to earlier, particular Christian Keysser, whom
they applaud enthusiastically. Keysser's major treatise, *Eine Papua-
Gemeinde* (first published in 1929), has recently been translated
into English and published by the Church Growth movement.(15)
And one is left with the question whether McGavran and his co-
workers do not in fact agree with Keysser's basic presuppositions,
for instance when he states categorically, *'Der Stamm is zugleich
die Christengemeinde'* ('The tribe is at the same time the Christian
Church').(16)

We do not have time to investigate thoroughly Warneck's and
the Church Growth movement's translation and understanding of
'panta ta ethne' in Mt. 28:19. I have recently attempted such an
in-depth enquiry elsewhere.(17) Suffice it to state here simply
that I could not find a single New Testament scholar of repute
who supported Warneck's exegesis. As a matter of fact, it is not
even entertained as a possibility. All agree that *'panta ta ethne'*
means essentially the same as *'hole he oikoumene'* ('the whole
inhabited world', Mt. 24:14) or *'pasa he ktisis'* ('the entire human
world as created by God', Mk. 16:15). Where New Testament
scholars do differ is on the question whether *'panta ta ethne'* refers
to Gentiles (non-Jews) only, or to all nations *including* the Jews.
This is, however, a completely different problem. The issue at
stake is theological, not socio-anthropological. 'Jew' and 'Gentile'
were in Matthew's time essentially religious and not ethnic terms.
G. Bertram writing on this period says, *'Judentum bedeutet nicht
Rasse sondern Religion'* ('Judaism does not mean race but
religion').(18) Similarly, in the Septuagint and Hellenistic Judaism
'ethne' is to be understood almost exclusively in a religio-ethical
sense, as 'Gentiles' or 'pagans', and not in an ethno-sociological
sense.

A 'THIRD RACE'

It is therefore indefensible to equate the tensions in the early Church between Jewish and Gentile Christians with those between different cultural groupings in our day. There is a tendency in some circles today to see the Antiochian question of whether Gentile converts should be circumcised or not as an issue of cultural adaptation or indigenization. However, it had nothing whatsoever to do with the modern homogeneous unit issue. At stake was not the question whether different Churches should be established for different cultural groups. The issue at stake was two different understandings of salvation. It was a matter of theology, not of communications theory. Paul and his co-workers passionately contended that the crucified and risen Messiah had superseded the Law as the way of salvation, and therefore to demand the circumcision of Gentile converts to the Christian faith was, in effect, crucifying Christ anew. Paul still accepted the principle of division of labour as far as the mission to Jews and Gentiles was concerned (cf. Gal. 2:7), but theological (or 'salvation-historical') difference between the two had been abrogated: the Law was a 'tutor' only until Christ came (Gal. 3:24).

As a matter of fact, an unbiased reading of Paul cannot but lead one to the conclusion that his entire theology militates against even the possibility of establishing separate Churches for different cultural groups. He pleads unceasingly for the *unity* of the Church made up of *both* Jews and Gentiles. God has made the two one, 'a single new humanity', 'a single body' (Eph. 2:14–16) (NEB). This was the mystery revealed to him, 'that through the Gospel the Gentiles are heirs together with Israel, members together of one body, and sharers together in the promise in Christ Jesus' (Eph. 3:6) (NIV). Paul could never cease to marvel at this new thing that had caught him unawares, something totally unexpected: the Church is one, indivisible, and it transcends all differences. The sociological impossibility (Hoekendijk) is theologically possible. And so the New Testament describes the Church as first-fruit, as new creation, as the one body of Christ the 'one new man'. The early Christians called themselves a *'triton genos'*, a 'third race', next to and transcending the two existing races of Jews and Gentiles, whose enmity was proverbial in the ancient world.(19)

THE ROLE OF CULTURE

All this most certainly does not mean that culture is not to play any role in the Church and that cultural differences should not be accommodated.

I have already said that there was a time in the Roman Catholic Church when romanity, symbolized by the universal use of the Latin language, was normative. Today relatively few would still subscribe to that view. Almost everybody now accepts that the Church should be indigenized, or, to use the modern word, 'contextualized'. The Church has to enter the very fabric of a local community, culturally, sociologically and otherwise. This is the legitimate element in Church Growth missiology and in the views of Warneck and his followers. Particularly in Protestant Churches, which purport to be Churches of the *Word*, the cultural dimension is of very great importance. The Church must do everything in its power to minister effectively and in a relevant way to a particular socio-cultural community. This cannot and may not be faulted.

However, cultural diversity should in no way militate against the unity of the Church. Such diversity in fact should *serve* the unity. It thus belongs to the *well-being* of the Church, whereas unity is part of its *being*. To play the one off against the other is to miss the entire point. Unity and socio-cultural diversity belong to different *orders*. Unity can be *confessed*. Not so diversity. To elevate cultural diversity to the level of an article of faith is to give culture a positive theological weight which easily makes it into a 'revelation principle'.

THE SOUTH AFRICAN SCENE

Against this background I now want to look at the situation in South Africa, particularly as regards the Nederduitse Gereformeerde (Dutch Reformed) 'family' of Churches.

In October 1981 the Nederduitse Gereformeerde Sendingkerk (Dutch Reformed Mission Church) celebrated its first centenary. Perhaps 'celebrated' is the wrong word, for much controversy and even boycotts characterized the centenary festivities of this Church that was formed a hundred years ago exclusively for the so-called 'coloured' people. Later similar separate Churches for black Africans and Indians were formed. Those who opposed the centenary celebrations referred to the DR Mission Church as 'a church born in sin' and as the product of 'sinful intolerance'.(20) To this we have to add that leading figures in the three 'black' Dutch Reformed Churches have in recent years consistently pleaded for a (re-)unification of all four Churches. Various sessions of the General Synod of the 'white' Church, however, have expressed very little interest in such a union and have tended to write the whole idea off as being politically motivated. So, as far as the 'white' Church is concerned, the idea of union appears to be a dead issue. In fact, many white church members and church councils object even to the presence of occasional black worshippers in white Churches.

How has this state of affairs come about? Without reiterating the entire history–a great deal has been written about this in recent years–I would like simply to highlight a few relevant events and issues.

At an early stage of the Dutch settlement at the Cape it became customary to make special provisions for ministry among the indigenous Khoikhoi people as well as the slave population which came from Indonesia, Madagascar, and East and West Africa. This was in line with the basic Reformation principle of preaching the Gospel in the language of the people.

At no stage, however, was there even the faintest suggestion of a theological justification for the idea of creating separate congregations–let alone a separate church structure (*'kerkverband'*)–for converts from these groups. Once they became Christians they were to enjoy their privileges as members together with the Dutch Christians.

It is true that, by the beginning of the nineteenth century, suggestions were made from time to time that Holy Communion should be administered separately to converts from paganism and Islam, yet still within the orbit of the same church affiliation (*'kerkverband'*). This was, however, rejected. An 1829 resolution of the Cape Town Presbytery in this regard is illuminating. It resolved, 'that it is compulsory, according to the teaching of Scripture and the spirit of Christianity, to admit such persons simultaneously with born Christians to the communion table.' The Synod of 1834 endorsed this viewpoint 'as an unalterable axiom which is founded on the infallible Word of God . . . and all Christian congregations and each Christian in particular have to think and act in accordance.'(21)

If we now jump from the 1830s to the second half of the twentieth century, we find a completely different climate and type of theological reasoning. In 1951, for instance, the Natal Synod of the Nederduitse Gereformeerde Kerk resolved to establish a separate Church for Indians, as it was felt that 'according to our policy of apartheid we should minister separately to these groups'.(22) In 1974 the General Synod of the NGK stated, 'The existence of separate Dutch Reformed Church affiliations (*'kerkverbande'*) for the various population groups is recognized as being in accordance with the plurality of church affiliations described in the

Bible.'(23) Many similar resolutions over the past forty years could be quoted.

How does one account for the shift in the past century and a half? It is generally accepted that the turning of the tide can be traced to a fateful resolution of the Synod of 1857. Of course, this resolution must be seen as one among many, as part of an historical process. And yet there is something pivotal about it. The full resolution, in the English translation, reads as follows: 'Synod considers it to be desirable and in accordance with Scripture that our converts from paganism be received and incorporated into existing congregations, wherever possible; however, where this practice, because of the weakness of some, constitutes an obstacle to the advancement of Christ's cause among pagans, congregations formed or still to be formed from converts from paganism should be given the opportunity to enjoy their Christian privileges in a separate place of worship.(24)

Of importance for our subject is that the Synod of 1857 (a) confessed that it was 'desirable and in accordance with Scripture' for all to worship together; (b) did not even remotely consider the possibility of the founding of separate *Churches* (denominations); (c) made some concessions, not because of theological arguments, but 'because of the weakness of some'.

However, since 1857, and particularly in this century, the situation has changed radically. Today, in the view of many Dutch Reformed churchmen, it is considered (a) to be 'desirable and in accordance with Scripture' that whites and blacks do *not* worship together, (b) that separate Churches (denominations) be established along racial lines, and (c) that the plea in some Dutch Reformed circles for common worship and church union is to be ascribed to the 'weakness of some'! Indeed, a volte-face of 180 degrees!

The question is whether this development is simply due to an increase in racial prejudice within the circles of the white Dutch Reformed Church during the past century and a half. Many people explain the whole development in these terms. And I believe that there is an undeniable element of truth in this view. It is, however, not the full story.

In two recent articles on the 1981 centenary of the Dutch Reformed Mission Church, published in *Die Kerkbode*, Ds Charles Hopkins is at pains to prove that racial prejudice was not a decisive factor in the creation of a Church for the so-called 'coloured' people.(25) He refers to the crucial role played in this regard by Ds J. C. Pauw of Wellington, and adds, 'nobody would ever have suspected the venerable and godly Father Pauw, as he was widely known, of prejudice, uncharitableness and haughtiness towards [coloured] church members.'(26) I am fully prepared to accept this; nevertheless, Hopkins has erred in his attempt to gloss over the reality of racial prejudice in his apology.

Be that as it may, the real reason for the creation of the Neder-duitse Gereformeerde Sendingkerk and of several other ethnic Churches in the decades that followed, may indeed not have been racial prejudice but, rather, a weak ecclesiology. The nineteenth century was, in Protestantism as a whole, not a great century as far as the understanding of the Church was concerned. It was the century of denominationalism, when all kinds of groups broke away and new denominations were spawned. This was true of church life in Southern Africa as well.

As far as the Nederduitse Gereformeerde Kerk was concerned, two theological currents influenced ecclesiological thinking.

The first one was *Pietism*. The emphasis here was on the individual. The Church as a body is of minor importance. The invisible unity of all believers is paramount. The true Church is therefore also the invisible, not the empirical one.

The second influence was that of *Liberalism*. Here the Church is viewed as a man-made society or *collegium* in which like-minded people can gather of their own free will. If you and your little group do not agree with others, you leave and form your own new denomination. If you do not feel doctrinally at home, even on minor issues, you separate yourself and those who agree with you. Likewise, if there are cultural differences, they become an excuse for the formation of separate denominations. The utility principle thus weighs most heavily.(27)

In this respect W. D. Jonker writes, 'It is a sign of deformation if the Church forgets its own nature and starts thinking and speaking about itself as though it were an ordinary human organization to which the same guidelines of human wisdom apply as is the case with other organizations. It was the typically liberal thinking of the Enlightenment that first led to the idea that the visible form of the Church was of lesser value, so much so that any rules could be made as long as they "worked" without caring about the indissoluble unity that ought to exist between the invisible, inner being of the Church and its visible form.'(28) Robert Recker, in discussing the Church Growth approach, puts it even more strongly. He warns against 'a growing virus in the body of Christ' that fosters the formation of different denominations 'upon the basis of very questionable distinctives'. He adds, 'When individual believers refuse any longer to entertain the biblical injunction to be reconciled to their brothers but rather simply run off to find some congregation which mirrors their own foibles, fears, suspicions, prejudices or what-not, in the name of feeling "at home" or comfortable, then something is radically wrong in the body of Christ.'(29)

The acceptable Christian way, so it appears to me, is rather to bear with one another even to the point of suffering, to forfeit some of our efficiency, for the sake of our unity. But this is perhaps a rather negative reason! There is also a far more positive one: to regard our cultural differences as mutual enrichment, as aids to a broadening of our horizons, as object lessons on the richness of the unfolding of God's works among people.

It goes without saying that any specific local congregation should function primarily within the orbit of one cultural context—as long as we do not define that cultural context too narrowly. But it should always be a congregation with open doors, into which people from other cultural backgrounds are welcomed and in which they are made to feel welcome. If a local Church closes its doors to other worshippers, it ascribes soteriological significance to cultural distinctiveness and thus falls captive to an ideology.

This is the tendency I discern in the symposium volume *Veelvormigheid en Eenheid*, published in 1978.(30) In it F. G. M. Potgieter contends that a people as an ethno-cultural group 'structures' the Church, from which it follows that 'the members of an autonomous Church are elected from the ranks of an autonomous nation. ... It follows further that the boundaries between autonomous Churches for all practical purposes coincide with those between nations. History also teaches that a Church becomes independent when the nation becomes independent. Our own history confirms this.'(31)

Potgieter goes even further: within the same ethno-cultural grouping there is no room for more than one Church (denomination) for people sharing the same confession. On the other hand, Christians of the same confession but of different cultural backgrounds should be divided into different denominations.(32) The implication is clear: cultural differences count for more than the sharing of the same confession.

What we find in Potgieter and many other proponents of the idea of separate ethnic Churches is a tendency to declare the structural unity of the Church (*kerkverband*) as something *optional*. That this is the case has been shown clearly by Durand and Lederle in their contributions to the symposium volume on *Die Eenheid van die Kerk*.(33) They argue cogently that this playing down of structural and institutional unity (*kerkverband*) is not an outflow of Reformed ecclesiology. Rather, Reformed theology has a high view of the Church and its unity, as can be seen from the classic Reformed confessions (cf. the Heidelberg Catechism, Question 54, and the Belgic Confession, Art. 27). It is stated unambiguously that only faith in Christ and not biological descent or cultural distinctiveness constitutes the precondition of admission to the Church. What we find today in Potgieter and other Reformed exponents of the doctrine of the plurality of ethnic Churches is a later development, and as such an aberration.

WHY UNITY?

Those of us who plead for the re-unification of the four Dutch Reformed Churches, currently separated along racial lines, and for open church doors during the period that negotiations regarding church union are still in process, are often asked why we make an issue of these matters. The answer is simple. The breaking down of barriers that separate people is an intrinsic part of the Gospel. What is more: it is not merely a *result* of the Gospel, allowing us first to group people together in separate, homogeneous Churches, in the hope that one day they will reach out beyond their own narrow confines. Experience teaches us that this does not happen; rather, the homogeneous group simply entrenches itself more and more in its sectional Church. But more important than experience is the fact that the New Testament teaches us differently. Evangelism as such itself involves a call to be incorporated into a *new* community, an alternative community. As René Padilla puts it, 'It may be true that "men like to become Christians without crossing barriers" [McGavran], but that is irrelevant. Membership in the body of Christ is not a question of likes or dislikes, but a question of incorporation into a new humanity under the lordship of Christ. Whether a person likes it or not, the same act that reconciles one to God *simultaneously* introduces the person into a community where people find their identity in Jesus Christ rather than in their race, culture, social class, or sex.'(34)

In regard to the subject under discussion and the way it is viewed by the current white Dutch Reformed Church leadership, I cannot help sharing Paul's agony in respect to his fellow-Jews. In II Cor. 3:14–16 he says that their minds have been made insensitive, for there is a veil that obscures their reading of the Old Covenant. So they cannot see and hear what it really says. I observe a similar veil preventing the Afrikaans Reformed Churches from really hearing what the Bible says about the unity of the Church. I say this not in a spirit of judgement, but of shared guilt and deep concern. Of course, other denominations have their limitations and blind spots too, in regard to other central issues of the Gospel. But my concern here is with a specific blind spot, that of being unable to catch a vision of a Church truly transcending the divisions of mankind.

Let me add that I firmly believe that this particular form of blindness is not part of the true Reformed tradition. The Afrikaans Reformed Churches have only to return to their roots to discover that what they now cherish is nothing but a heresy that strikes at the very foundation of the Church. Because of this heresy the Afrikaans Reformed Churches have designed a missiology tailor-made 'for Churches and institutions whose main function in society is to reinforce the status quo', where the Church becomes little more than a pale reflection of its environment. It is a missiology 'that conceives the People of God as a quotation taken from the surrounding society' instead of one 'that conceives [the Church] as "an embodied question mark [John Poulton]" ' that challenges the values of the world.'(35)

In summary, then, I am not suggesting an easy solution to the issue that is the subject matter of this paper. There must be room for cultural distinctiveness in any specific Church. People must be able to feel 'at home' in their Church. But this should never be regarded as something that militates against, let alone excludes, the indestructible unity of the Church. This is the danger in the Afrikaans Reformed Churches today. Naturally neither should the argument in favour of unity be employed to bulldoze Christians into an amorphous sameness. This was the mistake made in times past by Rome. Rather, let us strive for a gentle yet dynamic tension between the particular and the universal, to the mutual enrichment of all and to the glory of Him who is the Head of his *one* body, which is the Church.

Notes

1 To give only one example: the 1981 Summer Course of the (Roman Catholic) East Asian Pastoral Institute was devoted, in its entirety, to 'Inculturation: Challenge to the Local Church' (see *East Asian Pastoral Review* 18:3, 1981, pp. 203-99).

2 Looking at the 1578 ruling from the perspective of the present-day context of the South African Reformed Churches, one might easily deduce that

the two situations are similar. They are not, however. Individual Dutch- and French-speaking Christians in the Netherlands were free to join congregations of their choice and pastors could be called to any congregation. Structurally, therefore, the Reformed Church was *one*. See my comments on '*kerkverband*' towards the end of this article.

3 G. Warneck, *Evangelische Missionslehre* III/1 (2nd edition) (Perthes, 1902), pp. 247–50.

4 Ibid., p. 251 (my translation).

5 Ibid., p. 250.

6 Ibid., p. 258 (my translation).

7 J. C. Hoekendijk's study of this aspect in his *Kerk en volk in de duitse zendingswetenschap* (Amsterdam, 1948) is still unsurpassed in scope and quality.

8 Cf. Hoekendijk, op. cit., pp. 150–2.

9 D. A. McGavran, *Understanding Church Growth* (fully revised, Grand Rapids, 1980), p. 22.

10 Ibid., p. 56, cf. p. 348.

11 Cf. C. Peter Wagner, *Our Kind of People: The Ethical Dimensions of Church Growth in America* (Atlanta, 1979), pp. 123–5, 130–1; see also pp. 118–19.

12 H. R. Boer, *Pentecost and Missions* (London, 1961), p. 179, cf. p. 169.

13 McGavran, op. cit., p. 223, and elsewhere.

14 Cf. Wagner, op. cit., p. 123.

15 C. Keysser, *A People Reborn* (Pasadena, 1980).

16 C. Keysser, *Eine Papua-Gemeinde* (1929), p. 235.

17 See my 'The Structure of Mission: An Exposition of Matthew 28:16–20' in Wilbert Shenk (ed.), *The Study of Church Growth* to be published shortly by Eerdmans in Grand Rapids.

18 G. Bertram, '*Ethnos, ethnikos*' in *Theologisches Wörterbuch zum Neuen Testament*, Vol. 2 (Stuttgart, 1935), p. 362.

19 Cf. Adolf Harnack, *The Mission and Expansion of Christianity in the First Three Centuries* (New York, 1961), p. 243.

20 Quoted in H. C. Hopkins, '*Die geboorte van die Sendingkerk*' in *Die Kerkbode*, 23 September, p. 7 (translation mine).

21 Both resolutions quoted in W. van der Merwe, *The Development of Missionary Attitudes in the Dutch Reformed Church in South Africa* (Cape Town, 1936), p. 149.

22 *Acta Synodi*, Natal, 1951, p. 148.

23 *Human Relations and the South African Scene in the Light of the Scripture* (Cape Town/Pretoria, 1976), p. 82.

24 In the original Dutch the resolution reads as follows: '*De Synode beschouwt het wenschelijk en schriftmatig, dat onze ledematen uit de Heidenen in onze bestaande gemeenten opgenomen en ingelijfd worden, overal waar zulks geschieden kan; maar waar deze maatregel, ten gevolge van de zwakheid van sommigen, de bevordering van de zaak van Christus onder de heidenen in*

den weg zoude staan, de gemeenten uit de heidenen opgericht, of nog op te richten, hare Christelijke voorrechten in een afzonderlijk gebouw of gesticht genieten zal.'

25 Cf. *Die Kerkbode*, issues of 23 Sept. and 30 Sept., 1981.

26 *Die Kerkbode*, 23 Sept. 1981, p. 7.

27 See further two important contributions in Piet Meiring & H. I. Lederle (eds.), *Die Eenheid van die Kerk* (Cape Town, 1979), viz. those by J. J. F. Durand, '*Kerkverband–wese of welwese?*' (pp. 73–7) and H. I. Lederle, '*Kerkbegrip en kerkreg op die pad na kerklike eenheid*' (pp. 135–46).

28 W. D. Jonker, *Die Sendingbepalinge van die Nederduitse Gereformeerde Kerk van Transvaal* (Pietersburg: Studiegroep '*Kerk en Wêreld*', 1962), p. 19 (my translation).

29 R. Recker, in a review of C. Peter Wagner's *Our Kind of People*, in *Calvin Theological Journal* 15:2, Nov. 1980, pp. 303–4.

30 Cf. J. D. Vorster (ed.), *Veelvormingheid en Eenheid* (Cape Town, 1978).

31 F. G. M. Potgieter, '*Eenheid en veelvormigheid prinsipieel verantwoord*' in J. D. Vorster (ed.), op. cit., p. 29.

32 Cf. ibid. pp. 29–30.

33 See footnote 27 above.

34 C. René Padilla, 'The Unity of the Church and the Homogeneous Unit Principle' in *International Bulletin of Missionary Research* 6:1, Jan. 1982, p. 24; cf. p. 29.

35 Padilla, op. cit., p. 30.

4 DESMOND TUTU
Christianity and apartheid

In this essay I wish to show that apartheid, 'separate development', 'parallel democracy' or whatever this racist ideology is currently called is evil: totally and without remainder. I will attempt to do this as dispassionately and as clinically as possible, though this approach may appear to make the analyst somewhat coldblooded —for we are not dealing with statistics, but with people who know that they too, despite all appearances to the contrary, are God's children and not His stepchildren.

The Bible reveals that God's intention for all His creation and for all humankind is harmony, peace, unity, fellowship, friendship, justice and righteousness—conditions summed up in the almost untranslatable Hebrew word '*shalom*'. C. F. Evans* has described '*shalom*' thus:

Shalom is a comprehensive word, covering the manifold relationships of daily life, and expressing the ideal state of life in Israel. The fundamental meaning is 'totality' (the adjective *shalem* is translated 'whole'), 'well-being', 'harmony', with stress on material prosperity untouched by violence or misfortune. Peace is 'the untrammelled, free growth of the soul (i.e. person) . . . harmonious community; the soul can only expand in conjunction with other souls . . . every form of happiness and free expansion, but the kernel of it is the community with others, the foundation of life' (Johs. Pedersen, *Israel*, I-II, pp. 263–335). . . . A final peace as the gift of God in the coming age is a constituent of Old Testament eschatology, and is envisaged either as the abolition of war and the rule over the nations of Israel's messianic king (Isa. 9:2–7, Zech. 9:9f., Micah 5:5, Haggai 2:7–9), or as a paradisal existence in which all forms of strife will have been removed (Isa. 11:1f., 2:2–4, 65:25, Ezek. 34:25–28).

In the view of the biblical storyteller in the first creation narrative, the climax is reached when God creates human beings, and the most important feature of that part of the story is that they are

* 'Peace' in Alan Richardson (ed.), *A Theological Word Book of the Bible* (London, 1950), p. 165.

created in the image of God (Gen. 1:26). This is man's most important attribute. The Bible at this point makes no reference to racial,
ethnic or biological characteristics—which is remarkable considering
that the piece of writing in which this information is found is in a
proper sense chauvinistic.

Apartheid denies not only the biblical truths referred to above
but more astonishingly denies the central act of reconciliation
which the New Testament declares was achieved by God in His
Son, Jesus Christ. Apartheid maintains that human beings, God's
own creatures, are fundamentally irreconcilable, flatly contradicting the clear assertions of Scripture that God was in Christ reconciling the world to Himself. Reconciliation could be said to sum
up aptly our Lord's ministry and achievement. To deny that He
effected this is to deny not just a peripheral and fairly insignificant
Christian truth, but the heart of the Christian message. Apartheid,
is, therefore, a heresy. It is moreover morally reprehensible on account of its exorbitant cost in terms of human suffering. It is for
these reasons that I believe apartheid to be intrinsically evil.

THE DIVINE INTENTION IN CREATION
The Bible is unequivocal in describing God's purpose for the whole
of His creation. It does so both positively and negatively. In poetic,
highly imaginative language it speaks about the state of affairs as
God intended it to be at the beginning of creation. The first creation narrative (Gen. 1:1-2:4) ends with a description of the universe at peace. Man rules over the created universe on God's behalf. There is order and harmony. The narrative alludes to this
poetically when it shows that all animate nature is vegetarian.
There is no bloodshed, not even for sacrificial purposes. Here we
find God's *shalom*.

The second creation narrative containing the stories of Adam
and Eve and their descendants describes the idyllic condition in
the paradise of Eden. Adam and Even live in childlike innocence
gambolling with the animals, none of which preys on the others.
Lion and calf live happily together. There is harmony between
God and man, between man and his fellow man, between man and
the rest of God's creation. And man is at peace with himself as
well (Gen. 2:5-25).

The negative descriptions depict the situation when God's intention has been thwarted for the time being. The picture we get is of
disorder, disharmony, alienation and estrangement. There is here
for the first time in the creation story separation and disunity.

Adam and Eve, on account of their sin, lose their innocence and hide themselves from God (Gen. 3:8). There is disunity as Adam blames Eve for tempting him to disobey God's injunction (Gen. 3: 12). There is enmity between man and the animal word. He will henceforth crush the serpent's head and it will bruise his heel (Gen. 3:15). Nature has become red in tooth and claw. The rest of creation cannot escape the consequences of Adam's fall. It too is now in bondage and brings forth thistles because its human steward has gone disastrously astray (Gen. 3:18). Creation must await the setting free of man when it too will be liberated to celebrate the glorious liberty of the children of God. Thus separation, disunity and division are all due to sin and are contrary to the divine purpose.

The Old Testament proto-history culminates in the fearful story of the Tower of Babel where, because of human sin (*'hubris'*), God confuses men's tongues so that they are unable to communicate (Gen. 11:7). Sin makes it impossible for human beings to have fellowship. They are dispersed to all corners of the earth. That is not what God purposed for His human creatures. Consequently, with the whole situation crying out for reconciliation, for at-one-ment. He sets in motion the divine process which was to culminate in the crucifixion and resurrection of Jesus Christ. We might say then that the rest of the story of the Bible is how God goes about repairing the damage that sin caused, restoring the primordial harmony and unity that sin destroyed.

It is salutary to note how descriptions of paradise regained, of the so-called Messianic age, echo descriptions of the time of the begginning. This is the case for instance in Isaiah 11 where it is predicted that the wolf will again lie with the lamb and the calf and lion will grow up together. The animals will again be herbivorous, not preying on one another. Considering what we know of the enmity between Adam and the serpent, it is important that this messianic prophecy speaks about the child (Adam's descendant) playing over the cobra's hole and dancing over the viper's nest without coming to any harm (Isa. 11:4–9). Hermann Gunkel, the German biblical scholar, noting this 'nostalgic' character of the predictions of the future, said *'Endzeit ist Urzeit'*–'The end time is the beginning time.'

Apartheid contradicts the testimony of the Bible categorically. Whereas the Bible says God's intention for humankind and for His entire universe is harmony, peace, justice, wholeness, fellowship, apartheid says that human beings fundamentally are created for

separation, disunity and alienation. The apologists of apartheid
have sometimes used the story of the tower of Babel as divine sanction for their ideology of 'separate development' and ethnic identity. There is, of course, nothing wrong with racial and cultural
identity; in fact, we should celebrate these divine gifts. But we
should not give them an importance God never intended for them.
It is surely a perverse exegesis to say that a story that clearly describes God's punishment for human sin, and depicts that punishment as an inability on man's part to establish communication and
community with his fellow humans, is in fact one that sets forth
God's intention for His human creatures. It really is to stand
words on their head and to evacuate them of meaning. The Old
Testament knows of only one legitimate separation among persons
and that is the separation between believers and pagans. Every
other kind is si..ful.

CHRIST'S CHIEF WORK

The Gospel of Jesus Christ is a many-splendoured thing. It is like a
jewel with many facets to it. It speaks about the infinite value of
each individual person, the very hairs of whose head are numbered,
and whom the Good Shepherd knows by name. It assures us that
evil and death cannot have the last word, that at the centre of the
universe is a heart pulsating with a love that will not let us go, loving us not because we are lovable, but making us lovable by first
loving us, because 'whilst we were yet sinners, Christ died for us.'
(Ro. 5:8) We could also speak about the costliness of our redemption, indicating our worth in God's eyes. But however we approach
it, the heart of the Christian Gospel is summed up in the word
reconciliation. This means that Jesus came to restore friendship
and fellowship between God and man, between man and man, between man and the rest of God's creation. He was sent into the
world to effect atonement, at-one-ment; where there was disunity,
division, alienation and estrangement, He established their oppo-
sites—fellowship, unity, togetherness, friendliness, community,
peace and wholeness.

Jesus, speaking about the consequences of His sacrifice, said, 'I,
if I be lifted up, will draw all men to me.' (John 12:32) He unites
God's children of all races, colours, cultures, sexes and nationali-
ties in one fellowship, thereby transcending all those barriers and
distinctions humans often regard as overriding. 'God was in Christ
reconciling the world to Himself.' (II Cor. 5:19)

The spectacle of this new organism, the Church, which united the most unlikely and most uncongenial people into a viable fellowship, a brotherhood where slave and master, learned and unlettered, man and woman exchanged the kiss of peace, the sign of fellowship, amazed the pagans so much that it served as the best means for evangelization. It drew people into the Church in droves because they exclaimed, 'How these Christians love one another!' It was an irresistible magnet. St Paul grew indignant when the unity of the Church was undermined because it denied a central verity of the new faith that he was proclaiming. To him, denying this unity was tantamount to crucifying the Lord anew.

St Paul is constantly at pains to assert that though the Holy Spirit diverse peoples have been brought into one fellowship. They may have different spiritual gifts, they may carry out different functions, but it is precisely because of their diversity that they can subsist as one body (I Cor. 12:12–26). Diversity undergirds and leads to unity and interdependence, with the different limbs of the body each needing the others in order to live fully for the good of the whole. No part of the body is self-sufficient. God has created us unable to do everything of ourselves, so that we must depend on others in order to become fully human.

Apartheid turns all this upside down. It claims that our different identities, our diversity, demand separation and disunity. That is to deny a central biblical truth. It is to say that Jesus Christ has not in fact broken down the middle wall of partition that used to separate the Jew from the Gentile, making of the two one people with a common access through the one Spirit to the Father. Apartheid denies this when it decrees that membership of a Church is not open to people of races other than white, when this Church consistently turns away people of different races from its services, even funeral services. The New Testament can give no sanction to such theological aberrations. St Paul constantly refers to the fact that something quite new had come into the world with the death and resurrection of Jesus Christ: the drawing together of those who had previously seemed irreconcilable. 'For indeed we were all brought into one body by baptism, in the one Spirit, whether we are Jews or Greeks, whether slaves or free men, and that one Holy Spirit was poured out for all Christians to drink.' (I Cor. 12:13) 'Baptized into union with him, you have all put on Christ as a garment. There is no such thing as Jew and Greek, slave and free man, male and female; for you are all one person in Christ Jesus.' (Gal. 3:27–8). Apartheid declares that human beings are fundamentally irreconcilable, and that this is one of the most important facts about us. Consequently political dispensations must be so ordered as to take this fact into account.

Most exegetes would say that the description in Acts 2 of the first Christian Pentecost represents a comprehensive reversal of what took place in the Tower of Babel story. The building of Babel resulted in a dispersal of peoples. At Pentecost there was a gathering in and bringing together of different peoples from the various parts of the globe. (Pentecost in the Jewish calendar celebrates the *gathering in* of the wheat harvest at the climax of the week of weeks after the Passover.) After Babel the people could not understand one another; at Pentecost all could understand the descriptions of the mighty works of God. In building Babel they had all attempted sinfully to storm heaven. At Pentecost they had all gathered to praise God. It is surely therefore strange to claim for an ideology so at variance with the Gospel—one that breeds disunity, estrangement, alienation, greater polarisation among people of different races and groups, that accomplishes exactly the same results as we have shown to be the consequences of sin according to the Bible—that such an ideology is actually consistent with the Scriptures.

THE DIVINE IMAGE

The first creation narrative was written during the Babylonian exile, and in part was meant to bolster the sagging morals of the Jewish exiles by showing just how much greater their God was than the Babylonian deities. In a proper sense therefore it was intended to be chauvinistic propaganda. The climax of the story occurs in Gen. 1:26 with the creation of human beings in the image and likeness of God. What is extraordinary is that this assertion that human persons are created in the divine image is meant to apply to all human beings at a time when it would have been understandable if the author had somehow indicated that it applied only to Jews. It is all the more remarkable then that no ethnic, racial or other biological factors are mentioned as significant in the make-up of human beings. The most important fact about us, says the author, is that we are created in God's image. For this reason every human being is God's representative. This is what endows us all with infinite worth and human dignity. It is a spiritual reality. It explains why all of us have moral freedom, why we can converse with God, why we have a 'God instinct'.

Apartheid says that the most important fact about us is our ethnicity, some biological attribute that is really an irrelevance in determining our human worth. It exalts a particular biological characteristic to a universal principle determining what it means to be human. Some are more human than others. 'Blacks are human, but. . . .' Skin colour and race assume an importance they never had in the Scriptures. Skin colour and race become salvation principles, since in many cases they determine which people can participate in which church services—which are believed to be of saving significance. It is not enough to be baptised after confessing that Jesus Christ is Lord and Saviour. One must possess yet another attribute, which in the nature of the case must be reserved only for a select few. It is as if St Paul never had the controversies with the Judaisers, who demanded that new Gentile converts had to be circumcised, thus undermining the fact that salvation was a gracious and unmerited gift from God. It is as ridiculous to insist that race and skin and culture are crucial factors about our human nature as it would be to say that, in addition to being baptised, converts had to have big noses. . . . You could then put up signs saying 'Big Noses Only', and have certain facilities reserved only for Big Noses. . . . Professor Kosuke Koyama, a Japanese theologian, on a recent visit to South Africa observed with great insight that racism was actually pornographic because it exalted a particular biological attribute (other than sexual) out of all proportion and removed it from a context where it was properly significant.

APARTHEID'S COST IN HUMAN SACRIFICE
When moralists are uncertain about the moral quality of an act or policy, they will often seek to find out what the consequences of such an act or policy are. If these are evil, then the probability is that the original act or policy is itself evil. Christianity is unhappy with the dictum that the end justifies the means, especially when what is involved is the happiness of human beings. The philosopher Immanuel Kant observed that human persons should never be considered to be a means to be manipulated, or used to achieve some end, however worthwhile. Persons are always ends in themselves.

In concrete terms, apart from the deep hurts that the apartheid policy daily inflicts on all its victims (what those who are not at the receiving end call the pinpricks of 'petty apartheid'), such as the assault on human dignity when a black adult is addressed as 'boy' or 'girl'; when any black over sixteen years can be accosted in the street and asked to produce a document proving his right to be there; when a black cannot expect the common courtesies as a right; when a shop assistant looks at him with dead eyes that light up when a white person is addressed with a smile—there is the agony of 'grand apartheid', the policy designed to turn blacks into aliens in their own land, so that there will be no black South Africans.

This policy demands the uprooting of millions (at the latest count over two million) blacks from their homes, to be dumped in arid, often inaccessible, so-called resettlement camps in the bantustans, those ghettos of poverty and misery, inexhaustible reservoirs of cheap labour. I have visited many such dumping grounds and will never forget the little girl who said that when there is no food to borrow, they drink water to fill their stomachs. People starve in a land of record crop surpluses, because of a deliberate government policy. A black man must leave his family to go to town as a migrant worker, to live an unnatural existence in a single hostel. Black family life is being destroyed by a policy that from its inception all other nations have condemned as a cancer in society. It is apartheid that decreed that blacks must have an inferior education, which state of affairs led directly to the 1976 riots that caused so much carnage and loss of life and property.

Because apartheid is utterly unacceptable to the vast majority of the population of South Africa, it has to be applied by using laws that would be the envy of a totalitarian state—laws that permit indefinite detention without trial, that abrogate the rule of law, that lead to the evil of mysterious deaths in detention, that sanction arbitrary banning orders, with the victim having no right of defence as he does not know what case he must answer, and being turned into a non-person living a twilight existence. It is the apartheid system which has decreed that South Africa should be involved in an unnecessary border war, which is really a civil war. It is apartheid that has led so many South Africans to go into exile and to suffer the lot of the exile. The catalogue is long. But I hope I have shown that apartheid deserves to be condemned as morally reprehensible because it has caused and continues to cause so much human suffering.

* * *

I have tried to show that apartheid is intrinsically and irredeemably evil. For my part, its most vicious, indeed its most blasphemous aspect, is not the great suffering it causes its victims, but that it can make a child of God doubt that he is a child of God. For that alone, it deserves to be condemned as a heresy. Real peace and security will come to our beloved land only when apartheid has been dismantled. I have no doubt that this will happen. If God be for us, who can be against us?

5 SIMON MAIMELA
An anthropological heresy: A critique
of white theology

The concept of man in white theology is very difficult for a black person to understand. This portrait of man is one that a black person cannot identify himself with, because this man is to him an incurably dangerous monster. Two major principles, one theoretical and the other practical, have contributed to the formation of this white anthropology.

THE THEORY OF MAN IN WHITE THEOLOGY
Wishing to remain faithful to the belief that South Africa is a 'Christian country' and therefore that its view of man should be Christian, white theology on the theoretical level consciously tries to present a consistently biblical anthropology. On this level, there are positive affirmations about the human self that even those who are not white can applaud and embrace. For instance, even the most conservative theological statement by the Dutch Reformed Church such as *Human Relations and the South African Scene in the Light of Scripture*(1) easily affirms that: humans are creatures of God; they are created in God's image and are also primordially interrelated; they have a fundamental unity as well as equality by reason of their common origin in the first human parents Adam and Noah; they are brothers who must live in stable and peaceful relationships with one another, being at the same time accountable to God to whom they are vertically related. Humans are all sinners (outsiders) in the family of God and therefore are offered the same salvation without distinction, that is, no human being is deemed worthier or better than anyone else. Since they are children of God by sheer grace alone, they are commanded to love one another because they are responsible for one another in love; they must accept their neighbours in their own right and accord them room for self-fulfilment, thereby working for social justice, which the 'golden rule' demands from each of them in their private and public interrelationships. Since their national, social and sexual differences are transcended by the fact of the 'new unity in Christ',

humans must work for mutual respect and understanding, thereby building bridges to prevent sinful 'spiritual' estrangement. To do this they should practise open church membership so that no believer is excluded on the basis of national grouping or race, for the only criterion for membership should be whether a person proclaims Jesus Christ as his/her Saviour and Head. In fact white theology goes so far as to encourage people to work for unity both in theory and application, because those who are redeemed in Christ are no longer individuals, strangers to one another or independent of one another; for in baptism they have joined one body which binds them into a unity with their Head, Christ. In this new unity, they are a provisional manifestation of the new humanity which is still being recreated in the image of God, and as such must, through the guidance of the Word and Spirit, strive to give expression to their newness in Christ through concord and brotherly love.(2)

The theory of man in white theology that I have tried to outline here, a theory affirming the human self as the child, son or daughter of God, is thoroughly biblical and positive. One wishes it was professed without heavy qualifications, without many 'buts' and conditions and brackets. Indeed if this theory of human selves was affirmed without equivocation, if it was affirmed not merely 'in principle and under certain conditions', if it was lived out and embodied in daily white Christian obedience, then blacks would have no difficulty appropriating and claiming it for themselves, and South Africa would have vindicated its claim as a 'Christian country'. Even more, if our profession that humans are God's children who are ineluctably related as brothers and sisters was applied in our daily lives, we would have ideal interpersonal relations. In short, we would not have a 'race problem'.

However, day to day life in South Africa tells a different story, a story suggesting that our real lives have not been moulded or informed by the theoretical affirmations of white theology. Consequently, a week never passes by without one reading about disputes and debates as to whether blacks and whites should attend the same cchurches. Congregants revolt against policies that promote Christian mutual acceptance between the supposedly 'new creatures' in Christ. An interesting example is the controversy that has recently rocked the little community of Boshoff in the Orange Free State, resulting in the resignation of church officials who disagreed with their pastor when he declared that blacks and whites must worship together because their racial differences are transcended in Christ.(3) One may also recall stories in the press of Churches that would not allow blacks to attend the funerals of their white friends. Debates are heard about new church policies regarding the opening of private schools to all races. Debates are heard about the undesirability of sharing parks, beaches, cinemas, restaurants and so on. Debates are heard about the undesirability of a unitary common fatherland and citizenship. Some even dream about a 'white homeland' so that whites might insulate themselves against blacks. Indeed, the glorification of isolationism has such an appeal that Christians have been tempted to believe that differences in languages and cultures are insurmountable absolutes that must be allowed to override any unity in Christ that believers claim they have. Not surprisingly we read that racial division is itself Christian or biblical teaching.(4)

To sum up: the history of South Africa, both past and present, shows that whites have never put into practice their theories about our common human origin. They have not accepted blacks as brothers and sisters in Christ to whom they are united and related through their common God and Father. They have never put to practice their theories about human equivalence by virtue of human solidarity in sin. Refusing to practise their professed belief that no one is better than any other, they have always wanted to separate themselves.(5) Indeed, it is one of the strangest twists of logic that the Christian faith should be used as the strongest tool to divide rather than to weld together and reconcile.(6) This is exactly what happened in South Africa when Christians allowed physical and cultural differences to become barriers to wipe out any meaningful trace of biblical influence on white anthropology.

What I am claiming here amounts to this: biblical anthropology and white anthropology are mutually exclusive. To explain this, it is necessary to delve more deeply into the unargued, hidden and unconscious anthropological presuppositions of white theology, presuppositions that shape, inform and dictate white behaviour.

THE WHITE CHRISTIAN'S PRACTICAL VIEW OF MAN

A fully-fledged white anthropology is beyond the scope of this paper, but I shall try to give a broad outline as it strikes a black reader. If a distortion should arise it may be that white theology has not communicated itself clearly to those who are not white.

A good place to locate what the white South African Christian believes the human self to be is in his past and present *praxis*. An examination of this will reveal both his conscious and unconscious ideas, both his private and public understandings of himself and others. And thus we shall be led on to the socio-political, cultural and economic facts of life as these relate to the questions of apartheid, integration, white survival and self-determination. Here we meet not theories but historical agents in whom white Christianity is embodied, and an analysis of their actions reveals the real white anthropology as it works itself out in the history of South Africa. It is here that the *locus* of white anthropology is to be found.

Penetrating deeply into this layer of hidden, undeclared presuppositions of man in general, presuppositions that mould white thoughts about and behaviour towards themselves and towards people of other races, one is startled to discover that at its core the white Christian concept of the human self is not informed and shaped by biblical principles, but by principles that are decidedly heathen and unchristian. I am aware that this assertion will strike most whites as an unfair, unfounded allegation. However, I believe my contention can be borne out by the facts of white historical praxis, facts that strongly suggest that the white Christian's concept of man is much more Hobbesian than Christian. Agreeing with Hobbes (and Marx?(7)), the white Christian's view of the human self portrays man as a creature who is dominated by self-centred social drives, seeking to acquire as much wealth, power and prestige as he can for himself or his group or class, and caring for no others except as they are necessary tools for his personal gratification. True to its Hobbesian (Marxist?) orientation, white anthropology depicts a world in which every human self is the enemy of every other self. Not surprisingly the government becomes the only power capable of preventing the 'war of each against all and all against each.'(8)

It is against the background of these negative, cynical and pessimistic anthropological presuppositions, presuppositions much more heathen and unchristian than biblical in their orientation and content that we should try to understand white historical praxis in South Africa. Faithful to its creed, white anthropology holds the view that human interrelations can never be creative and positive because ultimately each human poses a danger to all the others. Nourished by this white 'spirituality', it is not surprising that white Christian historians want to see history through Hobbesian spectacles. Predictably, white history books are full of stories about African fratricidal rivalries before the white man came to secure peace between various ethnic groups. And as soon as the whites had settled, history becomes one in which the crude brutalities that either blacks or whites suffered at the hands of one another must necessarily predominate. The accent is always on the negative aspects of these inter-racial contacts, as if no positive, friendly interrelations had taken place. Details of stock-thefts, misconstructed treaties, cheating and heinous crimes that blacks are alleged to have perpetrated against innocent whites fill the pages of history-books. Nothing good or creative was to be found among blacks, because they were 'barbarous, . . . beasts in the skins of men; as they may appear by their ignorance, habit, language; with other things, which make them brutish'(9), beings with 'no order in Nature, no shame, no truth.'(10) This kind of historical framework which makes selective use of data to present a negative view may very well fit into the negative white Christian's presupposition of the human self, and may be of interest to those whites who are fascinated by strife and the conflictual dimensions of human relations, but, by the deliberate exclusion of the cooperative, friendly, and creative efforts that have made South Africa into what it is, it does not tell our children the whole story.

It is to be regretted that this view prevails today. Hence the white press and white alarmist religionists(11) dwell on the demonic nature of man and on the human readiness to destroy others rather than on the goodwill and readiness among humans to co-operate, help each other and promote the well-being of all. White anthropology teaches us that humans have uncontrollable fratricidal drives which even the Gospel and conversion cannot tame. Consequently, it teaches both whites and blacks, adults and children, to project on to others the capacity to wound and destroy. And it is this projection that makes our police panicky when dealing with unarmed, peaceful demonstrations. They may appear trigger-happy but they really believe and have been taught to fear humans by the white practical view of man.

Having been taught to presuppose the worst in human relations, it should not surprise us that white Christians will easily and without reflection work to discourage contacts between black groups who for their own good must be separated into self-enclosed entities.(12) The white Christian cannot conceive of a situation where blacks and whites can meet and work jointly for their common good. This explains the fury of some conservative whites at the suggestion that blacks should serve on the President's Council, or that a national convention be held so that blacks and whites can hammer out their common future. To these whites, the coming together of blacks and whites necessarily invites the dangers that should be avoided at all cost, the dangers that we will cut each other's throats and that whites will get the worst deal leading to their extinction.(13) Indeed, the negative presupposition is so predominant among whites that even the so-called liberals of the Progressive Federal Party cannot conceive of a unitary state and one-man-one-vote without postulating all kinds of dangers that might befall the minorities. Thus they implicitly subscribe to the view that humans are by design and nature bent on destroying each other. And thus the power of the government is invoked to impose safeguards for minorities: imposing order because left to themselves humans cannot be good neighbours. And indeed there are even people who have concluded not only that the whites have the *'swart gevaar'* and the 'race problem' on their hands, but also that each 'ethnic group' poses grave dangers for every other—and so it becomes a risky business to marry and live among Zulus if one is a Sotho, etc.

To be sure, it cannot be denied that our world is a dangerous place, that people can and do destroy others. An objective reader of South African history cannot remain unmoved by the violent aspects of the initial encounters between blacks and whites leading to destructive confrontations and the loss of lives of both blacks and whites. Even today there continue to be clashes and killings, a good example being the conflicts of June 1976. But the temptation and the tendency here is to overreact to both real and fantasy dangers, to distort reality. This is largely due to fear and a sense of vulnerability. But a fair reading of our history both past and present does indicate that there have been positive and creative relations between people, that people are not programmed by nature to destroy others.

It may perhaps be unfair to expect the white Churches and Christians to be other than advocates of a very pessimistic view of human nature, in the face of the hard practical experience of life in this country. Seeking resources to deal with new situations that appeared threatening, they fell back upon the tradition they knew, the Paul-Augustine-Luther-Calvin theological tradition.(14) Unfortunately this tradition had the effect of darkening or blurring white perceptions of what is truly human. The theological tradition from which they sought ethical guidelines is itself notorious for taking a rather dim and pessimistic view of the human self. It teaches that as a result of the fall man is a totally depraved being who has had all his powers crippled. Humans are inherently not good and cannot perform good works; they cannot act justly, creatively and responsibly towards their fellows and therefore cannot be relied upon for help and promotion of lives of others. It is a tradition that often delights in rebuking social activists for their optimism about human possibilities to change and to do good. Rather it tends to remind humans of how low, useless, rotten and sinful they are, thereby cultivating a low self-esteem. Its goal is not to make humans feel good about themselves and others. Even less does it aim to teach people through preaching and counselling that fellow humans can be trusted, can be regarded as friends who mean well for us by the virtue of the fact that they have been commanded by God to care for, protect and love us. It cannot do this because it is a theological tradition that is 'grounded in self-hate rather than in self-love and brother-love'.(15) And once people begin to believe that there is no good that they can do, does it come as a surprise that white Christians, nurtured in this tradition, project on their black countrymen and women the capacity to hurt and destroy them, and therefore to feel themselves justified in advocating the unbiblical, pessimistic, practical view of man that has just been outlined?

To sum up: we have two strong historical forces, the hard practical experiences of South African life on one hand, and a theological tradition on the other hand, that have collaborated to reinforce a very negative white anthropological presupposition of the human self in general. It became a short step not to seek Christian solutions but to look to the government to come up with ultimate principles and solutions, namely, a final salvation or protection of one's race or group from other humans who are looked upon as dangerous, to be avoided through a series of separations. In order to implement these principles, a government with an unquenchable thirst for the control of human lives and movement was instituted, with a machinery of functionaries to direct the country's talents, resources and energies towards

... discovering and creating boundaries, legalities, rules, contracts, protective devices, and various structures that will embody the controls that seem necessary to keep life in order.(16)

These devices, such as the Pass Laws, Group Areas Act, Separate Amenities Acts, Mixed Marriages and Immorality Acts, Population Registration Act, emanate from a philosophy of group survival in a world believed to be populated by monstrous human selves.(17) Being pre-occupied with final solutions and principles, white South Africans have made the truly human, the ordinary persons of blood and flesh that they meet on the street, victims, objects of manipulation, things, to be shoved around and strategized about. Indeed, as De Klerk points out, principles are often preferred to concrete persons.(18) People seem rather slow to learn that these principles, which claim to care much about 'race relations' or 'group survival', are nothing but abstractions existing in the heads of theorists, and in fact look past ordinary human beings and have no feeling for the agony of the people they purport to help.

These principles stem from a white theological anthropology whose grip will lead blacks either to death or to revolt. Black Christians have little option but to reject it in the name of Christ, who did not come to die for abstract and impersonal forces or things such as race or group but for concrete individual men and women who, not as a conglomerate and undifferentiated race, group, *'volk'* or mass, but as single persons, accept Him as Saviour.

THE ALTERNATIVES TO WHITE THEOLOGICAL ANTHROPOLOGY

It has already been said that white theological anthropology must be rejected on the basis of its own historical praxis. But if we were to rest our rejection on historical grounds alone, we would not have said much because human culture and activities are ambiguous: beauty and good are interpersed with evil and the demonic. The white Christian's practical view of man must also be rejected on biblical grounds; for it is in the Bible where the truly human has been revealed. The Bible teaches us something specific about human selves; it sets limits about what can be said about man. It teaches us that humans, though originally good creatures of God, have through the fall become corrupt, twisted, misdirected and are deeply immersed in sin that pervades their lives and work (Gen. 8: 21; Ps. 51:5; 58:3; Jn. 3:6; Rom. 5:12-21, 7:7-20). Because of sin humans do not love and serve each other as they should; they love and relate to each other wrongly; they organize their communities in irrational paths (Gen. 4:8-14; I Jn. 4:7-12, 19-21). But the Bible does not conclude that humans are by nature wholly evil. There is nothing natural about their inability to love and care for each other. There is nothing natural about sinning, about their tendency to destroy themselves and others. If there were, the Creator would not be treating humans so differently from brute animals, and would not be making each one morally accountable before Him.

The Bible teaches that humans are special and unique creatures

because of the dignity and value that God has conferred upon
them (Gen. 1:26f; 2:7). They are endowed with glory as those
who are created in God's image (I Cor. 11:7). They are valued
beings in the eyes of their Creator and, despite their insignificance
by appearance or abilities, despite their immersion in sin and faults,
God is committed to and wills to be with them as their Father.
Humans are God's trusted and loved creatures into whose hands
He joyously and with no hesitation delivered the entire creation
(Gen. 1:28–30, 9:1–3; Ps. 8:6–8), risking thereby the entire world
with them and staying by them, surrounding them with love, and
reproving them as a father would his son in whom he delights
(Prov. 3:12). Furthermore the Creator also gave them enough authority to care and manage creation with minimum interference,
provided they are responsible and answerable in their actions to
Him. As valued creatures whom He trusts, God believes humans
can act responsibly, decide and act maturely in relation to other
creatures.

By stressing the fact that we belong to each other and are
related as those who are brothers and sisters, the Bible wants us to
assume a posture so trusting as to regard all human relationships—
regardless of race or group affiliations—as potentially nourishing to
all who meet as persons. It wants us to assume that coming together in human fellowship is benign and enriching to both sides.
It wants us to believe that because the world is full of brothers and
sisters it is hospitable and is our home, a world in which

... all persons are available to me if I can learn how to contact them; all wisdom is available to me if I can learn how to see it; all help is there for me if I
can learn how to accept it; all love is there for me if I can be in it.(19)

Some of you might be feeling uneasy about the optimistic anthropology that is being advocated here; you might even complain
that I am crediting humans with too much ability to bring about
humane interpersonal relations. You might charge that this is an
unrealistic and utopian view of man which does not take seriously
the consequences of fall. My only defence is that this positive and
optimistic view of humankind is taught by the Bible itself. We as
Christians have little choice but to embrace this positive view of
human selves as the basis of human interrelations here and now.
Not that we must not take seriously the perversion of sin, but we
happen to believe that God's redemption in Jesus Christ is able to
heal even the most stubborn and virulent human diseases of the
heart. To be sure, sin is deeply rooted in human hearts and all human works, but the entire Christian message of conversion and

reconciliation is premised on the understanding that humans have been and continue to be changed by God, who continues to mould them into new creatures. We are not free to deny that the power of God's Word and Spirit can turn enemies into brothers and sisters in Christ. For Christ died in order to heal what sin has infected with sickness and death, to renew the entire human race and all human relations.

Christians cannot both believe in the possibility of Christ's and our ultimate resurrection from the dead and continue to remain sceptical about God's ability to overcome evil in human relations here and now. For if God's power is sufficient to bring about a great miracle of resurrection and ushering in the coming Kingdom, it surely cannot fail to change us into the beings He intended us to be, beings capable of loving community. This is then the basis of the Christian justification for the proclamation of a positive anthropology, which we must not only believe and pray for, but work hard to realise in our dealings with our human fellows—to whom Jesus Christ is related as their Brother and God as their Father (Rom. 8:14–17).

Notes

1 Cf. *Human Relations and the South African Scene in the Light of Scripture* (Pretoria, 1975).

2 Ibid., pp. 18–19, 30–34, 37, 47, 71, 85.

3 David Jackson, 'Three NGK Officials quit over Open-door Policy on Blacks' in *Sunday Times*, 26 October 1980, p. 24. Boesak lamenting over this Church apartheid writes: 'We share precious little, we do not worship or live together, so we do not know each other. . . . Their sons they send to work in the black Church have, with few notable exceptions, not identified with the black Church; they remain strangers', in the *Rand Daily Mail*, 1 August 1980, p. 10.

4 This is the main claim of *Human Relations and the South African Scene in the Light of Scripture.*

5 Jane M. Sales, *The Planting of the Churches in South Africa* (Grand Rapids, 1971), p. 19.

6 Johann Strauss, *Sociology II, Book 3* (Unisa, 1971), pp. 64–5, 68.

7 Commonly Marxism and South African white Christian anthropology are believed to be mortal enemies, yet there is something that they agree on: both stress the fact that humans (in Marxism one class is in mortal struggle with another, in white Christian anthropology one group, people or race poses a danger to others) are locked in a death struggle against one another. Their practical view of man is essentially the same, hence the tendency to wish to control human thought and movement is discernible in both systems.

8 The best summary is found in Alex Inkeles, *What is Sociology?* (Englewood Cliffs, 1964), p. 49.

9 Sales, op. cit., p. 13.

10 Ibid., p. 13.

11 Cf. Dominee Senekal of Bronkhorstspruit who uses Scripture to support Church apartheid, arguing that any meaningful intergroup relations would necessarily lead to mass integration and the total annihilation of the Afrikaners (*Rand Daily Mail*, 26 November 1980, p. 15).

12 M. Buthelezi, in 'The Ethical Questions raised by Nationalism' in *Church and Nationalism in South Africa* (Johannesburg, 1975), complains about the legislative destruction of all Christian efforts to strengthen the bonds of fellowship between people, and writes: 'It is not considered a healthy thing for Zulus to be together with Sothos, let alone Indians or coloureds, and further still let alone white people' (p. 102).

13 Cf. *To The Point*, 13 October 1980, p. 20.

14 Cf. G. D. Scholtz, cited by Strauss in *Sociology II*, op. cit., pp. 64–5, and W. A. de Klerk, *The Puritans in Africa* (London, 1975), p. 3, agree that Reformed ethics determined white attitudes in their dealings with blacks, attitudes that held to the belief that Christians (synonymous with whites) and barbarians (synonymous with blacks) do not mix.

15 W. Brueggemann, *In Man We Trust* (Atlanta, 1972), p. 102.

16 Jack Gibb, *Trust: A New View of Personal and Organizational Development* (The Guild of Tutors Press, 1978), p. 30.

17 *To The Point*, op. cit., p. 20.

18 De Klerk, op. cit., p. 121.

19 Gibb, op. cit., p. 83.

6

CHARLES VILLA-VICENCIO
An all-pervading heresy: Racism and the 'English-speaking Churches'

Dr Allan Boesak has recently observed that 'the white Dutch Reformed Churches must assume special responsibility' for the prevailing apartheid policy of South Africa. 'Apartheid has been born in the womb of the white NGK. Details of the policy were worked out by that Church and it has provided moral and theological justification for apartheid.'(1)

There was a time when the NGK would have welcomed an allegation such as this. Shortly after the election of the National Party to power in 1948, *Die Kerkbode*, the official newspaper of the NGK, noted with pride: 'As a Church we have always worked purposefully for the separation of the races. In this regard apartheid can rightfully be called a church policy.'(2) And Dr Boesak quotes 'an Afrikaner churchman' as saying, 'After 1948, it was not necessary for the NGK to make policy pronouncements, because the government was faithfully executing apartheid—the NGK's own creation.'(3) Yet there have of course been some classic pronouncements of this nature since 1948. In 1970 Dr J. D. Vorster, the then Moderator of the NGK in the Cape, defended apartheid thus:

Our only guide is the Bible. Our policy and outlook on life are based on the Bible. We firmly believe the way we interpret it is right. We will not budge one inch from our interpretation to satisfy anyone in South Africa or abroad. The world may differ from our interpretation. This will not influence us. The world may be wrong. We are right and will continue to follow the way the Bible teaches.(4)

Then there are the views of Dr A. P. Treurnicht, a former minister of the NGK and now leader of the Conservative Party, with its apparently broad-based white grassroots support. He has defended apartheid in numerous statements such as the following:

I know of no other policy as moral, as responsible to Scripture, as the policy of separate development. . . . If the . . . Christian Afrikaner can be convinced there are no principles or biblical foundations for this policy of separate development, it is but a step to the conviction that it is un-Christian. And if we believe it is un-Christian or immoral it is our obligation to fight it.(5)

The pertinent question is whether these are statements of an age past or perhaps an extremist fringe group, or whether they are reflective of the contemporary mainstream position of the Afrikaans Reformed Churches. Since the historic Ottawa statement declaring apartheid a heresy, the leadership of the NGK has certainly made a concerted effort to justify the racial policy of their Church in relation to that decision. Dr Pierre Rossouw, the Chief Executive Officer of the NGK, is careful to point out that the official documents of his Church state that a person may not be denied entry to a service of worship on the grounds of colour. Professor Johan Heyns has in turn said that if apartheid is a policy which safeguards the political and economic privileges of whites at the cost of blacks it is both 'sinful and heretical', and if his Church were guilty of turning away black members and denying black people access to the communion table he would already have resigned from that Church. Even Professor Albert Geyser, who was driven out of the NHK more that twenty years ago because of his protest against Article 3 of the constitution of his Church, which explicitly excludes black people from membership, has said a word on behalf of the NGK, to the effect that it has not written racial segregation into its constitution in a similar way.

This endless discussion of policy statements, doctrinal presuppositions and idealistic superstructures for the co-existence of people of different colour has, however, been brushed aside by the WARC as evasive and irrelevant. The emphasis of world-wide Christianity today, while not denying the importance of 'correct doctrine', rejects its isolation from life. Doctrine and faith are inextricably bound up with ethics and behaviour; put differently, 'ortho-belief' cannot be separated from 'orthopraxis'. This is the heart of the significance of the WARC decision: which involves more Churches than the NGK and the NHK, and turns what could have been a parochial, 'in-house', ecclesiastical squabble within the Dutch Reformed family of Churches into a *status confessionis* which challenges all Christians in and beyond South Africa.

Those Churches that have given birth to and nurtured apartheid, which condemns millions of black people to a sub-human form of existence in re-settlement camps and ghettos, stand condemned by this decision. Other Churches in this country, notably the so-called English-speaking Churches, face a different form of challenge and moral condemnation. Their stance on apartheid has been different. They, and especially the member Churches of the SACC, together with the Roman Catholic Church, have constantly and explicitly condemned apartheid as being contrary to the Word of God. Yet the life-styles, the socio-political values and practices of their members have not been vastly different from those of their counterparts in the Afrikaans-speaking Reformed Churches.

This is not to suggest that there is no fundamental theological or political difference between the two groups of Churches. There *is* a significant difference. The Afrikaans Reformed Churches continue to create the atmosphere for the implementation of apartheid as a 'Christian' policy. The English-speaking Churches have allowed this practice to continue but have repeatedly called it un-Christian. It is significant, however, that when Bishop Tutu said that one could not support apartheid and continue to regard oneself as being a Christian he was condemned by Afrikaans- and English-speaking clergy alike. By shifting its attention from policy to practice the WARC strikes at the heart of the witness of both these groups of Churches. Its concern is with the contradiction between word and practice, and this has direct implications for the church–state relations of both groups.

The decision of the WARC is that the membership of the NGK and the NHK stands suspended until: (a) black Christians are no longer excluded from church services, especially from holy communion; (b) concrete support in word and deed is given to those who suffer under the weight of apartheid ('separate development'); (c) unequivocal synod resolutions are made which reject apartheid and commit the Church to dismantling this system in both Church and state.

An important question concerns the extent to which the other Churches in South Africa have a clean bill of health in regard to these matters.

WHERE CHURCHES DIFFER

Leaving aside the manifold ideological divisions within and between Churches, this essay will concentrate on a particular tension, namely, the traditional political strain that exists between the Afrikaans-speaking Reformed Churches and the member Churches of the SACC.

Afrikaans-speaking Reformed Churches

The WARC statement adopted in Ottawa provides an accurate

description of the ideological position of these Churches: 'The Nederduitse Gereformeerde Kerk and the Nederduitsch Hervormde Kerk, in not only accepting but actively justifying the apartheid system by misusing the Gospel and the Reformed confession, contradict in doctrine and in action the promise which they profess to believe.' Since this decision, the NHK has withdrawn from this body stating that it 'cannot comply with the requirements set out by the WARC'. This Church has clearly declared itself to support apartheid by saying that 'A policy of separate and equal opportunities is not in conflict with the Scriptures.' The full text of the statement released by the NHK is included among the appendices included in this volume. It needs also to be added that the third Afrikaans Reformed Church in the country, the Gereformeerde Kerk, has never been a member of the WARC. The exclusivist doctrine of this church has isolated it from ecumenical influences, but it is often pointed out by its members that their 1961 synod rejected discrimination on racial grounds and instituted a General Synod where synods which are 'ethnically different' are given equal representation. A Gereformeerde theologian, Professor B. Spoelstra, has said:

Officially, therefore, the Gereformeerde Church rejects any suggestion that racial discrimination should be legitimated within the Church. In practice, however, problems as the result of non-ecclesiastical factors may lead to a renunciation of the principle.(6)

Calvin taught that it is within the womb of the Church that Christians are born and that they are nourished at her breast in order that they may be one in Christ, the only Lord of the Church.(7) Yet it can be shown beyond all doubt that the Afrikaans Reformed Churches gave birth to and have nourished the policy of apartheid. No honest and serious student of South African politics and theology would try to deny that. At most, those who seek to promote the Christian and Reformed integrity of these Churches would argue that they no longer seek to justify apartheid theologically, and that there is a restlessness within for renewal and moral reform.(8) To such pleading one can respond by identifying certain undeniable facts:

1 In the stormy aftermath of the Sharpeville shootings in 1960 the WCC called its South African member Churches (including the NGK of the Cape Province and the Transvaal) into consultation at Cottesloe. This was to become a major watershed in normative NGK ideology. The consultation came to conclusions which amounted to a complete rejection of the biblical and theological justification

of apartheid. The importance of these conclusions takes on even greater significance when one realizes that they were basically in accordance with certain study projects that had already been undertaken by the NGK.(9) Although mild by today's standards, this was probably the most serious theological threat to apartheid in the history of Afrikaner church–state relations. W. A. de Klerk tells of the events that followed this threat from this unexpected quarter.

Magisterially, Verwoerd [the Prime Minister of the time] in effect called the Dutch Reformed theologians to order. They had been unduly influenced by the World Council of Churches, in the end submitting to their liberal views.... Theologians, too, had to keep a single mind, remembering the high purpose of apartheid.... Neither would he allow this group of leading [NGK] churchmen to confuse the nation. They would have to recant. And they did: enough of them and in sufficient measure to undo everything that had taken place at Cottesloe.(10)

Enough NGK theologians were tamed to ensure the continued support of apartheid. Some quietly withdrew from the political challenge of the day, others busied themselves with changing 'individual attitudes', leaving the necessary structural changes to others, and still others became the high priests of the Afrikaner civil religion that would justify apartheid, not only for Afrikaners, but for many English-speaking whites who would happily take comfort that they could be both Christians and racists. There were few—Beyers Naudé was one—who would eventually break their ties with the white NGK in order to be obedient to God. The NGK still stands by its rejection of the findings of the Cottesloe conference, and has since withdrawn from the WCC and shared in the government's attack on this organization, the SACC and other ecumenical bodies.

2 In 1970 the General Synod of the NGK appointed a commission under Ds W. A. Landman to prepare a statement on race relations. The 1974 General Synod did not approve the entire report and chose simply to note certain more progressive findings, which were deleted from the final report, *Ras, Volk en Nasie en Volkereverhoudinge in die lig van die Skrif.* There are two essays in response to this report included in this book, which makes it unnecessary to comment on it any further. Suffice it to say that the report is firmly grounded in the framework of apartheid and provides a Scriptural basis for apartheid and white domination. In spite of the numerous critiques of this report by individuals and other Churches it is still the official statement of the NGK on race

relations.(11) The 1982 General Synod of this Church has, however, referred this document to a revisions committee, and although
it was suggested that this committee should include members of
the black NG Churches, this was rejected by the Synod.

3 Calvin stated that 'Wherever we see the Word of God purely
preached and *heard*, the Sacraments administered according to
Christ's institution, there, it is not to be doubted, a Church of God
exists.'(12) When debate has ended on the extent to which the
Afrikaans Reformed Churches theologically support apartheid, it
cannot be denied or questioned that they are *heard* by the overwhelming majority of their members and others to be supporting,
justifying and promoting it. A milieu has been created and nurtured
for generations in these Churches which has, generally speaking,
both modified the proclamation of the Word and caused congregations to *hear* it as promoting government policy. It is not therefore
without cause that the NGK has been referred to as 'the government at prayer'. Likewise, whatever the policy of the NGK may
be, *in practice* black and white members do not normally receive
the Sacrament of Holy Communion together. In fact, when an
Afrikaans Reformed preacher attacks apartheid as being contrary
to the Scripture or objects to a black person being turned away
from worship, this inevitably elicits protest from local church
councils, and is regarded as significant enough to make newspaper
headlines. The Ottawa conference concerned itself therefore not
only with principles and doctrines, but with the manner in which
such formulations are applied and practised—that is, *heard* and
administered.

The Afrikaans Reformed Churches are now universally recognized as supporting apartheid and have therefore been rejected as
heretical. To what extent, it needs to be asked, does this *status
confessionis* affect the English-speaking Churches, and notably
those that belong to the SACC?

SACC Member Churches

In contrast to the ideological support for apartheid from the
Afrikaans Reformed Churches, the SACC member Churches and
the Roman Catholic Church have consistently condemned apartheid as being contrary to the will and purpose of God.

It was Prime Minister Verwoerd who cast the die that was to
characterize the continuing pro-apartheid stance of the Afrikaans
Reformed Churches, and it was he who evoked intense opposition
from the English-speaking Churches. If he prevented the NGK from

breaking out of its programme of theologized apartheid, he motivated the English-speaking Churches to intensify their struggle
against this ideology of racism. In 1950 Dr Verwoerd became the
Minister of Native Affairs, and his vision of separate development
began to make demands on these Churches. In 1957 the Native
Laws Amendment Bill was promulgated, making it virtually impossible for black people to worship in Churches located in so-called
white areas. *Die Transvaler*, an official mouthpiece of the ruling
party, of which Verwoerd had himself been an editor, stated the
government position clearly:

As long as liberalistic bishops and canons, professors, students and politicians
can freely attend Church and hold meetings and socials together with non-
Europeans, apartheid will be infringed in its marrow. It is high time for this to
end.(13)

In his famous open letter to the Prime Minister, the Anglican Archbishop of Cape Town, Geoffrey Clayton, declared:

The Church cannot recognize the right of an official secular government to
determine whether or where a member of the Church of any race . . . shall
discharge his religious duty of participating in public worship. . . . We feel
bound to state that if the bill were to become law in its present form we
should ourselves be unable to obey it or to counsel our clergy and people to
do so.(14)

The intensity of the opposition to the bill compelled Verwoerd to
modify his stance slightly, but the bill was passed with a strong
majority, allowing the Minister to prevent black people from worshipping with their fellow white Christians if anyone complained
that they were a 'nuisance' or worshipping in 'excessive numbers'.
A pastoral letter from Clayton was read in all Anglican Churches,
calling on all clergy and people to ignore the so-called 'church
clause' of the new legislation, stating:

Before God and with you as my witnesses, I solemnly state that not only shall
I not obey any direction of the Minister of Native Affairs in this regard, but I
solemnly counsel you, both clergy and people, to do likewise.(15)

Other English-speaking Churches responded in similar vein protes-
ting the passage of the bill, but the editorial of *Die Kerkbode* was
compliant. The English-speaking Churches were criticized for their
attitude concerning this legislation, the Afrikaans Churches were
praised by Verwoerd because they 'did not allow themselves to
become implicated' and the members of the delegation of the NGK
which interviewed the Minister assured the people of his good
Christian intentions.

The Methodist Church made a similar stand in the wake of the Verwoerdian demands. It became clear that it was the next logical step in the life of this Church to elect the Revd Seth Mokitimi, a black minister, to the presidency. With this the latent fears of white Methodists surfaced. This could have meant that the Church might be declared 'black' by the government, meaning that it could not own property, which by constitution is vested in the name of the president, in 'white' areas. The fact that the apartheid mindset was beginning to influence white Methodists and the reaction of black Methodists to the hesitation concerning Mokitimi came to a head at the conference of 1958. After serious consideration of the possible consequences of establishing four separate Methodist Churches (white, black, 'coloured' and Indian) in compliance with the apartheid policy of the land, the breakthrough came with the adoption of a resolution which was to determine the future character of Methodism—and challenge the demands of Verwoerd:

The conference declares its conviction that it is the will of God for the Methodist Church that it should be *one and undivided*, trusting to the lead of God to bring this ideal to ultimate fruition, and that this be the general basis of our missionary policy.(16)

At the conference of 1963 Seth Mokitimi was elected president amidst widespread speculation of white defection and government persecution. But the 'one and undivided' resolution held, although since then black Methodists have consistently used this resolution to point to inconsistencies between word and deed in this Church. Methodism, together with the other Churches, has since those days made further progress toward normalizing (deracializing) its structures. These moves have, however, been too cautious, too hesitant and too tentative to escape the impact of the WARC resolution.

The English-speaking Churches have adopted numerous resolutions condeming racism since the early days of apartheid rule. Among the most significant statements of the Churches in this regard is the *Message to the people of South Africa*, published in 1968, calling apartheid a 'false faith', a 'novel gospel' and a 'pseudo-gospel'. Since then the SACC has passed a resolution in support of those who conscientiously disobey laws which they believe to contradict the Law of God and several member Churches have passed similar resolutions of their own. The Catholic Bishops Conference has in turn made several courageous stands condemning all forms of racial, political and economic discrimination. Yet it also needs to be said that this tradition of opposition to apartheid legislation has not always been enthusiastically and unanimously supported within the English-speaking Churches. For example, a resolution at the conference of the SACC held early in 1982, declaring apartheid to be a heresy and terminating dialogue with the NGK, was only narrowly accepted after some spirited opposition from white delegates. Nevertheless, all the member Churches of the SACC have since affirmed this resolution.(17)

History shows the Afrikaans Reformed Churches to have consistently and repeatedly supported apartheid and the English-speaking Churches to have condemned apartheid as being contrary to the will of God. In terms of doctrine and principle the English-speaking Churches cannot be faulted, and they have produced numerous courageous leaders, both black and white, who have endured both the wrath of the government and the opposition of the Afrikaans Reformed Church leaders for their stance. But it is in their general *practice* that the English-speaking Churches are found wanting.

AN ALL-PERVADING HERESY

The heresy of racism, separatism and apartheid is all-pervading in South Africa. In spite of the declarations of principle and belief (important as these are at the level of prophetic witness and as ideals to be striven for), separate worship, segregated holy communion services and racially constituted fellowship and service organizations (whether in youth work, women's associations or men's fellowships) are also the hallmarks of all the English-speaking Churches in this country. In this respect the English-speaking Churches are almost as racially divided as the Afrikaans Reformed Churches. John de Gruchy's comment in this regard is worth noting:

Although blacks have increasingly taken on leadership roles, many remain sceptical about the seriousness of the Churches in combating racism. They point to a wide range of discriminatory practices that have existed over the years, and which are only now being slowly and painfully removed.

This gap between word and deed has been exploited by the government as blatant hypocrisy. Many a deputation to the state has floundered on the mere fact that the Churches' own lives have not been beyond reproach. Indeed, on occasion the state has exercised a prophetic ministry to the Churches. For example, the Churches soon learned that they could not justly criticize wage discrimination between whites and blacks in society or in state employ because there was similar discrimination in the Churches.(18)

The racially integrated decision-making process of conferences, assemblies and synods, and the resolutions and statements of these bodies, have not borne fruit in the practice of local congregations.

Neither has this all-pervading heresy left the black congregations of these Churches unscathed. So-called 'coloured' congregations have often been as reluctant as white congregations to employ a black minister. Then too one has seen the effects of apartheid manifesting itself in the attempts made within the Methodist Church to establish geographically and racially integrated circuits or groupings of Churches. Invariably black congregations have opposed such moves with as much determination as, and often more determination than, their fellow white Methodists. There are often sound cultural and language reasons advanced for this reluctance, and it can also be ascribed to black reaction to white racism or even to black consciousness and political liberation strategy—but the question that needs to be asked is to what extent this reaction can be regarded as also heretical.

It would appear that a new complacency has emerged in the English-speaking Churches. With the stormy and aggressive sixties and seventies behind us, it is not uncommon to hear of a 'new conciliatory spirit' spoken of in the official decision-making bodies of these Churches. This can probably be attributed to two factors. The one is that black people have been elected to leadership positions. This has, to some extent, satisfied the demands of black caucuses and power groups within these Churches. Then too, because this leadership is still required to operate within what is largely a white power structure and be dependent on white funding, it is a relatively moderate and cautious leadership. The other factor is that local white congregations are beginning to learn to live with the anxiety created by their leadership's rhetoric. While at one time a large section of the white clergy and laity used vociferously to oppose the 'liberal' white and 'radical' black leadership, they have now learned largely to ignore their pronouncements. A quiet *quid pro quo* is being agreed. Conservative whites 'tolerate' black leadership and black leadership and black leaders are compelled to allow grassroots whites to continue in their former ways. The English-speaking Churches are in danger of drifting into a period of 'ecclesiastical neocolonialism'. Black leaders are replacing white leaders while the white congregations continue to cling to the habits once delivered to them by their fathers in the faith.

There is a new black leadership in these Churches which can determine the future direction of the witness of these Churches. The question is whether it will, by acquiescence, allow insidious and residual forms of racism to continue, or whether it will call the blacks and whites who form the grassroot membership of these Churches to repentance.

TOWARDS SPIRITUAL RENEWAL

The Gospel links spiritual renewal and conversion to a confession of guilt and the evidence of a renewed life. It summed up in the notion of *repentance*. This is always more than remorse and regret and involves a turning away from the past to a new future in Christ and in fellowship with one's fellow-believers. But such a conscious programme of renewal needs to begin with an awareness of the prevailing situation. In relation to the present debate it means that the Church of Christ in this country needs to confess its sin, acknowledge the all-pervading nature of racism and consciously apply itself to the eradication of this heresy.

The Afrikaans Reformed Churches stand guilty before the judgment of the World Reformed Churches. To stubbornly seek to justify a policy of apartheid which has been consistently condemned on every reputable platform of opinion in this world is a futile and ridiculous exercise, and Christians throughout this land and the world need to use all the persuasive powers at their disposal to bring these Churches to their senses. To rephrase this theologically, the Afrikaans Reformed Churches have been declared heretical and have therefore become the object of conversion.

The English-speaking Churches, not being without their guilt, need to open themselves to the renewing of God's spirit, trusting in Him alone and denouncing the gods of this society—paternalism and dominance, economic success and social status. This means that they need to express a *solidarity of sinfulness* with the Afrikaans Reformed Churches and in so doing create a new basis for fellowship with all who confess their sin in awareness of their racism. This means that the English-speaking Churches cannot sit in judgment on the Afrikaans Reformed Churches, but together with them need to seek renewal according to the will and purpose of God made known in the Scriptures, which calls people to love one another, to remove the 'middle wall of partition' and to build a society of justice and truth.

There is a pressing need to spell out in the most concrete terms what this means. At this point, the long-standing debate as to whether the basic problem in South Africa is a racial or an economic one comes to the fore. Churches need to commit themselves to state what justice and truth mean in terms of definite political options in this land. Karl Rahner has warned that

> . . . the Church can be wide off the mark in such imperatives and directions . . . more palpably than in theoretical declarations. But this is a risk that must be taken if the Church is not to be seen to be pedantic, to be living in a world

of pure theory, remote from life, making pronouncements that do not touch the stubborn concreteness of real life.(19)

This is the challenge facing the English-speaking Churches. They need to confess to their heresy of practice in solidarity of guilt with the Afrikaans Reformed Churches and to seek to translate their many principles of non-racism into a society built on political guarantees of non-discrimination and liberation from oppression.

The significance of the Ottawa resolution is not to be underestimated in this regard, primarily because it has altered the theological and political climate for the majority of Christians in this country. It has produced a consensus among the mainstream Churches, with the exception of the three Afrikaans Reformed Churches, against apartheid, and perhaps now for the first time in South Africa the main theological thrust is zealously against the present government. The Churches have stated theologically, and the Reformed Churches by way of confession, that any system which discriminates against people in any way is irreconcilable with the Christian faith. This statement is rich with political implications. The famous 1934 Barmen Declaration of the Confessing Church against Hitler was no more politically concrete and yet everyone understood its political implications. A Confession of Faith is an instrument against which to test, for example, a political policy. The Churches have declared themselves *theologically*, but if they are to do more than create vague expectations they must begin to explain what this theological commitment means, in political and economic language. They will presumably have to say, in addition to much else, that any political or economic system which excludes anyone from full participation in any aspect of it on the grounds of race is morally unacceptable. When one takes the context of the Ottawa resolution into account, and certainly when one reads the Confession of Faith of the NG Mission Church within the reality of the prevailing political situation in South Africa, one is quite justified in interpreting these pronouncements to advocate a vote for every person in one political system in this country. Churches are merely contributing to political confusion and obscurantism if they do not declare themselves clearly and openly on such matters.

THE CHURCH AT THE CROSSROADS

South African society has always been an intensely religious one. The Church has always operated on the central stage of political debate and the present government has always enjoyed the support of the three Afrikaans Reformed Churches. But this situation may now be poised to change.

The WARC decision can only contribute to the growing split within the NGK. It will probably cause a backlash among the more conservative members, hardening their attitude against theological and political reform and inclining them towards the traditional *'volksteologie'* of Dr A. P. Treurnicht's Conservative Party. A leading NGK theologian has recently, for example, said privately that if there is any move by the NGK to the left this will precipitate a major schism on the right. At the same time, the WARC resolution will possibly motivate the reformists within this Church to push for further reform. What can be said is that the monolithic political nature of the NGK will no longer be able to be assumed. There is already a clear indication that the National Party is becoming increasingly impatient with the conservative elements of this Church. Editorials in newspapers supportive of the government point out that the NGK is in danger of hopelessly lagging behind current theological thinking in the rest of the world, which is concerning itself not with the question, 'What do you believe?' but 'How do you live with the implications of this belief?' The Minister of Constitutional Development has recently made a thinly-veiled attack on those theologians and politicians who promote 'theological racism', and the Prime Minister has repeatedly reminded his followers to practise a Christianity that is grounded in love for one another. There is every indication that the government will no longer be able to count on the broad-based support of the powerful Afrikaans Reformed Churches for its cautious programme of reform.

The role of the reformists within these Churches could be a significant one. The problem is that most reformists in the Afrikaans Reformed Churches have in the past not been allowed to be too influential. The Afrikaner's sense of identity is inherently related to his sense of loyalty to the *volk*, and few have been prepared to break with Church, culture and family in order to be obedient to their theological and political convictions. People like Beyers Naudé, who have been prepared to do this, have ultimately been prevented by the government from exercising a creative role in society, and Naudé himself is repeatedly criticized by those who like to regard themselves as 'reformists' within the white NGK for having excluded himself from being an influence within Afrikanerdom by having been too radical, and for having ultimately resigned from the Church. Preferring to adopt '*'n klip in die skoen mentaliteit*' ('a stone in the shoe mentality'), the voice of such *verligte* critics of the Afrikaans Reformed Churches has been insignificant in relation to the powerful voice of the spokesmen and leaders of these Churches. It is partly this realization that has caused Professor Johan Degenaar, the political philosopher of Stellenbosch University, to identify *verligtheid* as being the stumbling block to a new Afrikanerdom, which will not be dependent on Afrikaner power.(20) Clearly the reformists in the white Afrikaans Reformed Churches have a difficult choice. In declaring themselves openly to be in opposition to the present system, both in Church and state, they need to spell out what their alternative is or else they will simply be absorbed into P. W. Botha's total strategy. The significant and disturbing factor is that most of these reformists have not joined the *Broederkring* or ABRECSA, which have declared themselves to be in favour of one united NGK and rejected apartheid as a sin.

The white English-speaking Churches face a similar dilemma. Recent events have made it clear that the government is not prepared to tolerate a radically prophetic witness by the Church. The sustained attack by the government on dissident clerics and the appointment of the Eloff Commission to investigate the activities of the SACC is enough to confirm that.

What then is the role of the English-speaking Churches? There is every indication that they will not be prepared to capitulate entirely before a government onslaught. There is also, however, a real danger that their prophetic role will become less explicit in the years ahead. Opposition from the Church will be tolerated if it does not strike too hard at the confidence of whites and undermine their will to resist the growing political demands of black people. The Churches will be persuaded to confirm that 'there are changes taking place in South Africa'. Gradually, as the proposed constitutional reforms take place, this will result in a society which appears to be less obviously racist. A black middle class will be partially integrated and there will be so-called 'coloured' and Indian cabinet ministers, within a society less obviously bolstered by bad theology and biblical exegesis. In such a situation the Churches could become more acquiescent. White church members will be increasingly reluctant to have their Churches destabilize a situation which is less obviously racist and which they will argue 'is changing'. Black ministers and laity in the black 'homelands' may, in turn, be less inclined to make political demands which could strike at the structures of these homelands. This possibility has already been anticipated by some of the most outspoken and radical black and 'coloured' members of the English-speaking Churches opting for high positions in the central and homelands governments. Ultimately this willingness by some black leaders to co-operate with the present government through their homelands policy and the President's Council may well yet prove to be the single most important factor militating against black liberation in this country. While the government may be able to eradicate most aspects of petty apartheid, the major political hurdle which it cannot negotiate without black co-operation is the one concerning the vote and political power-sharing. It is this factor which makes the 'bantustan' mentality of some blacks every bit as divisive as apartheid.

The English-speaking Churches will repeatedly need to reconsider their position and the extent to which they are promoting the spiritual, psychological, social, economic and political liberation of their people—or merely giving credence to and 'baptizing' reform politics ultimately designed to ensure the future hegemony of whites in this country. The Church stands at the cross-roads. Either it is to be radically theological and in so doing be radically obedient to God regardless of what it may mean concerning puny ambitions and privileges that have been buttressed by years of indoctrination, or else it will become part of the oppressive system of this new ideology of privileged white and 'honorary white' survivalism.

Karl Barth's radical theological-political directive for the Church, born out of his struggle against Nazism, has a high relevance for us in this country:

No sentence is more dangerous or revolutionary than that God is One and there is no other like Him. All the permanencies of the world draw their life from ideologies and mythologies, from open or disguised religions, and to this extent from all possible forms of deity and divinity. It was on the truth of the sentence that God is One that the 'Third Reich' of Adolf Hitler made shipwreck. Let this sentence be uttered in such a way that it is heard and grasped, and at once 450 prophets of Baal are always in fear of their lives. There is no more room now for what the recent past called toleration. Beside God there are only His creatures or false gods, and beside faith in Him there are religions only as religions of superstition, error and finally irreligion.(21)

This is why the WARC had to declare apartheid a heresy. This is why the Church in this country needs to reassess its role in relation to the state. There is every danger that it could be co-opted yet again into the creation of a new ideology of oppression designed to slightly improve the lot of some black people (at the expense of others who are dumped in the resettlement camps 'outside South Africa') but ultimately to guarantee the continued domination by a minority group of whites.

The Christian offer of liberation provides no guarantees, only opportunities and hope. This requires a brave heart and real faith.

But the alternative is not even worth considering because apartheid guarantees only chaos.

Notes

1 Unless otherwise stated quotations such as these have been taken from statements and press interviews given by Dr Boesak and others in relation to the recent WARC meeting in Ottawa.

2 *Die Kerkbode*, 22 September 1948, pp. 664–5.

3 Allan Boesak, 'The heresy of apartheid' in *Dialogue*, May 1981.

4 *Sunday Times*, 8 November 1970.

5 A. P. Treurnicht, *Credo van 'n Afrikaner* (Cape Town, 1975), pp. 20 and 13.

6 B. Spoelstra, 'Denominationalism, with reference to the Three Afrikaans Churches' in W. S. Vorster (ed.), *Denominationalism–its Sources and Implications* (Pretoria, 1982).

7 John Calvin, *The Institutes of the Christian Religion*, ed. John T. McNeill (Philadelphia, 1960), Book IV, ch. 1, para. 4.

8 Several statements of protest from within the NGK, including the 'Reformation Day Witness', the 'Forty-four Statements' first published in *Stormkompas*, and the 'Open Letter' signed by 123 members of the NGK are printed and discussed in J. H. P. Serfontein, *Apartheid, Change and the NG Kerk* (Johannesburg, 1982).

9 A. H. Lückhoff, *Cottesloe* (Cape Town, 1978), pp. 146, 256, 158 and 161–2; also Elfrieda Strassberger, *Ecumenism in South Africa 1936-60: with special reference to the mission of the church* (Johannesburg, 1972).

10 W. A. de Klerk, *The Puritans in Africa* (London, 1975), p. 254.

11 The official translation of this report is entitled *Human Relations and the South African Scene in the Light of Scripture* (Cape Town and Pretoria, 1976).

12 John Calvin, op. cit., Book IV, ch. 1, para. 9.

13 Alan Paton, *Apartheid and the Archbishop* (Cape Town, 1973), p. 283.

14 Ibid, pp. 279–80.

15 Ibid, p. 286.

16 *Minutes of the Seventy-sixth Annual Conference of the Methodist Church of South Africa*, 1958, p. 65, para. 12.

17 See, for example, the resolutions of the Methodist Church of Southern Africa, the United Congregational Church of Southern Africa and the Church of the Province of South Africa (Anglican) in the appendix.

18 John de Gruchy, *The Church Struggle in South Africa* (Cape Town, 1979), p. 61.

19 Karl Rahner, *The Shape of the Church to Come* (London, 1974), p. 79.

20 Johannes Degenaar, 'Is vreedsame fundamentele verandering moontlik in Suid-Afrika?', an unpublished paper read to POLSTU, 29 June 1982.

21 Karl Barth, *Church Dogmatics* (Edinburgh, 1957), 11, 1, p. 444.

7

JOHN W DE GRUCHY
Towards a Confessing Church: The implications of a heresy

The dehumanizing fruits of apartheid have increasingly revealed its evil character. This has long been recognized by the world-wide Church, including Churches within South Africa. But racism has continued to abound in the Churches, and has even been theologically sanctioned by some. It has thus become necessary not only to recognize apartheid as a sinful policy, but also to reject it as a heresy that is dividing the Church and compromising its proclamation of the gospel of Jesus Christ. No Church, indeed, no Christian is exempt from taking a stand on the issue. To choose Jesus Christ implies rejecting apartheid; to choose apartheid means rejecting the implications of his gospel. The alternative is as stark as that, and the choice must be made. To choose Jesus Christ is a liberating step, and in this instance it frees both the Church and the Christian from the idolatry of racism and enables them to begin confessing him as Lord with new power. This confession must necessarily go beyond words, but it cannot be silent or hidden. It must be proclaimed from the housetops, and demonstrated in the marketplace.

RE-OPENING THE DEBATE ON A CONFESSING CHURCH
Whether appropriate or not, parallels between South Africa's apartheid society and the German Third Reich have often been drawn since 1948.(1) Within church circles, especially after the failure of the Cottesloe Consultation in 1960(2), this comparison also sparked off debate on whether or not a South African equivalent was needed of the Confessing Church that opposed Nazism in Germany in the 1930s.(3) The idea was first articulated publicly by Dr Beyers Naudé, a former NGK moderator and director of the Christian Institute, in an article published in *Pro Veritate* in July 1965.(4) Entitled *'Die Tyd Vir 'n "Belydende Kerk" is Daar'* ('The Time for a "Confessing Church" has arrived'), it was written shortly after Naudé's home and the offices of the Christian Institute had been searched by the Security Police for documents relating to Com-

munism and the banned African National Congress. To Naudé the
event smacked so strongly of Nazi-style tactics that he became convinced that the time had arrived for a Confessing Church in South
Africa.

Naudé's article sparked off considerable debate, particularly
amongst NGK theologians and ministers. This led him to spell out
in greater detail in subsequent articles both the parallels that he
saw between the South African and the German situations, and
what he meant by a Confessing Church. The parallels were racism
(i.e. anti-semitism in the case of Germany); a false unity between
Church and *volk*; ideological pressure on, intimidation of, and an
attack on the Church; and a sinful silence in the face of injustice.(5)
With regard to the question of a Confessing Church, Naudé was at
pains to make clear that this did not mean the formation of a new
denomination, nor did it require members of any Church to leave
their denomination in order to become part of the Confessing
Church. What he had in mind was a Confessing movement within
the Churches, binding together in faith, study and action those
who sought to be obedient to Jesus Christ within apartheid society.
And in fact he concluded by stating that in this sense the Confessing Church had already come into existence.(6)

The debate about a Confessing Church in South Africa continued
throughout the sixties and gained considerable momentum with the
publication by the SACC of the *Message to the People of South
Africa* in 1968.(7) Indeed, the *Message* was regarded by many within the circles of the Christian Institute and the SACC as the confessional basis for the formation of a Confessing Church. It was also
understood in this way by many overseas observers of the South
African church scene, particularly in the Netherlands and West
Germany. The SPROCAS report, *Apartheid and the Church*(8)
spelt out what the *Message* implied for the Church in South Africa.
Its conclusions, if put into effect, would have led to a Confessing
Church.

When Eberhard Bethge, the friend and biographer of Dietrich
Bonhoeffer, visited South Africa in 1973, he found the issue very
much alive. After returning to Germany he discussed the matter in
an article expressly called 'A Confessing Church in South Africa?',
which began:

'Are we involved in a "church struggle" like that in the Third Reich and do we
have to create a "Confessing Church" as you did in Germany?' This question
was raised in almost every discussion I had in South Africa. The term 'Confessing Church' is indeed current in South Africa today and excites and troubles

friend and foe alike. In many quarters the view now is that a *status confessionis* now exists, and some individual Christians sacrifice themselves to draw public attention to this fact.(9)

In his response to questions such as the one he mentions, Bethge wondered how helpful, in fact, the example of the Confessing Church was for those involved in the struggle in South Africa.(10) His answer was ambivalent, not because he saw no parallels between the two situations (on the contrary), but because the situation of the Church in South Africa was structurally so different from that in Germany, and it was seldom helpful or appropriate to try to re-create something proper to one situation in another. But he concluded:

Yet the fact that people in South Africa are talking about a 'Confessing Church' shows how deeply they realize that they cannot stand for a multiracial Church unless at the same time they work openly together for a multiracial society, and that they would become hopeless accomplices of this apartheid society if they were to retreat to some imagined third, neutral position, in which, instructed by the 'Church', they would keep quiet about political matters.(11)

The question of a Confessing Church in South Africa did, however, seem to pass away during the following years. Indeed, little was heard of the idea until 1980 when the SACC convened a Consultation on Racism at Hammanskraal that February. At the end of this Consultation the black delegates issued an ultimatum to their respective Churches. They called upon 'all white Christians to demonstrate their willingness to purge the church of racism' and declared that

. . . if after a period of twelve months there is no evidence of repentance shown in concrete action, the black Christians will have no alternative but to witness to the Gospel of Jesus Christ *by becoming a confessing church*.(12)

Precisely what was intended was not indicated. Perhaps the major reason for this was the fact that the delegates came from differing denominational backgrounds so that what might be an appropriate step for a black Dutch Reformed minister to take would not necessarily be the same for a Catholic priest or a Methodist minister. Unlike the pastors and congregations which constituted the Confessing Church in Germany, they neither share a common confessional standpoint nor belong to structurally similar denominations. But in spite of this lack of clarity, and also in spite of the fact that the ultimatum does not appear to have been put into effect, the issue of a Confessing Church was once again on the agenda of theological and Church debate. And it was soon to become a focal concern with the emergence of the Alliance of Black Reformed Christians in Southern Africa (ABRECSA).

ABRECSA was launched at its first conference, held at Hammanskraal, in October 1981, under the chairmanship of Allan Boesak.(13) In his opening address to the conference, 'Black and Reformed: Burden or Challenge?', Boesak showed how the Reformed tradition in South Africa had become a travesty of what it was clearly meant to be, but that when correctly understood, 'black Christians who are reformed have no reason to be ashamed of this tradition'. He went on to say:

It is my conviction that the Reformed tradition has a future in this country only if black Reformed Christians are willing to take it up, make it truly their own, and let this tradition once again become what it once was: a champion of the cause of the poor and the oppressed, clinging to the confession of the Lordship of Christ and to the supremacy of the Word of God. It will have a future when we show an evangelical openness toward the world and toward the worldwide Church, so that we will be able to search with others for the attainment of the goals of the Kingdom of God in South Africa. In this I do not mean that we should accept everything in our tradition uncritically, for I indeed believe *black Christians should formulate a Reformed Confession for our time and our situation in our own words.*(14)

Boesak then went on to spell out what this would mean, and much of what he said was later taken up and included in the Charter of the Alliance.(15) For the first time since the debate on a Confessing Church began, the Charter spelt out in some detail what this could mean.

It is unnecessary to repeat what is in the ABRECSA Charter, but several comments may be helpful. Firstly, while the word 'Black' in the title clearly refers to ethnicity, it is understood 'to mean a condition and an attitude and not merely the pigmentation of one's skin'. In other words, the confessing community envisaged by ABRECSA is not confined to one racial group but open to all those Christians and Churches that are committed to its theological basis. Secondly, while the theological basis is unashamedly 'Reformed', it is not confessionalistic. The authority of Scripture; the Lordship of Christ; Christian responsibility for the world; obedience to the State, but only under God; the visible unity of the Church transcending all human barriers—these are all clearly Reformed emphases, but they are not exclusively so. They provide the substance for a confession of faith in the South African context to which most, if not all, Churches could give their allegiance.

But then, thirdly, the Charter arrives at the point of division, that is, that decisive element in a confession which separates the true Church from the false.

We, as members of ABRECSA, unequivocally declare that apartheid is a sin, and that the moral and theological justification of it is a travesty of the Gospel, a betrayal of the Reformed tradition, and a heresy.

While many may affirm the theological basis articulated by ABRECSA, not all are prepared to condemn apartheid as a heresy. Yet it is precisely this dividing line which is of fundamental importance in the situation because it provides the basis for rediscovering the true identity and expressing the real unity of the Church in South Africa.

It is always a risky business trying to distinguish the true Church from the false Church. As the Westminster Confession reminds us: 'The purest churches under heaven are subject both to mixture and error.'(16) But certainly from a Reformed perspective it is necessary to accept the risk and move from abstract definitions of the Church to a concrete recognition of its boundaries. We are indebted to Dietrich Bonhoeffer for his clarity on the subject:

The knowledge of the extent of the Church is never theoretically at the Church's disposal but must always be ascertained at any given moment. . . . This brings the element of living decision into the determination of the boundaries of the Church. The boundaries of the Church are always decided only in the encounter between the Church and unbelief; the act is a decision of the Church. (17)

Which brings us back to the WARC decision regarding apartheid as a heresy and the status of the NGK and the NHK within the Reformed family of Churches. This family has, after a long period of searching and struggling, found it necessary to draw the boundaries of the Reformed Church. This has not been done in an arbitrary manner. Indeed, *the boundaries have revealed themselves in the struggle for the truth of the Gospel*, and the WARC has finally been forced to acknowledge and articulate them. In a real sense, the NGK and NHK created the boundaries by choosing to support apartheid in the first place, but their initial choice and their present refusal to acknowledge apartheid as a heresy places them on the wrong side of their own creation. They who determined the boundaries now find themselves on the outside, and those who were on the outside now find themselves at the centre of the Reformed community. That is the irony of the Ottawa decision.

The ABRECSA Charter, which paved the way for the WARC decision regarding apartheid, also provides the possibility for a fresh initiative for expressing the unity of the Church in South Africa. Throughout this century various denominations in South Africa have sought to unite.(19) Some unions have been consummated, but the uniting of the major denominations, whether of the so-called English-speaking Churches or the Afrikaans Reformed family of Churches, has remained elusive. Although theological differences such as those concerning episcopacy have played a role in preventing union, more generally it has been the non-theological factors of race, culture and ethnicity.

While it is painfully true that the divisions which separated Christians from one another in Europe were transplanted into South Africa, it is equally true, and more painful, that these confessional divisions have been exacerbated by separation along racial, cultural and ethnic lines. These issues, normally regarded as non-theological, must now be seen as equally confessional, because they have to do with the truth of the Gospel as much as those that, for example, traditionally separate Catholics from Calvinists. In seeking to express the unity of the Church in South Africa it is therefore clearly inadequate to try and resolve the inherited confessional differences without at the same time, and even more urgently, attending to the contextual confessional issues. If the Churches seriously begin to confess Jesus Christ as Lord in South Africa in terms that relate to the critical issues of our society, that is, the real issues which divide them, they will begin to discover their unity in a new way. Indeed, Naudé noted that this had already begun in the sixties. It may be argued that it has been gathering momentum ever since. There is a confessing *movement* in South Africa, and one which includes Christians from virtually all denominations who regard apartheid as a heresy and who strive for true justice and peace.

But perhaps the time has come to go one step further. ABRECSA has laid the foundation for a new initiative in the search for Christian unity in South Africa. Without being exclusive, it has called on those Churches within the WARC in South Africa to come together in a new way, to unite 'in organization, in action and in witness'. From a Reformed perspective, this is possible because they all share a common confessional basis. In other words, there is a similar situation to that which pertained in Germany. The member Churches of the WARC are theologically and structurally related because of their Reformed heritage. And this, in turn, enables them to go further and confess that faith in terms which relate explicitly to South Africa today, not just in rejecting apartheid, but in affirming the full significance of Jesus Christ as Lord for the social, economic, political and ecclesiastical life of the country. In this way the unity of at least a part of the Church in South Africa could be restored as a truly Reformed and Confessing Church comes into being. But first the Churches must be willing to declare, as some have now done, that apartheid is indeed a heresy, and that a *status confessionis* has arrived which requires decision and action.

APARTHEID AS A HERESY

The word 'heresy' originally meant making a choice or taking sides. In that sense we are all heretics. But already in the New Testament it begins to be understood in a pejorative way. The heretical person causes division and leads the Church astray. (Titus 3:10; II Timothy 3:6f.). It was Ignatius of Antioch who, in the second century, took the further and decisive step and declared that heresy is the denial of 'the simple truth about Jesus Christ'.(20) Heresy thus came to mean, for Christians, the distortion of the truth revealed in Jesus Christ, and something that not only leads to division within the Church but also to a false witness in the world.

There are several possible objections to the charge that apartheid is a heresy. In the first place the hurling of theological anathemas seems both antiquated and odd to modern people living in a secular world where religious pluralism is a fact and religious tolerance a necessity. The accusation that a particular religious belief is a heresy and its adherents therefore heretics not only sounds self-righteous and authoritarian, but also seems to close the door to meaningful dialogue which might bring about a change of heart. The second objection to the charge that *apartheid* is a heresy is that we are dealing here, not with an article of Christian belief held by a church, but with political ideology and government policy. This being so, is it not inappropriate, indeed confusing nonsense, to call it a heresy? The third objection is whether it is really helpful in the struggle against apartheid to label it a heresy. The World Council of Churches' conference on Racism in Theology and Theology against Racism in 1975 recognized 'that some of the theories and beliefs advanced to justify racism may be heretical', but went on to plead that the discussion on racism not be 'side-tracked' into an academic discussion of what is or is not a formal heresy'.(21) We may go even further and ask, finally, whether this is not just another ecclesiastical smokescreen created to hide the real issues facing South Africa today from view. Is it in any way releavant to the contemporary debate and struggle? Many would argue, and we would agree with them, that the real issue is economic exploitation, quite as much as—if not more so than—racism, and that even if apartheid does finally crumble into the dust such oppression would remain.

While we must beware of witchhunts, self-righteousness, and anything which is destructive of persons and genuine human relations, in answer to the first objection it must be said that if the Church is no longer concerned about heresy it has lost its passion for the truth revealed in Jesus Christ. Bonhoeffer recognized this in the midst of the Church struggle in Nazi Germany:

A church which no longer takes the rejection of false teaching seriously no longer takes truth, i.e. its salvation, seriously, and ultimately no longer takes the community seriously, no matter how pious or well-organized it may be. Anyone who follows false teaching, indeed who simply supports it and furthers it, no longer obeys Christ.(22)

To be concerned about heresy does not mean being intolerant towards other religious traditions; it means being committed to the struggle for truth within the life of the Church. It is a concern for the integrity of the Gospel in the midst of, and for the sake of, a sceptical world.

The obvious questions which follow from this relate to the second objection. Can political ideology and government policy be labelled heresy if the latter has to do with a struggle within the life of the Church? And in what way does apartheid deny the truth revealed in Jesus Christ and thus undermine the Christian faith?

In answer we must say at once that apartheid, or its progeny 'separate development', is not just a government policy. It is a policy which was to a large extent conceived and born within the Afrikaans Reformed Churches. It is a policy which has subsequently been nurtured within them, and, let it be clearly said, also within the so-called English-speaking Churches. Furthermore, and this is the crux of the matter, apartheid has been justified and defended as a Christian policy based on the Bible, especially by the Afrikaans Reformed Churches. The Christian faith has thus been misused in providing moral under-pinning and theological legitimation for a racist ideology. In other words, it cannot be argued with any honesty that apartheid is simply a political programme unrelated to theology or the life of the Church.

In what sense, then, is apartheid a heresy? We maintain that it is, in the first instance, an anthropological heresy. It is based on a false view of man. This, in turn, leads to a false doctrine of the

Church and of the reconciliation which God has achieved in the death and resurrection of Jesus. We shall reflect on these dimensions of the apartheid heresy as we consider those marks which have generally been considered the marks of heresy.

In his discussion of *The Four Great Heresies*(23) that confronted the Church in its early history, J. W. C. Wand writes of the three marks of a heresy that were used by the church fathers in determining whether or not a particular belief was heretical. In the first instance, and fundamentally, a heresy was something novel. This is not the same, of course, as re-interpreting the faith in new situations. All heresies whether ancient or modern introduce something new and alien into the faith and life of the Church. When the NGK at the Cape decided in 1857 on a policy that finally led to a segregated Church, it legitimated a path for the Church at variance with its own previous decisions, the confessions of the Reformed faith, and, as it itself acknowledged at the time, with Scripture. A policy that so clearly had no theological justification, ran counter to the Reformed tradition and led to the division of the Church on ethnic and cultural lines should have been recognized immediately for what it was, an ecclesiological heresy. It implied that Christ had not created the new humanity to which the New Testament bears witness (cf. Ephesians 2). But, as Karl Barth has noted, 'No heresy has ever had the original intention of being a heresy; it has become so only when and where a first unintended lapse from obedience has not been noted and resisted in time.'(24)

While the heresy of apartheid manifested itself initially in the way in which the Church in South Africa structured its life and pursued its missionary task, that is, as an ecclesiological heresy, its roots lays much deeper. The Church was not just pursuing a pragmatic missionary policy: it was in fact succumbing to the racial attitudes and economic interests of much of its white constituency. The false values of the world had crept into the centre of the Church's life, ironically at the very point in time when the NGK was becoming most concerned about preserving its Calvinist orthodoxy and combating heresy!(25) How more subtle could the 'principalities and powers of this world' be? Without realizing it, the Church was allowing itself to be captured by a false theology, a theology determined by its white members, which denied the revelation of God in Jesus Christ in practice even while it affirmed it most strongly in theory.

The God in whom Christians believe shows no partiality towards anyone on the basis of race or culture. To deny this, is to reduce

God to a tribal deity and turn him into a national idol. God becomes 'our god'. In the opening paragraph of his *Institutes of the
Christian Religion* John Calvin reminds us that a true knowledge
of God is bound up with a true knowledge of man. It follows, then,
that a false doctrine of God is inextricably bound up with a false
and unchristian view of man. A false theology leads to a perverted
anthropology. It gives credence to the view that some races and
cultures are innately superior to others. In practice, of course, it
generally works the other way round. A false view of man, implicit
in the way in which people regard and treat others, betrays a false
view of God irrespective of the orthodox views which may be held.
It is in this context that we can see most clearly the significance of
what Visser 't Hooft correctly called 'moral heresy'.(26) Wrong
practice reveals bad theology.

   Indeed, as the *Message to the People of South Africa* stated in
1968, the ideology of apartheid is fundamentally a pseudo-gospel:

There are alarming signs that this doctrine of separation has become, for
many, a false faith, a novel gospel which offers happiness and peace for the
community and the individual. It holds out to men a security built not on
Christ but on the theory of separation and preservation of racial identity. It
presents separate development of our race groups as a way for the people of
South Africa to save themselves. Such a claim inevitably conflicts with the
Christian gospel, which offers salvation, both social and individual, through
faith in Christ alone.(27)

The fact of the matter is that apartheid makes a person's ethnic
identity, the colour of his or her skin, *the* crucial factor in determining human relations and ordering society. It is ethnicity that
prescribes, for example, whom you may marry, where you may live,
where you may work, what kind of education you may receive, and,
in some cases, to which Church you may belong. This is a denial of
the truth revealed in Jesus Christ. Apartheid not only brings the
Gospel into disrepute in this way, it also denies the efficacy of the
Gospel, maintaining in principle and producing in practice something quite contrary to it. For while the Gospel reconciles people
from different cultures and enables them to live together, apartheid
denies this possibility at the outset, even in the Church.

   It has taken a hundred years and more for apartheid to be seen
for what it really is, a heresy, a novel departure from the truth
revealed in Jesus Christ. Because the NGK and NHK have not
recognized their error, an immense amount of hurt and suffering
has been and is being caused. For this reason alone, and for the sake
of the future of the Church in South Africa and its integrity

throughout the world, it is essential that at last apartheid be named a heresy without any equivocation. And this is our response to the third objection we listed above. Christianity can no longer be used to justify unjust policies; apartheid is theologically untenable and therefore morally bankrupt. We must say so once and for all. This is not an academic issue, but one of great practical significance. It is fundamental to the struggle against apartheid because it destroys any claim that it has a Christian basis.

The attempt to justify apartheid in Christian terms is now virtually universally rejected by the Church. This relates to the second characteristic of heresy to which Wand points us. A heresy is something partial, that is, it belongs only to certain localities rather than being something confessed by the universal Church. Racism in the Church is not confined, of course, to South Africa. It is a universal phenomenon. But it is condemned by all confessions within the Christian Church today as wrong and unchristian. And it is condemned not only because of the particular situation in which it is found but because it inevitably affects the life of the Church as a whole.

This leads to our response to the final objection against labelling apartheid a heresy. Increasingly it is being recognized by the universal Church that the struggle against apartheid is part of, as well as symbolic of, the struggle for justice between affluent first world countries (the 'north') and poor third world countries (the 'south'). It is, in other words, not unrelated to the struggle for economic justice, the struggle between rich and poor, which many regard as the primary issue whether in South Africa itself or in the world as a whole. Our response to the final objection would therefore be that the rejection of, and the struggle against, racism is fundamental to the struggle for a just South Africa.

. . . racism is in almost all cases connected today with economic exploitation and political tyranny. The apartheid system in Southern Africa is only the microcosm of the world system and is deeply implicated in that system in various ways. When, therefore, the Lutheran World Federation in Dar-es-Salaam declared that the situation in Southern Africa constituted a *status confessionis*, it *de facto* declared the North–South situation a confessional issue. It is all important that the one, holy, catholic and apostolic Church of Jesus Christ should declare this in a truly committed way and begin to act accordingly.(28)

If the first mark of heresy is novelty and the second partiality, then, according to Wand, heresy is thirdly 'characterized by an element of stubbornness and disobedience'.(29) The struggle against heresy should not be confused with attacking heretics as people.

Indeed, many heretics have not only been earnest seekers after the truth and more attractive personalities than their opponents, but some regarded as heretics have finally been proved right. If they had not been stubborn, the truth for which they valiantly fought would not have prevailed. So it is a risky business fighting heresy. It requires considerable discernment and humility. But the risk has to be taken for the sake of affirming the truth and practising what is right. The stubbornness of which Wand speaks is not that of standing for the truth, but of refusing to acknowledge the truth once it has become clear.

In all humility, and with a deep sense of shared guilt, it has to be said that the NGK and NHK have stubbornly defended apartheid even when it has been convincingly demonstrated(30) from Scripture and the Reformed Confessions that it is a denial of the Gospel. Some of its own theologians have made this clear time and time again.(31) Twenty years ago the WARC warned the NGK and NHK that apartheid was 'a form of idolatry' and contrary to Reformed theology.(32) This was reiterated by the WARC in 1970:

In the past few years much has been said in many quarters about racism. It is, however, incumbent upon the Church to recognize racism for the idolatry it, in fact, is. As the covenant community has historically clashed with Baalism and other idolatries, so must the Church root out racism with its insidious substitution of colour for the God of the covenant sealed in Christ Jesus. . . . The Church of Jesus Christ does not make room for walls, be they tribal, racial, cultural, economic, national or confessional. The Church that by doctrine and/or practice affirms segregation of peoples (e.g. racial segregation) as a law for its life cannot be regarded as an authentic member of the body of Christ.(33)

The WARC then went on to deal with specific issues which especially concerned it, one of which was:

. . . the impression which the Dutch Reformed Churches in South Africa give that they support the government in its policy and practice of racial segregation and white supremacy: and the lukewarmness of the other Churches in South Africa in opposing oppression and injustice.(34)

There can be no doubt that the overwhelming consensus of the universal Church today regards apartheid and racism in the same way. The Reformed family of Churches thus felt it could no longer refrain from declaring apartheid to be a heresy and suspending the full rights of the NGK and NHK until such time as they too regard apartheid in the same way. A *status confessionis* had arrived.

A *STATUS CONFESSIONIS*

When the Church is confronted by a novel and partial interpretation of the Gospel that is disrupting its unity and impairing its witness, it is forced to recognize that a situation has arisen which demands that it once again clarify its faith and confess it anew in relation to the issues at stake.

It is vital that the Church should determine in each situation the sort of struggle which is and should be going on. In other words, decide when a situation becomes a clear case for confession (*casus confessionis*), a situation calling for the *status confessionis*.(35)

Such situations have occurred repeatedly throughout the history of the Church when it has become aware of the ripening of heresy in its midst. And it has been on the anvil of the ensuing struggle for the truth of the Gospel that the great creeds and confessions of faith of the Church have been forged.

A Church confession with Church authority has always arisen in a definite antithesis and conflict. It always has a pre-history, which does not consist in the discussion of an academic or even an ecclesiastico-political desire to reconfess the common faith, or even in the discussion of the fulfilment of this desire. It consists rather in controversies in which the existing exposition and application of Holy Scripture is called in question because the unity of the faith is differently conceived, and there is such different teaching on the basis of the existing unity that the unity is obscured and has to be rediscovered. . . .(36)

In this century, the most celebrated *status confessionis* was that experienced by the established Evangelical Church (i.e. the Lutheran, the Reformed and the Churches of the Union) in Germany in their conflict with those 'German Christians' who wished to align the Church with Nazi ideology. Within the first year of this struggle the famous Barmen Declaration was drafted and adopted by the Synod of the Confessing Church (May 1934). The novel and partial character of the 'Gospel' according to the 'German Christians' was decisively rejected at Barmen, and later that year, at the meeting of the Universal Christian Council for Life and Work held at Fanö in Sweden, the position of the Confessing Church was recognized as the true voice of the Gospel in Nazi Germany. Though not an official delegate, Dietrich Bonhoeffer played a crucial role at Fanö, and clearly regarded it 'as the dawn of a new era in the ecumenical movement'.(37) Unfortunately, the ecumenical Church in the end failed the Confessing Church in its hour of need. But at least at Fanö, against considerable opposition (and not just from the

'German Christians'), the struggle for the truth of the Gospel and therefore the need to identify and combat heresy within the life of the Church were recognized and introduced into the emergent ecumenical movement.

The significance of Fanö for the unity and witness of the postwar contemporary church has only recently been recognized. In this regard, Ulrich Duchrow's recent study *Conflict over the Ecumenical Movement: Confessing Christ Today in the Ecumenical Movement* is of considerable significance. Both Duchrow and Eberhard Bethge, in his more recent paper on the meaning of the *status confessionis*,(38) point to the significance for the contemporary Church of the decision of the Lutheran World Alliance meeting at Dar-es-Salaam in 1977 to recognize that a *status confessionis* existed in Southern Africa.

In his address to the Dar-es-Salaam conference Manas Buthelezi, a Lutheran bishop and theologian from South Africa, stated that

The Church has reached a confessional situation, reminiscent of the Reformation, when a new Church alignment was called into being by theological and ethical trends that had led to the adulteration of the essentials of the faith.(39)

In response to this, the conference appealed especially to its 'white member churches in Southern Africa to recognize that the situation in Southern Africa constitutes a *status confessionis*'. This meant that 'On the basis of faith and in order to manifest the unity of the Church, churches would publicly and unequivocally reject the existing apartheid system.'(40) As yet, however, little concrete seems to have resulted from this decision.

What happened at Dar-es-Salaam for the Lutheran confessional family has now happened at Ottawa for the Reformed family of Churches. In the same way as Buthelezi raised the matter for the Lutherans, so Boesak placed it on the agenda of the WARC:

In South Africa apartheid is not just a political ideology. Its very existence as a political policy has depended and still depends on the theological justification of certain member churches of the WARC. For Reformed churches, this situation should constitute a *status confessionis*. This means that churches should recognize that apartheid is a heresy, contrary to the Gospel and inconsistent with the Reformed tradition, and consequently reject it as such.(41)

This is precisely what the Ottawa Assembly did.

If there is one thing the NGK would not have anticipated, it is that it would ever be accused of heresy by other Reformed Churches. The NGK has been perhaps more conscious of its confessional character than most other Reformed Churches, as several heresy trials during the course of the past century bear witness. How is it possible, then, that this Church, which, unlike the NHK, does not have any racial clause in its constitution and articles of faith, and which has been such an ardent defender of the faith, is being charged with heresy?

One major reason, we would suggest, is that the NGK has traditionally and officially regarded and treated its confessions of faith in a too static and scholastic way. As A. C. Cochrane has pointed out, a formal attachment to a Confession of Faith is 'no sure guarantee against heresy'.(42) Karl Barth's critique of unevangelical conservatism is appropriate here. Whereas for Barth the danger of theological liberalism was that of undermining the historical continuity of the faith, the danger of theological conservatism was that of denying the need for the living Word of God to speak afresh to the Church in every situation.(43) The Church comes to regard itself as the custodian of the truth, and, believing that the content of the Gospel is securely held, it passes it on from one generation to the next. In the process it assumes that doing this involves faithfulness to the Gospel. In fact, says Barth, 'In these circumstances it is not the Gospel which gives to the community the faith. . . . ; on the contrary, it is the community which imposes on the Gospel its own faith, mode of thought and outlook.' G. C. Berkouwer expresses the same insight when he writes that a concern for 'verbal conformity' to a confession 'can slacken concern for forms of heresy that penetrate under the seeming protection of orthodoxy: the life and thought of the Church can capitulate to particular ideologies, *frequently even with an appeal to the Gospel*'.(44) This makes it very difficult for a Church which adopts such a posture to hear any 'word of prophecy' which may be addressed to it even from within its own ranks. It is this, rather than simply the cumbersome procedures of the NGK, which at a deeper level explains why that Church was unable to respond creatively to the *Open Letter* addressed to it during 1982 by 123 of its own ministers and theologians.(45)

Confessing Christ in the world must always be historically concrete and specific because it is the living Lord of the Church who is being confessed in relation to contemporary issues. The Japanese theologian Yoshinoba Kumazawa has put this clearly:

Since the faith is to be confessed in relation to the historical acts of God, confessing the faith must bear an historical character. Specifically it should be *confessio in loco et tempore*: confessing the faith in a certain place and time. We are not going to 'repeat' statically what was confessed in the past within a particular situation.(46)

This means that the Church needs both to discern the meaning of the situation in which it presently exists, and to find the courage to risk confessing the faith anew in terms of that situation. A conservative confessionalism, while seeming to be less risky and more secure, is in fact in danger of erecting a false basis for security. In remaining faithful to the historic confessions by only verbally assenting to them in the present, a Church will end up denying their original intention and power and their meaning for today.

We must try to 'interpret' dynamically 'here' and 'now' what is going on in our present situation. The confessing attitude distinguishes itself from confessionalism through this character of historical act. In other words, not a superhistorical static *traditum*, but an historical dynamic act of succession, namely, *traditio*, is the basic attitude of confessing the faith, as distinct from confessionalism.(47)

'Confessionalism' prevents the Church from recognizing heresies that are not already dealt with in the historic confessions of faith, just as it prevented many of the Lutheran Confessional theologians in Nazi Germany from recognizing the threat to the Evangelical faith and Church at that time.(48)

The failure of the NGK and NHK to recognize apartheid as a heresy does not give the so-called English-speaking Churches any cause for self-righteous satisfaction or judgment. Their complicity in racism in practice (even if not, at least in recent times, in theory) is becoming ever more apparent as scholars begin to examine church history. For a variety of historical reasons, rather than through any innate theological purity or confessing courage, they have ended up by and large on the right side. Certainly this is true of those that belong to the South African Council of Churches. But the recognition by them that apartheid is a heresy must not be allowed, in turn, to become a slogan that prevents them from seeing other perhaps even more pertinent and critical issues facing the Church in South Africa today. Confessing the faith against the heresy of apartheid has, in view of what we have just been saying, the potential for a static confessionalism on the part of the English-speaking Churches. Together with the NGK they too must be called to repentance and openness to the living word of the Gospel for the whole Church in South Africa at this critical moment in the history of the country.

It is thus within this context of a *status confessionis* that we are forced to ask 'Has the time for a Confessing Church finally arrived?'

Our answer is yes. ABRECSA has pointed a possible way forward, in the first instance, for the Churches in South Africa that belong to the WARC. It may well be that as the sin of apartheid entered into the Church and into the social fabric of South Africa through a misrepresentation of the Reformed faith, so it shall be overcome, at least in part, by a rediscovery of the full meaning and implication of that faith for our situation.

The sixteenth-century Reformers were adamant: there can be no true Church unless it is continually in the process of reformation (*ecclesia semper reformanda*). This is why it has become so essential to recognize the *status confessionis* of the present time, for that is the first step to repentance and renewal. And it is fundamentally the renewal of the Church in the power of the Spirit that we are concerned about, not the criticizing or the judging of the NGK or any other Church. Indeed, all that we have said arises out of an ardent hope that the NGK itself will not remain outside the process, but that, in sharing in repentance together with the rest of the Church in South Africa for the hurts resulting from apartheid, it too may reject apartheid as a heresy, and play the role which, in the providence of God, it may yet fulfil in the healing of our land.

Notes

1 Cf. 'An Open Letter concerning Nationalism, National Socialism, and Christianity', supplement to *Pro Veritate*, July 1971. The letter was written by a group of ministers and theologians in Cape Town.

2 Cf. A. H. Lückhoff, *Cottesloe* (Cape Town, 1978); John W. de Gruchy, *The Church Struggle in South Africa* (Cape Town, 1979), p. 65f.

3 The question was probably first raised by Dr Robert Bilheimer, an American theologian, and one of the Secretaries at Cottesloe.

4 *Pro Veritate*, 15 July 1965, vol. IV, no. 3, p. 1ff.

5 'Nogeens die "Belydende Kerk" ', *Pro Veritate*, 15 November 1965, vol. IV, no. 6, p. 1ff; and 'Nou juis die "Belydende Kerk" ' *Pro Veritate*, 15 December 1965, vol. IV, no. 8, p. 1ff.

6 *Pro Veritate*, 15 December 1965, p. 4.

7 See John W. de Gruchy and W. B. de Villiers (eds), *The Message in Perspective* (Johannesburg, 1969).

8 *Apartheid and the Church* (Report on the Church Commission of the Study Project on Christianity in Apartheid Society), (Johannesburg, 1972).

9 Appendix in Eberhard Bethge, *Bonhoeffer: Exile and Martyr* (London, 1975), p. 167.

10 Ibid., p. 172; Cf. John W. de Gruchy, 'Bonhoeffer in South Africa' in Bethge, op. cit., p. 36f.

11 Ibid., p. 177.

12 Statement issued by Representatives at the Consultation on Racism, 14

February 1980, in *Ecunews*, 27 February 1980, 4/1980, p. 11.

13 Cf. ABRECSA Conference Report, Appendix p. 163.

14 'Black and Reformed—A Challenge or a Burden?' in ABRECSA Conference Report, p. 19 (our emphasis).

15 See below, Appendix p. 161.

16 Art. XXVII; cf. John W. de Gruchy, 'The Identity of the Church in South Africa' in *Journal of Theology for Southern Africa*, no. 8, September 1974, p. 38ff.

17. Dietrich Bonhoeffer, 'Zur Frage nach der Kirchengemeinschaft' in *Gesammelte Schriften II* (München, 1959), p. 222; English translation *The Way to Freedom* (London, 1966), p. 79. This essay is of considerable importance for the present discussion.

18 Decisions taken at the National Conference of the SACC, 20–24 June 1982.

19 Cf. Donald Cragg, 'The State of the Ecumene in South Africa' in *Missionalia*, vol. X, no. 1, April 1982, p. 3ff.

20 Letter to the Ephesians, 6.

21 *Racism in Theology and Theology against Racism* (Report of a Consultation organized by the Commission on Faith and Order and the Programme to Combat Racism), (Geneva, 1975), p. 14.

22 Dietrich Bonhoeffer, 'Unser Weg nach dem Zeugnis der Schrift' in op. cit. p. 340; English translation in op. cit., p. 189.

23 J. W. C. Wand, *The Four Great Heresies* (London, 1955). Cf. the discussion on heresy by G. C. Berkouwer *The Church* (Grand Rapids, 1976) p. 377f.

24 Karl Barth, *Church Dogmatics* I/2 (Edinburgh, 1962), p. 807.

25 Cf. the trial of the Rev. J. J. Kotzé at the Cape Synod in 1862/3.

26 W. A. Visser 't Hooft, 'The Mandate of the Ecumenical Movement', Appendix V in Norman Goodall (ed.), *The Uppsala Report 1968* (Geneva, 1968), p. 320; cf. Berkouwer, op. cit., p. 381.

27 *The Message* (Appendix p. 155).

28 Ulrich Duchrow, *Conflict over the Ecumenical Movement* (Geneva, 1981) p. 342.

29 Ibid., p. 16; cf. Berkouwer, op. cit., p. 383.

30 Cf. Douglas Bax, *A Different Gospel: A Critique of the Theology Behind Apartheid* (Presbyterian Church of Southern Africa, 1979). See pp. 112–43 below.

31 Cf. B. B. Keet, *Suid-Afrika Waarheen* (Stellenbosch, 1955).

32 WARC, Frankfurt, 1964; cf. Appendix to the Assembly Report III.

33 Nairobi 1970, *Proceedings*, p. 226.

34 Ibid., p. 227.

35 Duchrow, op. cit., p. 19.

36 Barth, op. cit., p. 628.

37 Cf. Duchrow, op. cit., p. 319; on the significance of Fanö, see Eberhard Bethge, *Dietrich Bonhoeffer* (London, 1970), p. 298ff.

38 Eberhard Bethge, '*Status confessionis*—was ist das?' (unpublished paper; April, 1982).

39 'In Christ—One Community in the Spirit' in *In Christ—A New Community: The Proceedings of the Lutheran World Federation 1977* (Geneva, 1977), p. 90ff.

40 Duchrow, op. cit., p. 75.

41 'He made us all, but. . . .', p. 1 above.

42 A. C. Cochrane, *The Church's Confession Under Hitler* (Pittsburgh, 1976), p. 196.

43 Cf. *Church Dogmatics* IV/3, p. 818.

44 Ibid., p. 819; Berkouwer, op. cit., p. 380 (our emphasis).

45 Cf. David J. Bosch, 'Die Ope Brief in Konteks' in David J. Bosch, Adrio König, Willem D. Nicol (eds.), *Perspektief op die Ope Brief* (Cape Town, 1982).

46 'Confessing the Faith in Japan' in *The South East Asia Journal of Theology*, July/October 1966, p. 161.

47 Ibid., p. 162.

48 Cochrane, op. cit., p. 186ff.

8 WILLEM VORSTER
The Bible and apartheid 1

An interpretative critique of *Human Relations and the South African Scene in the Light of Scripture*.

Recent meetings of the WARC have made it clear that the Church is deeply involved in the political situation in South Africa. It is furthermore evident that the Bible plays an important role in discussions on the Church and race relations in the country. This is not strange and there cannot be any objection to the involvement of the Church and of theologians in the relationship between peoples and social justice. I would, in fact, assert that the time has come for the Church in South Africa to speak out with a unified voice and for theologians to partake actively and positively in the making of the history of the country and its peoples. This does not imply, however, that all theologians should all of a sudden regard themselves as politicians. What I have in mind is the creation of a contextualized theology which is *credible* and will stand the test of time. Church and theology are not back-seat drivers for the state or any political party. Although the Church is not of the world it is in the world. That is why it has become absolutely necessary for theologians in this country to rethink the task of theology in the current situation.

In view of the important role the Bible seemingly plays in South Africa and the many different ways in which it is appealed to, it would seem that the interrelation between the Bible and politics needs to be investigated afresh. Loader recently analysed the use of Scripture in conventional Afrikaans theology.(1) In spite of the rejection of fundamentalism and biblicism by all three Afrikaans Reformed Churches, he showed how the Bible is misused by theologians of these Churches. He did not, however, analyse the use of Scripture by these Churches with regard to race relations.

The NGK, like the other two Afrikaans Reformed Churches, has paid a considerable amount of attention to the problem of the Bible and race relations, the history of which is illuminating. The current official views of the Church are incorporated in the synodal report entitled *Human Relations and the South African Scene in the Light of Scripture.* This report was drafted by a commission chaired by Ds W. A. Landman and approved as an official document of the Church by the General Synod in October 1974.

In an attempt to determine the nature of the use of Scripture by the NGK in the area of race relations, I shall analyse this report, keeping in mind that it is the work of a commission and not an individual. The sole purpose of my investigation is to test the *credibility* of the use of Scripture in this document in order to further discussion of the matter. I shall limit my analysis to: the use of Scripture; the Bible and history; the Bible as a book of norms.

THE USE OF SCRIPTURE

The report, *Human Relations and the South African Scene in the Light of Scripture*, did not originate in a vacuum. It has a history of its own and is dependent upon a tradition. On the former I will not comment. The latter reveals a kaleidoscopic picture of the making of an ideology. This report marks in a certain sense a watershed in this process. In comparison with earlier NGK documents of the same kind, it undoubtedly reflects a change in political premises and attitude. Although it remains to a great extent a plea for the status quo it is not, like earlier documents, simply an apology for all aspects of apartheid on biblical grounds. The change is nevertheless political and not interpretative.

The Relevance of the Bible

The relevance of the Bible for matters of race relations in South Africa is taken for granted by the NGK. All the documents I have consulted witness to the following presupposition: *the Bible is the Word of God containing eternal and unchanging norms that have to be applied by those who wish to do the will of God.* Although there has been a loss of certainty through the years with regard to the will of God as far as race relations in South Africa are concerned, the basic assumption remains: the Bible has in principle something to say about race relations in a plural society. The following statement of the *ad hoc* commission of the Council of Churches of the NGK and its so-called 'daughter' churches (1956) is, for example, quoted with approval in the report: 'To an increasing extent the Christian Church is becoming aware of the danger of acquiescing in race relations which possibly do not accord with the Word of God. That is why the Dutch Reformed Church is listening anew to what the Word of God has to tell us about the matter in the present-day situation.' (p. 7)

It is remarkable that the assumption of the Bible as a book that contains the principles normative for all spheres of life is nowhere *explained* in the report. Not even in the paragraph on the 'hermeneutic (i.e. interpretative) approach' does one find a trace of an exposition of this assumption (cf. pars. 5 and 2). It is simply stated that the Bible contains principles normative for relations between peoples to which the Church must unconditionally and obediently bow (p. 7). This assumption has a very long and interesting history. Even a well-informed New Testament scholar like Professor E. P. Groenewald could comment with great certainty in 1947 on 'Apartheid and guardianship in the light of Holy Scripture', and maintain that there are many statements in the Bible that give fixed principles with regard to race relations. He concluded that the Bible teaches the unity of mankind; that God consciously divided man into races, peoples and tongues; that apartheid is the will of God and that it leads to national, social and religious apartheid; that there is a spiritual unity in Christ.(2) He furthermore asserted that the race policy of the Afrikaner gives proof of their fear of God, and Scripture says, 'Happy is the nation whose God is the Lord'.(3) The lack of sensitivity regarding problems involved in interpreting the Bible in such a manner is evident from the influence of Groenewald and others on the growth of tradition. On the grounds of the authority and so-called all-sufficiency of Scripture it is believed that the Bible is a guide for all times and all problems of all natures.(4) This assumption is highly problematic. The Bible simply becomes an 'oracle book' of proof texts. Almost anything can be read into it when using it to establish an ideology like apartheid.(5,6) However, these interpretations formed the blueprint of the report as far as biblical principles were concerned.

It can be argued, as does the report, that this point of departure is a confession. This cannot be faulted as long as such a confession is open for discussion, validation and control. Most of the report's statements are followed by explanations and motivations. One would therefore expect some kind of explanation of statements 1, 2 and 5 (pp. 7–10) that would clarify the assumptions that form part of this point of departure. The acceptance of such a confession is in no way a guarantee of the correctness of its interpretation of Scripture or even a condition of the valid exposition of Scripture.(7) 'Just as others try to interpret the Bible "atheistically" or in a "Marxist sense", so here we find a biblical exegesis which elevates the concept of "people" (understood ethnologically) and that of "race" to the role of biblical keynotes. It is not surprising that the outsider finds evident "racist" features in what results.'(8) The report is the result of a history of uncritical hermeneutics, a hermeneutics of acceptance in which the relevance of the Bible is not questioned but simply accepted and confessed. This assumption needs thorough revision.

The Selective Use of the Bible

Most Christians, be they defenders of apartheid, feminism, materialism or liberation, tend to use the Bible selectively as a kind of proof text. It is necessary to note that there have for many years been a number of axioms, derived in this way, that have served as the scriptural basis for apartheid in the NGK. In 1948 Professor B. J. Marais objected to a report on racial and national apartheid in the light of Scripture, which in substance contained the ideas developed by Groenewald referred to above. A commission reworked the report(9) and in 1951 a number of axioms was subscribed to.(10) Thus our report is based on a selective use of the Bible which furnishes a basis for the political status quo: 'A political system based on the autogenous or separate development of various population groups can be justified from the Bible.' (par. 49.6, cf. 13.6) By using the Bible selectively, a major problem results. If it is true that there is no sign of a racial problem in the Bible (Report, p. 13), why should one then look for a scriptural basis for the so-called racial problem?

It is difficult to understand the logic of the 'hermeneutic approach' of the report (par. 5) when it says: 'A serious warning must be issued against the marked tendency which has always existed, namely to link up an understanding of the Bible with current tradition. The danger then exists of the Scriptures being interpreted according to what the "historical situation" prescribes—and therefore mostly on a selective basis.' It is exactly on this score that the report is self-contradictory. Clearly the 'historical situation' out of which the report grew is taken as a grid through which the Bible is read. It is this grid that provides the hermeneutical key for a selective reading of the Bible. There is no *objective* reading of the Bible. Many Christians would subscribe to this particular way of using the Bible(11) but this does not make a selective use of the Bible valid.

Bearing in mind that nothing in the Bible was written with modern man in view, and noting the cultural changes Christians have undergone since the days of the primitive church in Jerusalem, one is astonished to read in the report (par. 10) that 'The holy command that Israel should continue to exist independently *vis-à-vis* the other peoples cannot be applied directly, but certainly by way of analogy, to the situation of the present day. In the case of Israel the multi-national demand for isolation was motivated by religious and not by racial or ethnic considerations.' (p. 21) The dangers of so-called analogies between Israel and other nations are well known, and cannot be prevented by a 'salvation–historical' premiss. (p. 22)

The argumentation in the report runs in a vicious circle. It starts with an ideology which is introduced into Scripture and in the end it becomes an ideology based on Scripture. We do not need the Bible for this purpose. Common knowledge should suffice to judge the credibility of our decisions on human relations. Let me illustrate this with a few remarks on the exposition of 'development' in the report (cf. ch. 3 par. 48). The point of departure is unexceptionable: 'The Gospel is concerned with the man as a whole, with his spiritual as well as his material needs.' (p. 67) This statement is substantiated by a quote from the recommendations of the Reformed Ecumenical Synod of Lunteren (1968), which reads, 'Christians in general and the Church in particular bear a responsibility towards members of all races who suffer from poverty, underdevelopment and political oppression. Believers should be willing to bend every effort to alleviate the suffering of such peoples.' (p. 66) Scripture (Ps. 65:10f., 72:16, 104; Mt. 5:45; Gn. 2:15 and I Pt. 4:10) is invoked. The term is defined (par. 48.2) as 'a broad concept which comprises economic–technical, socio-political and cultural development, as well as the development of man towards the realization of the full potential with which God endows him.' Attention is drawn to the shift from the economic to the human aspect of development in Third World countries. 'Recently, however, the emphasis shifted to human development, and development came to be seen as the process of liberation and conciliation which enables people to realize their full human potential, as God intends them to do.' (p. 67) The share of the Church in development is limited to 'the instruments of grace, the Word and the sacraments, as well as the service of the diaconate.' (p. 67) On the ground of Mt. 6:33 it is asserted that in biblical terms 'development is in the first instance a spiritual concept' (p. 68), although the material aspect is not denied.

I do not want to challenge the truth of these statements. I am concerned with the way in which Scripture is used. If it is true that the Gospel is concerned with man as a whole and that development is a process of liberation and reconciliation which enables man to develop 'towards the realization of the full potential with which God endows him', the question arises how one can determine what God intends (cf. par. 48.2). Should one read the Bible from the perspective of a Christian who is an underdog or from that of the ruler; with the glasses of those who regard themselves as freedom fighters or of those who maintain the status quo? Should one infer from par. 48.2 that one can preach liberation from capitalism as development? Does one have the right to limit development to 'spiritual development' with an appeal to Mt. 6:33? While Mt. 6:33 indeed reads, 'Set your mind on God's kingdom and his justice before everything else, and all the rest will come to you as well', there is in the same Bible a verse that reads, 'Suppose a brother or sister is in rags with not enough food for the day, and one of you says, "Good luck to you, keep yourselves warm, and have plenty to eat", but does nothing to supply their bodily needs, what is the good of that?' (Ja. 2:15f.). Is the one statement then opposed to the other or should one pursue the one and leave the other? If it is preferred to use the Bible as is done in par. 48.4, one should replace, 'in biblical terms' with 'in one instance in the Bible'.

It is clear that the report is based on the assumption that a selective use of Scripture can substantiate a particular political policy and in that way make the Bible relevant. The basic framework consists of a few selected proof texts. D. S. Bax is most probably correct in his assertion, 'Although the report refers to a large number of texts (nearly 50), its case is really built on only a few texts. These are the same texts to which the NGK for years has traditionally appealed in support of apartheid: Gen. 1; Gen. 11; Dt. 32:6; Ac. 2: 5–13 and Ac. 17:26. All of them are basically misinterpreted.'(12)

The Hermeneutic Principles of the Report

I have already referred to the report's premiss that the Bible is applicable to all walks of life in all ages. In addition the following hermeneutic principles are also given:

1 The Bible must be interpreted in accordance with recognized Reformed, scientific, hermeneutic principles in keeping with its actual intention. It is not a scientific text-book of empirical sociology or anthropology.

2 The Scriptures must not be used 'biblistically'; they must be interpreted in their own context and in the context of the entire history of salvation.

3 In dealing with Scriptural data the Church will constantly have

to be aware of the central theme of its preaching, i.e. the way of salvation in Christ and the coming of the kingdom of God, and it will have to indicate and extol the norms that coincide with this theme in all spheres of life.

4 'The Church has a prophetic function in respect of the state and society when the Scriptural norms that should apply in all spheres of life are not respected.' (p. 11)

Principle 1 It is unfortunate that this principle is not explained in the report. Terms like 'Reformed', 'scientific', 'hermeneutic principles' can refer to many different things today, even in so-called Reformed circles. 'Reformed' it seems to me would be something totally different in the Netherlands from what it would be in South Africa. And what is regarded as 'scientific' in the report can hardly be related to any theory of science or any modern hermeneutic system. It is, however, evident from the report that Reformed, scientific, hermeneutic principles include matters like the following: The Bible as Word of God 'presents fundamental data and principles of normative significance in all spheres of life' (p. 11); the Bible should not be used selectively, or in a biblicist way. It should be interpreted in context in relation to the history of salvation. The Bible is a unity and there is both a continuity and a discontinuity between the testaments; the central theme of the Bible is the kingdom of God; reconciliation has a cosmic aspect; the Bible is not a scientific text-book for sociology or anthropology; no historical situation should function as a hermeneutic principle. Most of these 'hermeneutic principles' can be found in older books of a Reformed tradition(13); in that sense these principles are 'Reformed'.

I have indicated that I wish to contextualize these principles within the report. I shall therefore not subject them individually to scrutiny. Let us rather turn to the question of whether the report is true to its own point of departure. I shall limit my discussion to two examples.

The major part of the report is a contradiction of its own warning that the 'historical situation' should not be allowed to function 'as a hermeneutic principle according to which the Scriptures are interpreted' (p. 9). It is, however, the current race situation and political policy in South Africa that led the report's compilers to use Scripture selectively. Genesis to Revelation is explained within this hermeneutic frame of reference. This is illustrated by the question 'whether Gn. 11:1–9 can serve as a Scriptural basis for a policy of autogenous development' (p. 18). On page 10 the report refers to Bright who pointed out the 'efforts by an earlier generation to justify slavery on Scriptural grounds' while on page 12 there is an attempt to find a Scriptural basis for separate development.

A second very important principle in the report is *context*. But here again it fails to be consistent. One can only refer to the use of Gn. 6 (p. 20); Dt. 32:8; Am. 9:7; Ps. 147:19,20; Ac. 14:16, 17:30 (p. 23) in connection with the equality of people (cf. I Cor. 11:7, Jn. 1:14 on p. 30), to name but a few instances of the misuse of Scripture with regard to context.(14)

The second part of the first hermeneutic principle cannot be faulted. The question however arises why so much importance is attached to finding sociological and anthropological guidelines from the Bible if the possibility is denied on principle (cf. pars. 7 and 19.6).

Principle 2 'Biblicism' like 'fundamentalism' has become a convenient term of abuse. The first question to be asked therefore is what these terms refer to in the report. On pages 10 and 11 'biblicism' is limited to the use of 'context'. In the application of 'context', however, the report is a failure. 'Biblicism' can refer to more than taking 'context' seriously.(15) 'Someone might maintain that all problems of faith, life and theology were to be solved simply by use and exegesis of the Bible and conversely that no other consideration need be taken into account than the knowledge furnished by the Bible. He might maintain this without maintaining the characteristic fundamentalist tenet that the Bible is without error of any kind; he would simply be arguing that though the Bible contained errors of various sorts, mainly no doubt historical inaccuracies, it remained in fact the sole guide for theology and all theological effort should be devoted solely to the interpretation of it.(16) In view of this the use of Scripture in the report seems to be 'biblicistic'.

Principles 3 and 4 In the third main part of this article the Bible is discussed as 'a book of norms'. A quote from Von Allmen will therefore suffice here. 'In the nature of the case, general "principles" of this kind cannot be very concrete; they must necessarily disregard the "situation" if they are to be valid in every place, time and circumstance. We are not surprised to find, therefore, that the result of the search for biblical starting-points sounds very abstract

and general: a policy which tries to preserve the identity of the
various ethnic groups, cultures and races can be endorsed provided
that the ultimate goal remains "biblical", namely that love, justice,
truth and peace prevail.'(17)

THE BIBLE AND HISTORY

With regard to hermeneutics paragraph 9 of the report is one of the
most problematic in the whole document. Both its hermeneutic
principles and the pretension that it offers a scientific exposition
must be called into question.

The purpose of the analysis of Gn. 10 and 11:1-9 in paragraph 9
is said to determine 'whether the Scriptures also give us a normative
indication of the way in which the human race differentiated into
a variety of races, peoples and nations' and 'whether the diversity
of peoples accords with the will of God and whether it was God's
intention, from the outset, to differentiate the human race in this
way' (p. 14). From the very beginning it is evident that the analysis of Gn. 10-11 (also 9:24-27) is determined by the question on
page 18, namely 'whether Gn. 11:1-9 can serve as a Scriptural
basis for a policy of autogenous development'.

Let it be clear that it is in principle possible to interpret any
given text in different ways in accordance with the method of interpretation applied. The answer one gets depends upon the question you ask. One can inevitably also ask wrong questions. The
history of interpretation also teaches us that even, or perhaps especially, the Bible is interpreted in many ways. Some people regard
the Bible as a book which refers to realities outside the text, be
they theological (e.g. God, heaven, angels) or historical (e.g. places
and people in the real world). Others read the Bible with a view to
the 'intention' of the author, that is with reference to what the
'historical' authors actually had in their minds. Yet others wish to
read the Bible 'as it stands', as literature. It has become clear that
the Bible is a collection of *ancient* books which have to be interpreted in the light of their own character, that is, occasional religious
writings of different kinds which were written long ago over a long
period of time.

One of the most important problems we have inherited from the
Enlightenment is that of history and especially the Bible and history. This problem cannot be ignored or thought away. The report
states categorically and correctly that the Bible is not a scientific
text-book of sociology or anthropology. But the Bible is also not a
history-book. One can use the Bible as a source for the reconstruc-

tion of history, but that does not make the Bible itself a history-book. He who wants to make historical statements in the light of the Bible should realize that whether it is a history of Israel or the life of Jesus which is to be reconstructed, it will be a reconstruction of possibilities and probabilities and not of facts in the sense of 'how it actually happened'.(18) It is wrong to assume that the Bible presents reality in its naked (uninterpreted) form. Even the authors of biblical writings did not describe 'reality' as it actually happened. In this respect matters like text type and so on play a very important role. 'We recognize at once that there is no *one* significance to any event. There may be as many meanings attributed to it as there are persons who interpret it. But it is precisely this diversity of interpretation *that forces us to use the rough distinction between fact and interpretation.* By using this distinction, we indicate that although the death of Hitler meant many different things to different people, his death was a fact alike for Nazis, Jews, Germans, Russians and English historians.'(20)

Gn. 1–11 confronts us with difficulties in this respect. It is undoubtedly not 'history' in the sense of a logical story based on the weighing and selection of facts. It is a theological interpretation of *prehistory.* That is why both the motivation and the explication in paragraph 9 of the report are so problematic. One does at least expect interpreters who regard the Bible as a history-book to use an historical method when they make historical statements. What is found in the report points to the contrary. We come across the give-away phrase 'the event itself'. 'It is important to note that the situation presupposed in Gn. 11:1–9 goes back beyond Gn. 10 and in reality links up with the end of Gn. 9. The descendants of Noah's three sons remained in the vicinity of Ararat for a few generations (Gn. 10:25) before they decided to move in a [south-] easterly direction to [the later] Babylonia (11:12). In the first verse these people are described as "the whole earth" in the sense of "all the inhabitants of the earth". It is important to note this. *At the time therefore there were no other people on earth* [my italics]. It is also said that at that time they all spoke the same language. This state of affairs existed after their arrival in Babylonia and the commencement of their building program.' (p. 15f.) Furthermore, 'From the sequel to this history it is clear that the undertaking and the intentions of these people were in conflict with the will of God. Apart from the reckless arrogance that is evident in their desire to make a name for themselves, the deliberate concentration on one spot was in conflict with God's command to replenish the earth (Gn. 1:28; 9:1,7).' (p. 16) This *historical* argumentation is continued and it is asserted, 'That the differentiation of humanity into various language groups and "nations" was extended further to give rise to *race* differences is not, in fact, mentioned in the Scriptures in so many words, but is neverthess confirmed by the *facts of history* [my italics]. The ancient Egyptians were already familiar with a division of mankind into (five!) races.' (p. 16f.) What is here being described in the report as history is later referred to as 'story' (cf. pp. 17-19), and although 'race' is not mentioned in Gn. 11 as the report rightly states, a discussion thereof in the light of Gn. 11 is nevertheless given. 'The diversity of races and peoples, to which the confusion of tongues contributed, is an aspect of reality which God obviously intended for this dispensation. To deny this fact is to side with the tower-builders. Therefore a policy which in broad terms (as distinct from its concrete implementation) bears this reality in mind, is biblically realistic in the good sense of the word. We must not forget that Gn. 11 also tells us of man's attempt to establish a (forced) unity of the human race.' (p. 18) These quotations make it clear that in the report (a) Gn. 11:1-9 is read from the perspective of the current 'historical situation' in South Africa in order to find a Scriptural basis for that situation; (b) Gn. 10-11 is regarded as history in the sense of how things actually happened—a history which can be used to bring to light yet additional historical 'facts'; (c) context is ignored to such an extent that the sequence of a story can be changed arbitrarily for 'historical' arguments; (d) 'race' as an extra-textual entity is read into the text.

In the report the text of Gn. 10-11 is presented as a window through which the reader can see how things actually happened in order to establish a Scriptural basis for a political policy. 'The question we are faced with here is *whether the Scriptures also give us a normative indication* [my italics] of the way in which the human race differentiated into a variety of races, peoples and nations.' (p. 14). It is assumed that one can infer from the table of nations how things were in the beginning and what God's will and intention is. For this purpose the discrepancy between Gn. 10 and 11 in connection with the one and many languages had to be removed by saying that Gn. 10 presupposes Gn. 11 or, even stronger, presupposes the situation (an historical argument!). In order to solve the problem of 'chronology' and harmonize two parts of the story of prehistory, the text is reorganized and the order of events ('reality', according to the report) rearranged according to the views held by

the compilers of how things 'were' originally. First Gn. 11 then 10!
Undoubtedly a narrator can arrange events according to his will.
Nobody would deny that, and certainly scholars of the past have
attempted to argue the unity of the story of prehistory by rearran-
ging the material.(21) The problem with the report is, however,
that a reconstruction of prehistory is given without any historical
argumentation whatsoever, to serve a political purpose. Having
done the rearrangement all sorts of quasi-historical deductions are
made from Gn. 11. Since the 'will of God' had to be proved, it did
not cause any problem! Text type, problems of the history and
growth of these chapters and the relationship between these two
chapters and the remainder of Gn. 1–11 are simply ignored because
they are regarded as a historical review of how things really happened.

I do not wish to enter into all the problems involved in the origin
and growth of our present text of Gn. 1–11. However, research has
made it clear that these chapters are not a unity.(22) It is furthermore known that a large part of Gn. 1–11 is taken up by genealo-
gies which originated from different backgrounds and that they
represent an independent text type.(23) The function of Gn. 10 as
'genealogy' is related to the command given to Noah in 9:1, 'Be
fruitful and increase, and fill the earth.' It illustrates how his
ancestors were spread over many geographical areas.(24) The
report on the other hand maintains, wrongly, 'Thus the emphasis
falls here on the primordial relatedness of all peoples and their
fundamental equivalence.' (p. 15) There is no sign in Gn. 10 of
'fundamental equivalence' or 'primordial relatedness' (as historical
data) let alone of 'race'.(25) Gn. 10 should be read from the perspective of its *Gattung* (genre) and its relatedness to earlier genealo-
gies in Gn. 1–11 and not from the perspective of so-called norms
in connection with the 'views' of God on 'separate development'.

As to Gn. 11:1–9 there is little doubt among contemporary Old
Testament scholars about its text type. Since the days of H. Gunkel
it has been regarded as an aetiological saga which explains the origin of the diversity of languages.(26) Two motifs are present,
namely the confusion of tongues and as a result the dispersion of
man because of his arrogance. These motifs have nothing to do with
the 'origin' of 'ethnic diversity' in the sense of the report. In view
of the fact that Gn. 11:1–9 is read (a) out of context, (b) as history
from the perspective of 'separate development', (c) to prove that
'separate development' is according to God's will, deductions are
made in connection with the current 'historical situation' in South

Africa! The transition from Gn. 10 to 11 is not smooth. This has to do with the purpose of the two parts of prehistory.(27) This is why it is not necessary either to change the present sequence of Gn. 10 and 11 or to harmonize the two chapters. In the first a genealogy is used to explain how the ancestors of Noah, that is the nations and peoples, filled the earth, and the latter is a saga to explain the origin of the diversity of languages and the dispersion of peoples.(28)

Paragraph 9 of the report has in the first place to do with the problem of the Bible and history, as I have indicated. Harvey speaks of 'the morality of historical knowledge', something which is totally absent in the report. The compilers of the report were compelled to ignore their own 'hermeneutic principle' and point of departure the moment they started reading Gn. 10–11 as history and disregarding the context of these chapters. Context is more than the relationship between two parts of a text. Intertextual relationships often form a network of 'intersignification' as we have seen above. He who wishes to treat biblical data as history has to take into account the relationship between form and content. In the case of Gn. 10 and 11 it is a problem of history, genealogy and saga. These forms determine the rules of the game.

THE BIBLE AS A BOOK OF NORMS

The mere appeal by an individual person to biblical utterances always carries with it the danger of biblicism. This situation becomes all too easily obscured since what is elevated to the status of a revealed norm has always served simultaneously as a justification of personal conduct. The truth is that Scripture has been replaced by an exegesis which accords with domesticated and longstanding particular interests.(29)

This remark gives, to my mind, an adequate description of what happens in the report. The Bible has the function of a book of rules and regulations, norms and principles by which church and society are organized in a plural society where the rulers have opted for 'separate development'.

There are two matters which are very problematic in connection with the use of the Bible as a book of norms in the report. The first is the view of Scripture, i.e. what Scripture actually is, and the second is the application of this view. On page 10 the report says, 'Although the Bible is no scientific text-book, it nevertheless does present fundamental data and principles which are of normative significance in all spheres of life. This is linked up with the fact that the central theme of Scripture is the kingdom of God and that Christ's incarnation and sacrifice of atonement also have wider cosmic significance. In assessing the directive principles for all spheres of life as derived from Scriptural data, we must take into account the timely warning of the Reformed Ecumenical Synod of Grand Rapids, 1963, against an "incautious use of the term 'principle'. . . . When the Synod uses the term 'principle' in this context the term shall mean 'a regulative rule of conduct expressive of God's will as revealed in Scripture, and demanding application regardless of place, time and circumstance'." (Acts, p. 37)' The 'same' definition is given on page 12. There it reads, 'In terms of race relations the Scriptures never present "a regulative rule of conduct expressive of God's will . . . and demanding application regardless of place, time and circumstance".' The greatest part of the report is, however, a search for principles and norms in connection with race relations and 'separate development' in order to legitimize the current 'historical situation' in the Republic of South Africa. The Bible becomes a book of overt and hidden norms. One can speak of such a 'normative' interpretation as a method of interpretation in the same way as one would speak of a marxist, sociological, or historical-critical interpretation of the Bible. Behind every story, psalm, letter or whatever form or statement there is a norm. This approach to the Bible should be questioned (even though such a method is not alien to the history of interpretation of the Bible).

Over the ages Church and theology have been regulated to a great extent by the Bible. Many techniques were developed to bridge the gap between the text of the Bible and the situation within which it was used. In addition to a literal interpretation, the application of the Bible in new situations was made possible by allegorical, typological, spiritual and other types of interpretations. With the aid of the so-called *'sensus spiritualis'* concept, amongst others, the Bible was applied directly to Christian 'life-situations'.(30) Although the techniques mentioned above are not applied in the report, the compilers nevertheless make use of a so-called 'deeper' meaning of biblical data. Behind the 'message' of any part of Scripture there might be a deeper normative meaning, the will of God, it is assumed. The Bible as a whole, in all its parts, not only the ethical statements, provides us with norms.

This approach has its background in the doctrine of the authority of the Bible. Already in the seventeenth century a distinction was being made between the 'historical' and 'normative' authority of the Bible. Even a person like the Reformed systematic theologian

Bavinck, however, asserted that everything in the Bible does not have normative authority.(31) Heyns (32), whose influence in the report is significant and clear, on the other hand introduces the artificial distinction between 'peripheral' and 'scopic' authority in an attempt to solve the problem of the normativeness of the Bible as a whole. Thus for the compilers of the report the Bible as a whole is a book of norms, even though it is not explained how these norms are to be discovered.

I do not think that any of the compilers would conceive of Christianity as a religion of the law. It is, however, difficult to expel the impression that they handle the Bible in a rabbinic manner, seeming to think that what Christians need is a Mishna and a Talmud. Their search for norms and what I have called a 'deeper' meaning makes the Bible a new book of law. We are here confronted with the problem of the relevance of the Bible. For them the Bible is

... a work to which one could turn with one's problems and receive directions about what was right or what should be done. The idea that the Bible ought to work in this way is probably a survival of fundamentalism. I am not thinking only of crude and obvious matters such as looking into the Bible to find guidance on whether women can wear trousers or go to church without a hat; I am thinking of the more sophisticated questions, often discussed in ecumenical gatherings, such as whether Christians should in certain circumstances support revolutionary movements, or whether they can offer insights which would help towards peace in an area of severe conflict. To me it seems not perhaps impossible, but certainly exceptional, that even a sophisticated consulation of the Bible can lead directly to decisions about such things. The Bible is not in fact a problem solver. It seems to me normal that the biblical material bears upon the whole man, his total faith and life, and that out of that total faith and life *he* takes his decisions as a free agent.(33)

The question arises whether the report's transformations of the norms and principles which are found in the Bible are credible. To put it another way: how are these meta-historical norms of the report applied in practice?

There is a remarkable difference, as far as the application of the Bible is concerned, between chapter one and chapters three and five, which deal with 'social justice' and 'marriage and mixed marriages' respectively. The situation in the latter chapters is much more 'open', perhaps because the 'Scriptural commandment of neighbourly love' (46.4) is decisive, and the policy of 'separate development' is partly shifted into the background. The result is that different adjustments are made to matters which had previously been regarded in the NGK tradition as matters that are based on scriptural grounds (cf. 47.2). In a changed situation these matters are interpreted in a different manner *in the light of Scripture* (cf. pp. 78 and 99). The *norms* of Scripture are in other words applied differently in a changed situation with regard to the *same* problems (e.g. mixed marriages).

The report refers to the search for norms that are to be applied in changing situations. Applicability of the Bible, like the relevance of the Bible, is, however, a very complicated matter.(34) The vast difference in culture between the people spoken of in biblical texts and those of Christians in South Africa underlines the strangeness of biblical data. Even in the Bible we find that the same problem is viewed from different perspectives by different authors (cf. *law* in Mt. and Paul, or Mt. and Mk. on *divorce*), not to speak of the difference in frame of reference between a modern Christian in South Africa and any author of any book in the Bible. This gives rise to the hermeneutical problem of *applicability* of the Bible.

The exegete is extended beyond his limits when he seeks to solve this problem solely with the norms of the Christian tradition. The crucial problem is clearly not the translation of Scriptural norms, but rather a reaction to any contemporary situation whatsoever, against which Christianity is measured. . . . Christian conduct exists only when it is a manifestation of the salvation which has already taken place. . . . The distinctive character of Christian conduct is dependent on the redemption which has already been made a reality.(35)

Application here does in any case not mean application of *norms* in new situations. It has to do with the whole problem of understanding. That is why the application of the Bible is a matter of decision and action. On the ground of his salvation a Christian can decide and act from *his* understanding of a situation and not on account of meta-historical norms. These actions and decisions are determined by the tension between the salvation a Christian already has and the hope in Christ. They can be 'in line' with what the Bible teaches but need not flow from or relate to any aspect of the Bible.(36) The Bible is a living witness that is not to be 'copied' slavishly, for it seeks to enter into a dynamic, inspiring relationship with us.(37) The sensitivity in the report for the present situation where the compilers made their own decisions—often without or even with an irrelevant appeal to Scripture—is praiseworthy. Understanding the Bible can also mean getting involved with the Bible and the world.

Bibliography

1 J. A. Loader, 'The use of the Bible in conventional South African theology' in W. S. Vorster (ed.), *Scripture and the use of Scripture* (Pretoria, 1979), pp. 1–25.

2 Cf. E. P. Groenewald, 'Apartheid en voogdyskap in die lig van die Heilige Skrif' in G. Cronjé, *Regverdige rasse-apartheid* (Stellenbosch, 1947), p. 65.

3 Ibid.

4 Cf. A. B. du Preez, *Die Skriftuurlike grondslag vir rasseverhoudinge* (Pretoria, 1955), p. 5.

5 Cf. Agenda of the Transvaal Synod of the NGK, 1944, p. 57, on the so-called 'armament of the blacks'. In view of the guardianship of whites, it is argued that blacks and 'coloureds' should not be armed during war.

6 Groenewald, op. cit., pp. 55–7, on Mt. 28:19; Ex. 9:1, 10:3.

7 J. Barr, *The Bible in the modern world* (London, 1973), p. 31, note 14.

8 D. von Allmen, *Theology–advocate or critic of apartheid? A critical study of the 'Landman Report' (1974) of the Dutch Reformed Church (South Africa)* (Berne, 1977), p. 8.

9 Cf. NGK, *Handelinge van die een-en-twintigste sinode* (Johannesburg, 1948), pp. 280–84, 368–9, 446.

10 Cf. J. F. du Toit, *Die NG Kerk in Suid-Afrika en rasseverhoudinge. Opsomming van belangrike uitsprake en besluite vanaf 1950–60* (Pretoria, 1961), p. 7f.

11 Cf. D. Nineham, *The use and abuse of the Bible. A study of the Bible in an age of rapid cultural change* (London, 1976), p. 42.

12 D. S. Bax, *Memorandum for the regional consultation of the WARC, 1979, on behalf of the Presbyterian Church of Southern Africa* (1979, not published).

13 See e.g. S. Greijdanus, *Schriftbeginselen ter Schriftverklarung en historisch overzicht over theorieën en wijzen van Schriftuitlegging* (Kampen, 1946).

14 Von Allmen, op. cit., p. 16.

15 G. Gloege, 'Biblizismus' in *Die Religion in Geschichte und Gegenwart*, vol. 1 (Tübingen, 1957), p. 1263.

16 J. Barr, *Fundamentalism* (London, 1977), p. 6.

17 Von Allmen, op. cit., p. 8.

18 Cf. Leopold von Rancke's axiom *'wie es eigentlich gewesen ist'* ('as it actually happened'), which is a category central to his historiography.

19 Cf. F. E. Deis, *Historiese heuristiek, teologiese hermeneutiek en Skrifgesag* (Port Elizabeth, 1976), p. 22.

20 Van A. Harvey, *The historian and the believer* (London, 1967), p. 217.

21 C. Westermann, *Genesis 1–11* (Darmstadt, 1972), p. 95.

22 Cf. J. Wellhausen, *Die Composition des Hexateuchs und der historischen Bücher des Alten Testaments* (Berlin, 1963), p. 11f.

23 Cf. Westermann, op. cit., p. 56.

24 Cf. G. von Rad, *Theologie des Alten Testaments. I. Die Theologie der geschichtlicher Überlieferungen Israels* (München, 1966), p. 67.

25 Cf. Von Rad, op. cit., p. 175.

26 Cf. Westermann, op. cit., p. 104.

27 Cf. Wellhausen, op. cit., p. 11.

28 Von Rad, op. cit., p. 177.

29 K. Berger, *Exegese des Neuen Testaments. Neue Wege vom Text zur Auslegung* (Heidelberg, 1977), p. 254.

30 E. Otto, 'Die Applikation als Problem der politischen Hermeneutik' in *Zeitschrift für Theologie und Kirche* (1974), pp. 145-80.

31 J. A. Heyns, *Brug tussen God en Mens. Oor die Bybel* (Pretoria, 1973), p. 129.

32 Ibid.

33 Barr, op. cit., p. 142.

34 Cf. Otto, op. cit., pp. 145-80.

35 Berger, op. cit., p. 255.

36 Berger, op. cit., p. 256.

37 J. S. Krüger, 'Theological Ethics' in I. H. Eybers *et al.* (eds.), *Introduction to Theology* (Pretoria, 1978), p. 225.

9 DOUGLAS BAX
The Bible and apartheid 2

Christians in South Africa are fundamentally divided over what the Bible teaches about race relations. On the one side stand the three Afrikaans Reformed Churches. Traditionally these Churches have all understood the Scriptures to support the policy of apartheid both in the missionary policy of the Church and in politics. This is still the understanding of the leaders of these Churches and the bulk of their ministers and ordinary members. They accuse those who understand the Bible differently of being misled by a 'liberal' and 'humanistic' ideology which exaggerates the *gelykheid* (sameness) and unity of the human race. The presuppositions of this ideology, they maintain, prevent those who understand the Bible differently from seeing or taking seriously what the text of Scripture actually says.

On the other side of the fundamental divide stand the so-called 'English-speaking' or 'multi-racial' Churches, the black, 'coloured' and Indian 'daughter' (now preferably called 'sister') Churches of the white Afrikaans Reformed Churches, and a growing minority of theologians, ministers and ordinary members within the white Afrikaans Churches themselves. All these in turn accuse the traditional teaching of the Afrikaans Churches of being misled and corrupted by the presuppositions of a nationalist and racist ideology.* In the background, supporting this side of the divide, is the international Christian community, including the member Churches of the World Alliance of Reformed Churches overseas. This the WARC made clear in August 1982, when it adopted its forthright statement *Racism and South Africa*, accusing the white Afrikaans Reformed Churches of 'theological heresy'.

In this essay we shall examine in some detail the actual interpretation of Scriptural texts on which the NGK, as the largest and most important of the white Afrikaans Churches, bases its support

---

* In practice, of course, many English-speaking Church people are also guilty of racism.

for apartheid. In doing so we seek to redress the general failure in the past of English-speaking Church people to grapple with the Afrikaans Reformed Churches' interpretation of Scripture in any depth or detail. One reads with a little embarrassment, for instance, of the way in which English-speaking delegates attempted to counter the typical NGK exegesis of Scripture at an inter-Church conference in 1953, when the Afrikaans- and English-speaking Churches were still in dialogue. Indeed one must confess that these delegates did resort to arguments based more on 'liberalism' or a liberal theology than the text of Scripture.(1)

In examining the NGK's interpretation of Scripture we also seek to make a contribution to the continuing dialogue with the NGK. At its General Synod in October 1982 the NGK, partly in reaction to the WARC's stand, set up a commission to re-examine its theology of race relations. It is to be hoped that this commission will not ignore criticism of the NGK's interpretation of Scripture as much as its previous commission seems to have ignored such criticism, expressed, for instance, in the 1972 SPROCAS Report, *Apartheid and the Church*.

The most important recent statements of the NGK, and the most comprehensive, are:

1 A report adopted by its General Synod in 1966. This was published under the title *Studie Stukke oor Rasse Aangeleenthede*, and in English as *Human Relations in South Africa*.

2 A report published in 1975 under the title *Ras, Volk en Nasie en Volkereverhoudinge in die Lig van die Skrif*, and in English as *Human Relations and the South African Scene in the Light of Scripture*. This report was the final product of a commission that the General Synod had constituted in 1970. The chairman of the commission was Ds W. A. Landman, and the report is sometimes called the Landman report. The commission, partly with the help of NGK theologians other than its own members, produced a long report whose original text was printed in the *Handelinge* or Acts of the 1974 General Synod of the NGK. This Synod, however, did not approve the entire report: it decided merely to note some parts that were not in line with traditional NGK theology or were critical of the status quo in South Africa. The parts that it actually endorsed it then left to the *Breë Moderatuur* or executive council of the NGK to give final form to.

The 1975 report has since been endorsed again by the NGK, for instance at its Cape Synod in 1979, and for the time being it remains the official standpoint of the NGK. It is also considerably longer and more comprehensive than the earlier one. We shall therefore focus on the 1975 Report in our examination.

SCRIPTURE TEXTS PRO APARTHEID?

Although the Report refers to a large number of texts (nearly 50), it cites most of them incidentally, and those on which it tries to build its essential argument are really only a few. These are the same texts to which the NGK for years has traditionally appealed in support of apartheid: Gn. 1:28, Gn. 11:1–9, Deut. 32:8, Ac. 2:5–13 and Ac. 17:26. The question then is whether the Report correctly interprets these texts to support its theology of race relations.

Genesis 1:28
And God blessed them and God said to them, 'Be fruitful and increase, and fill the earth and subdue it.'

The Report asserts that the 'diversity' of *volke* (peoples) and races 'was implicit' in this command of God to multiply and fill the earth, i.e. mankind was to fill the earth by diverging into different *volke*.(2) Because the Report identifies the diversity of *volke* and races so much with diversity of culture, it calls this command 'the cultural injunction'. That this was God's command, given to man at the time of his creation and repeated to Noah and his sons (Gn. 9:1,7), shows how fundamentally it is meant to condition mankind's existence. Thus 'ethnic diversity is in its very origin in accordance with the will of God for this dispensation', and must be incorporated 'in our ideas on relations between races and peoples (*volkere*)'.(3)

This is *eisegesis*, however, not *exegesis*: it reads into the text what is just not there. Contrary to the Report's argument about what it sees as 'implicit' in this text, calling mankind to increase and fill the earth by no means necessarily presupposed ethnic diversity, let alone keeping the *ethnoi* (peoples or *volke*) and their different cultures apart. The wording of Gn. 1:28 is quite clearly not a 'cultural injunction' to this effect. It calls mankind to fill the earth by multiplication, not by division.

It is true that reputable scholars have linked this verse to the idea of culture. But for them the point of this is in man's being called to 'subdue' the earth and (in the words that follow) 'rule over the fish of the sea, the birds of the air and over every living creature that moves on the ground'. It is by the development of the tools and artefacts of culture (civilization) that men will accomplish this.

In this sense then 'in Gn. 1:28 man is given a cultural task at the Creation'.(4) Gn. 1:28 envisages 'a programme of human history and culture, when it describes man's divine commission as to replenish the earth and have dominion over the creatures'.(5) These scholars nowhere suggest that any diversity of cultures is implicit anywhere in this text.

Contrary to the Report's interpretation, what Gn. 1:27f. stresses is the homogeneity of those who are to live all over the earth, for they are all descendants of the same original parents. That this unity and homogeneity is far more fundamental for the Bible than any subsequent differentiation (e.g. in Gn. 11) is shown precisely by the way Genesis pictures it as a fact of man's very creation and origin.

Gn. 1 stresses this homogeneity equally clearly in the contrast it makes between the way in which God created the vegetation, the creatures of the sea, the birds of the air and the animals on the ground, on the one hand, and the way God created mankind on the other. In creating the plants, the fish, the birds, and the animals on the land, it stresses each time, God made them each 'according to their various kinds' (v. 11f., 21, 24f.). When God makes mankind, however, any such words are excluded. Thus mankind is understood, in contrast with the plants, fish, birds and animals, to be of *one* kind.

Genesis then, in chapters 2 to 10, goes on to stress yet further that all mankind is descended from the same parents and is therefore of one kind. It does this again and again: Gn. 2:4ff. (Adam and Eve are created as the common parents of all mankind, 'Adam' itself actually being the Hebrew word for 'mankind'), 3:20 (Eve 'was the mother of all who live'), 4:1ff. (the descendants of Adam make up mankind), 6:5ff., 9:1,7 and 10:1ff. (after the flood all mankind descended from the one man, Noah, just as previously all descended from Adam). As Karl Barth remarks, 'From Adam to Noah the *Volke* as such are not yet there.'(6) And Gerhard von Rad, 'Therewith the idea of the unity of mankind derived from creation is expressed more clearly than anywhere else in the whole of the ancient world.'(7)

In all these ways Genesis stresses that all people are fundamentally united, because all belong to one family, that of Adam and then that of Noah; all are fundamentally of the same kind.

The Report is even wrong in interpreting Gn. 1:28 and 9:1,7 as *commands*; in fact they are all really in the form of a *blessing* and a promise spoken with the effective power of the Creator. The form 'And God blessed them and God said to them . . .' is merely a literal translation of the typical Hebrew idiom of 'parataxis' (the placing side by side of co-ordinate main clauses, here linked together by 'and') that in other languages would ordinarily be expressed in some such way as, 'Then God blessed them, saying . . . .' Claus Westermann interprets the words 'Be fruitful and multiply, and fill the earth' as a 'blessing on mankind phrased as imperative',(8) and Von Rad remarks, 'Man received from the hand of God also the blessing that empowers him to reproduce and multiply.'(9)

Only in a very special sense can this text be called a 'command': in the same sense as God's words that go forth to effect His creative purpose in Gn. 1:3,6,9,11,14f.,20,22 and 24, or to effect His providential or redemptive purpose elsewhere may be called 'commands' (Isa. 55:11). It is not an ethical command, however, not a commandment. That is also why it is never repeated in any of the lists of God's commandments in Scripture.

It is important, moreover, to stress that Gn. 1:28 does describe this as a blessing, for this aspect of Gn. 1:28 contrasts it with the later story of the Tower of Babel in Gn. 11:1–9 (see below). What God does in Gn. 11 is not to bless mankind but to frustrate it by imposing on it a confusion of languages. The diversity of languages or *volke* at Babel is therefore quite a different thing from God's blessing at creation.

If all this is so, we may well ask how on earth the NGK came to this strange interpretation of Gn. 1. There seem to be three aspects to this:

1 As the Report in many places makes clear, it really attempts to argue from what *is* to what *ought to be*, i.e. from the observed fact of diverse *volke* and races in mankind to the conclusion that God must will that we maintain this diversity by keeping the races separate. This argument, however, is based on natural revelation and natural law rather than Scripture. As members of a Reformed Church, therefore, these scholars needed to find some sort of Scriptural support for it. The numerous texts they cite from Scripture to show that it acknowledges that there are different *volke* of course fail to prove this argument. They were therefore driven to read the 'ought' back into God's 'command' when He created man. As it is not there in any explicit way, however, they had somehow to deduce that it is 'implicit'.

2 The 1966 report tried to argue that from the beginning 'diversity and pluriformity were present within . . . mankind' as well as among the plants and animals. In what way? In that two human sexes were created and 'the woman differed physically from the

man'.(10) The 1975 Report, apparently realizing that it is quite irrelevant to compare this sexual difference (which is in any case a
basis for intimate unity, not separation) to the differences between
the various kinds of animal and plant, abandoned this parallel.
Nevertheless the 1975 Report seems to have retained from this
abandoned argument the idea that this differentiation must be
somehow 'implicit' in the story of the creation of mankind.

   3 The key Scriptural passage in the Report's argument is the
story of the Tower of Babel (Gn. 11:1–9). In order that the differentiation of mankind described there should not be theologically
a much less fundamental characteristic of mankind than the unity
and homogeneity described and emphasized in Gn. 1–10, however,
it was necessary to read this differentiation back into the creation
story itself somehow.

Genesis 11:1-9

*(1) Now the whole world had one language and a common speech.
(2) As men moved eastward, they found a plain in Shinar and settled there. (3) They said to each other, 'Come, let us make bricks
and bake them thoroughly.' They used brick instead of stone, and
tar instead of mortar. (4) Then they said, 'Come, let us build ourselves a city, with a tower that reaches to the heavens, so that we
may make a name for ourselves and not be scattered over the face
of the earth.'*

*   (5) But the Lord came down to see the city and the tower that
the men were building. (6) The Lord said, 'If as one people speaking the same language they have begun to do this, then nothing
they plan to do will be impossible for them. (7) Come, let us go
down and confuse their language so they will not understand
each other.'*

*   (8) So the Lord scattered them from there over all the earth, and
they stopped building the city. (9) That is why it was called
Babel—because there the Lord confused the language of the whole
world. From there the Lord scattered them over the face of the
whole earth.*

Not only in the 1975 Report but throughout the whole tradition
of this NGK theology of race relations this has been in effect the
cardinal text.(11)

   Leaving aside whether we should regard this text as literal history
in the fundamentalist way the NGK reports seem to, two basic
questions emerge from it: What sin does it portray mankind as

having committed on the plain of Shinar? What did God intend in His reaction to this sin?

The 1975 Report, like that of 1966, interprets the sin as a deliberate attempt to defy God's command, given at creation (Gn. 1:28) and repeated to Noah (Gn. 9:1,7), that mankind should divide into separate *volke* with different cultures. Because such division is the indispensable basis for them to spread apart, this defiance frustrated God's plan that mankind should 'fill the earth'.(12) Hence the Report asserts that the unity of the people on the plain of Shinar (described in v. 1 as well as v. 6) was already itself contrary to God's will, 'artificial' and a 'humanistic attempt at unity based on the arrogance of man'.(13)

The Report interprets God's reaction to this sin as *reasserting* His original command that mankind should split up into different *volke* with different languages and therefore different cultures.(14) Moreover it adds that in re-establishing this process of 'differentiation'(15) God now extended it by dividing mankind into different *races* as well. This we know, it says, from 'the facts of history'. 'The ancient Egyptians were already familiar with a division of mankind into (five!) races.'(16) Therefore, the Report adds,

The diversity of races and peoples to which the confusion of tongues contributed is an aspect of reality which God obviously intended for this dispensation. To deny this fact is to side with the tower builders. Therefore a policy which in broad terms (as distinct from its concrete implementation) bears this reality in mind, is Biblically realistic in the good sense of the word.(17)

On this basis the Report concludes that 'the policy of separate development retains . . . validity' for relations between different cultural and racial groups.(18)

This, however, is neither the traditional nor the usual present understanding of Gn. 11 in the Christian Church as a whole. An alternative interpretation that accords with the usual understanding is the following.(19)

The sin of the people on the plain of Shinar is expressed in their resolve, 'Come, let us build ourselves a city, with a tower that reaches to the heavens, so that we may make a name for ourselves and not be scattered over the face of the earth.' In other words as they migrate through the world they experience *angst* as in their finitude, frailty and individual mortality they face its vastness. The result is pride and ambition, and a resolve to use their (cultural–technological) prowess to establish a security for themselves. It is to be a security centred on a corporate identity, solidarity and fame of their own, based on their own achievements.

In the Bible, however, to rely on one's own ability like this always means to abandon Yahweh (Jer. 17:5-8).(20) It means to cease calling on the name of the Lord (Gn. 4:26). Thus they forget and deny their only true security: 'The name of Yahweh is a strong tower; the righteous run to it and are safe.' (Prov. 18:10). In their arrogance they aspire to the heights of heaven, seeking to take over the providence of God, to make themselves the captains of their corporate fate. In this sense they too wish to 'be like God' (Gn. 3:5. Cf. Isa. 14:4,12). 'Man wants to run the world in his own way. He wants to put himself at the centre of his civilization on a pedestal inscribed with his name: "Glory to MAN in the highest".'(21)

Moreover, the time of the composition of Gn. 11 is relevant. It was composed when Babylon was a splendid metropolis with high walls and perhaps a great temple or an early *ziggurat* (an artificial holy mountain).(22) It represented the acme of cultural life to the early Hebrew tribesmen, who had emerged from the desert not very long before. The story projects the metropolis back into prehistory for the aetiological reason of explaining the origin of languages and because the story is a theological satire on the pretensions of all civilization without God—of which Babylon is the paradigm. (In the same way 'Babylon' in the New Testament comes to stand for Rome with its pagan civilization.)

But God has, as it were, to come down to see what mankind has built. The writer means that from the perspective of the real heaven where God dwells in His transcendence mankind's most pretentious achievements are so insignificant as to be almost invisible. They are after all only made of perishable bricks (11:3)! Seeing that mankind's pretentiousness is unbounded (11:6), however, God confounds men's speech and scatters them to remind them that they are mortal: 'particular creatures and not budding angels or universal minds'.(23) 'Utopia is stillborn', and 'man's common purpose becomes a wrangle of warring interests'.(24) God's reaction thus corresponds to that in Gn. 3:22-24. Just as there He deprives Adam and Eve of the Paradise in which He originally set them, so now He deprives mankind of the unity and mutual understanding which He gave them through their common origin but which they have misused.

However, this is not God's final word.(25) Just as in His reaction to mankind's previous sins His judgment was not bereft of grace, so now. He not only punished Adam and Eve but also showed them

His grace by making garments of skin to clothe the nakedness of which they had become ashamed through their sin. He not only punished Cain but also placed His mark of protection on him. In response to the 'angel marriages' and the general wickedness of mankind He not only sent the flood to destroy mankind but also spared Noah and his family and made a covenant with them never again to destroy mankind. In the same way He now not only punishes the people on the plain but again acts in grace. He calls Abram out of his country and his people and his father's household, in order that He might, through Abram, bless 'all peoples on earth' (Gn. 12:1–3). His blessing will be a salvation in which they will recover their unity, as the new people of God.

This time, however, they can no longer find unity in the pretensions of human culture. The ground of their unity will be in God and His grace alone. They will therefore learn to boast not in their own pretensions but in the Lord (Jer. 9:23f., I Cor. 1:31). Babylon the Great will finally fall (Rev. 18), but mankind will in the end attain the true City of God that endures for ever (Rev. 21).

Which of these two interpretations is correct? We shall give six reasons why the Report's exegesis is a misinterpretation that depends on incorrect assumptions.

1 The Report's exegesis depends on what we have already seen to be an incorrect interpretation of Gn. 1:28. Gn. 11 itself moreover in no way interprets the fragmentation of mankind into different, conflicting language groups as merely giving 'a new momentum and character' to any former 'cultural injunction' in 1:28. On the contrary, whereas 1:28 is called a blessing, 11:6–9 is clearly the opposite of a blessing: it is a curse that frustrates and punishes men. Just as God's wrath following the sins of Adam, Cain and the 'angel marriages' and the general wickedness of mankind in Gn. 3–6 frustrated and punished men, so after the tower-builders' sin in Gn. 11 it does the same.

Whereas earlier God blessed men so that they would gradually fill the earth (1:28), now (but only now) by confusing their language He divides them into separate, alienated and potentially conflicting groups, and thereby now (but only now) *scatters* them abroad over the face of all the earth (11:8f.). Thus Gn. 1:28 and 11:7–9 are not continuous but discontinuous: the one speaks of the order of God's creation, the other of the disorder that follows mankind's sin. Men lose their unity (and their common language and culture) *not* because God was reasserting what He originally willed at all, but because they have misused this unity and their cultural prowess, and have sought their security in their own group identity, culture and power of achievement, instead of in God alone.

2 In locating the sin of the tower-builders in Gn. 11:1 rather than 11:4, the Report quite misses the point that the story itself presupposes the linguistic unity of men as a prior, *given* cultural fact (11:1). It was the state all people naturally enjoyed *before* and up to when they built the city and the tower on the plain of Shinar, not something they accomplished or somehow regained by their humanistic arrogance. It is something they lost for the first time only after and as a result of what happened at Babel (11:6–9). It was not, therefore, men's unity or their linguistic, cultural or ethnic homogeneity that was 'artificial' or contrary to God's will or command, but their Promethean attempt to use this unity to achieve a cultural and technological identity and greatness and fame of their own, and so by their own achievement to save themselves from the threat of finitude, dispersion and insignificance in the face of the vast and mysterious world (11:4). Were this not so, mankind would have been punished long before they reached the plain, for they had unity and homogeneity long before they arrived there (11:1). (All this again confirms how mistaken the Report's interpretation of Gn. 1:28 is.)

Thus the story of Babel in fact directly and radically *opposes* the Report's attempt to make so much of cultural identity and achievement. Indeed the text warns that it is precisely an attempt like that of the Afrikaner *volk* to secure its own future as a *volk* or nation by attempting to secure its cultural identity from the threat of the finitude or eventual dissolution that brings upon itself the judgment of God and disaster, because it is a titanism that seeks security in that which is its own (*die eie*), instead of in God alone. This is why the cultural *angst* that typically has motivated nationalism in modern history parallels the *angst* of the tower-builders so much; why Dr Malan's attempt to cast the history of the Afrikaner *volk* as 'the highest work of art of the Architect of the centuries'(26) so much parallels the tower-builders' ambition.

3 The Report asserts that race differences are an extension of 'the differentiation of humanity into various language groups and nations'.(27) For evidence, as we have seen, it cites 'the facts of history', and specifically that the ancient Egyptians already classified mankind into five races.(28) This, however, involves a forced and elementary fallacy:

The identification of race and language is one of the more obvious fallacies in the lexicon of racialism. The two terms are used interchangeably without the slightest justification. . . . Historically, race, in its only intelligible (that is, *biological*) sense, is altogether indifferent to the development of language. . . . The structure of language is determined by factors quite apart from racial considerations. A nation may include people who speak the same language yet are of varied ethnic strains.(29)

'The facts of history', moreover, certainly do not show that mankind has been or can be divided into separate national states that each comprise natural units made up of homogeneous linguistic or racial groups. This is an entirely fictitious idea invented by the Romantic movement of the eighteenth and nineteenth centuries, and it gives rise to the delusions of nationalism, racialism and tribalism. As a principle of political policy it is obviously inapplicable on this earth. In Europe, for instance, the different peoples and language groups are far too densely packed and entangled with each other to be sorted out in this way. Karl Popper points out that the failure of the Versailles settlement after the First World War, with all its terrible effects, was mainly due to President Wilson's attempt to apply this Romantic principle to European politics.(30) Only a maniac like Hitler could dream that one should or could apply this principle down the line by means of large-scale group-areas removals.

Since the dawn of history, men have been continually mixed, unified, broken up, and mixed again; and this cannot be undone, even if it were desirable. . . . The principle of the national state . . . owes its populatity solely to the fact that it appeals to tribal instincts and that it is the cheapest and surest method by which a politician who has nothing better to offer can make his way. . . . Human individuals and not states or nations must be the ultimate concern.(31)

This argument from so-called 'facts of history' in the NGK Report shows to what an extent its thinking is an example of 'Cultural Protestantism' rather than Reformation theology. It abandons the Reformation principle of arguing on the basis of *sola Scriptura* (by Scripture alone) for a mess of historical pottage and natural revelation cooked in Pharaoh's Egypt. No one denies that from the beginning of recorded history there have been different races, but Gn. 11 in no way connects this with what happened at Babel.

Not only does the Report, without any support from the text itself, 'extend' it to refer to race, it actually makes race rather than language the fundamental issue of the text. It uses the text to justify the separation of races but not the separation of different language-groups; it uses the text to attack marriages between different racial groups, but not marriages between different language-groups. It would be hard to think of a more illogical perversion of the text of Scripture.

4 The Report confuses two quite .different things: providence and ethics. The fact that *God* in His providence has punished men by confusing their languages, so that they divide into groups that misunderstand and are alienated from each other, does not mean that *we* should seek to exacerbate this. There is no commandment whatsoever to this effect in Gn. 11. A theology that does confuse providence and commandment in this way, however, would, if it were consistent, end up by allowing such absurdities as, for instance, the logically similar inference that because God punished man with death (Gn. 3:19, Rom. 6:23), He must want men to kill each other. Moreover with particular regard to Gn. 11 it would oppose members of any one group learning the language of any other group, on the grounds that for them to do so would be to frustrate the alienation that God had willed in His providence.

Ethics, however, can never be based on general providence; as every ethicist worth his salt knows, 'ought' can never in principle be derived from 'is'. On the contrary Christian ethics must always be directed towards, and derived from, what *will be* in God's eschatological Kingdom, in which His will will be perfectly revealed and accomplished. Thus it must be derived from the revelation of that future Kingdom in the person and work of Jesus Christ.

5 Because in fundamentalist fashion it tends to read Scripture passages out of context, the Report misses the whole point that Gn. 11 is the climax of the sinful prehistory of men and so leads up to the climax of God's response to man's sin in this prehistory: His call to Abram in Gn. 12:1-3. This call is God's intervention in history to save man from his sin and its consequences; it is the beginning of God's 'saving history'. And this intervention means that God calls Abram to do just the opposite of the tower-builders: not to trust in, but to abandon his own (*die eie*)—his country, his kindred, his father's house. God calls Abram to abandon all that ties him to his cultural identity and security, so that thereby God may establish a different people, one whose trust is not in their culture or their cultural identity or greatness but in Himself. Therefore God says to Abram, Leave all these things (all that the tower-builders counted on when they set out to make a name for themselves), and *I* will make your name great. Moreover in doing this Abram becomes the paradigm of all people who trust in God alone in their pilgrimage through the world and are saved by grace alone.

6 In the Old Testament Yahweh promises that when He fulfils the process of salvation (which He began in Abram), He will reverse the curse of Babel. He himself will come down not to punish and frustrate men (as in Gn. 11), but to be in the midst of His people as 'the King of Israel' who will bless men.

At that time I will change the speech of the peoples to a pure speech that all of them may call on the name of the Lord and serve him with one accord. . . . On that day you shall not be put to shame because of the deeds by which you have rebelled against me; for then I will remove from your midst your proudly exultant ones. . . . (Zeph. 3:9,11)

This text seems to refer back to the story in Gn. 11, as does Isa. 66:18–23, where Yahweh proclaims, 'I . . . am about to come and gather all the nations and tongues', so that 'they will come and see my glory'. Even more probably than the text in Zephaniah this is a promise that God will reverse what He did at Babel.

This then is God's ultimate plan in response to man's sin, including the sin of the tower-builders. As His plan for the future it is also what reveals His ultimate will towards which our ethics in the present must be directed: the *unity* of the *volke*, but a unity based on the grace of God, for since mankind's separation into different nations such unity can no longer be based on man's cultural achievements and pride. Thus it is in fact the Report's claim that the cultural and racial diversity of *volke* is 'designed to serve the advancement of the kingdom' of God that is a 'false humanism'.(32)

Deuteronomy 32:8–9
(8) When the Most High portioned out the nations,
when he dispersed the sons of mankind,
he set the limits of the peoples
according to the number of the sons of God [or *sons of Israel*],
(9) while the Lord's share was his own people,
Jacob was the portion he allotted himself.

This has been another favourite text in the NGK to support apartheid. Like the other texts it was used in the 1966 report.(33) Dr J. D. Vorster, particularly, used to quote it as decisive. Such quotation depends on an interpretation of its Afrikaans translation, which is different from the way we have translated it above: *Toe die Allerhoogste aan die nasies 'n erfdeel gegee het, toe Hy die mensekinders van mekaar geskei het, het Hy die grense van die volke vasgestel volgens die getal van die kinders van Israel.*

The 1975 Report uses this text more tentatively, maintaining that it 'seems to indicate' that the destinies (*lotgevalle*) of *volke* are 'not beyond the will and intervention of God'.(34) Linking this text with Amos 9:7, it goes on to argue that these two texts indicate that 'on occasion He even assigned each (*volk*) its own homeland'.(35)

In the first place we should note the variant readings in the fourth line. (The Report itself notes that 'the text is subject to dispute'.(36)

The traditional Masoretic Hebrew text here reads 'sons of Israel', and this is the reading adopted by AV, RV, RSV(margin), NIV and the Afrikaans translation (1933, revised 1954). Scholars have interpreted this text *either* as meaning that when the Most High distributed the nations he set their limits in such a way as to leave an adequate territorial area or living space for Israel among them, *or* as meaning that when the Most High distributed the nations He made the number of nations correspond to the number of the sons of Israel, i.e. seventy (Gn. 46:27, Ex. 1:5).(37) The first is an older interpretation.(38) In a more modern commentary like that of Von Rad's, however, it is accepted that the second meaning is the correct interpretation of the Masoretic text.(39)

The Septuaguint indicates that its translators followed a different text which read 'sons of God'. This reading has long been preferred by many scholars as fitting the context better. Moreover it has now received very strong support from the discovery of an ancient fragment among the Dead Sea Scrolls that also reads 'sons of God'. This reading is therefore followed by most modern translations, especially since the discovery of the Scrolls, including RSV, NEB and GNB. A recent commentator like Von Rad thinks it 'as good as certain' that this is the correct reading.(40)

The meaning of this latter reading is that when the Most High portioned out or distributed the nations, He decided how large they would be on the basis of dividing them up into a number of peoples or *volke* corresponding to the number of 'the sons of God', (i.e the heavenly beings referred to in Gn. 6:2,4, 28:12; I Ki. 22:19–22; Job 1:6, 38:7; Ps. 29:1, 82:1,6, 89:6f.); meanwhile He chose Israel as His own people. The sense appears to be, then, that Yahweh assigned one heathen nation to every heavenly being, for the latter to rule over as vice-regent and watch over as guardian angel, in the same way as an ancient emperor placed a satrap or viceroy over each province of his empire.(41) Meanwhile Yahweh chose Israel as His own people whom He would rule over directly without such mediation. (Cf. Ps. 82; Dn. 10:13,20f., 12:1; Ecclus. 17:17.)

Deut. 32 as a whole seems to identify these supernatural beings with the gods that the heathen nations worshipped (cf. Deut. 32:8 in GNB and v. 12, 15–21, 37–39 and 43). This is then a remnant of the radically weakened or reduced polytheism that occurs in places in the Old Testament (Deut. 4:7, 10:17; Josh. 22:22; I Sam. 26:19; II Ki. 3:26f.; Ps. 33:12,82, 136:2; Dn. 2:47, 11:36) alongside the more categorical assertions of exclusive monotheism such as the one which this chapter itself then goes on to make (Deut. 4:35, 32:39; I Ki. 18:39; Ps. 47, 86:10; Isa. 43:10, 44:6, 46:9 etc.).

This reading fits the context better in the following ways:

1 The use of the term 'the Most High' in line 1 is appropriate to distinguish Yahweh as the Supreme God from the lower gods.

2 Line 1 reads a little more naturally if it speaks of Yahweh distributing 'the nations' (to the sons of God) rather than of Yahweh distributing 'to the nations' an object whose nature has to be inferred from the following lines (their territories).

3 This reading gives verses 8 and 9 together a much clearer line of thought. (The Report in fundamentalist fashion again pays no attention to context.)

4 This reading also ties in, as we have seen, with verses 12, 15–21, 37–39 and 43 in a way that the other does not.

5 Deut. 32:1–43 records the song that Moses recited 'from beginning to end in the hearing of the whole assembly of Israel' (31: 30). This was while they were still in the desert, before entering the land of Canaan. Moreover Moses is here referring to what happened long before, in 'the days of old' (v. 7), and how Israel *in spite of this act of God's grace* has become a corrupt and warped generation which no longer acts as His children (v. 5). It makes much more sense, therefore, if 32:8 refers to something they have already experienced, not to the occupation of a territory of their own in Canaan that still lies in the future. Thus even though it is quite possible to translate the Hebrew of line 3 of Deut. 32:8 'He marked out the borders (*grense*) of the peoples', as though it referred to territory, such a translation fails to fit the context of the whole chapter so well. In the context the much more natural translation is 'He set the limits of the peoples', referring to their sizes as groups of mankind, not their territories.(42) This is further borne out by what follows: from 32:10 Moses goes on to speak of God's finding Israel in the desert and protecting and caring for him *there* by Himself. 'The Lord alone did lead him, and there was no

foreign god with him' (v. 12). The song nowhere refers to the settlement in Canaan.

What is clear from the above is that the Septuagint and Dead Sea Scrolls reading is almost certainly the original one. But this reading has nothing to do with 'homelands' or even territories, if the above points hold water: its concern is the aetiological question, 'How did the relationship between Yahweh, the God of all the world, and Israel come to pass?'(43) And it answers in terms of God's gracious election of His people in the desert. (Cf. Hos. 9:10.)

Moreover even if we were to adopt the Masoretic reading in line 4, the context still makes it much more likely that the meaning of line 3 is that God determined the original sizes of the peoples as groups of mankind, so that there were seventy of them, rather than that He marked off the *grense* of their territories. (This meaning, with either reading in line 4, also takes away any reason for translating the Hebrew verb in line 2 *'van mekaar geskei het'*, as the Afrikaans version does. *'Versprei het'* or *'verdeel het'* would be at least as precise a translation of it and fits the parallelism with line 1 better.)(44) It is important to emphasize, therefore, that *neither* of the readings supports the Report's argument.

Indeed, neither of the readings, and neither of the meanings which scholars have attached to the Masoretic text, supports the Report's argument, for several other basic reasons. The aim of the text on *either* reading, the context makes clear, is merely to assert God's special relation with the people of Israel. It says absolutely nothing, in *either* reading, to imply that the individual members of any two nations (let alone the members of two different races within one national area like South Africa) should not migrate or mix or integrate, or should be confined to their own separate (national) areas. Moreover, even to attempt to read such an imperative into the text is to make the fundamental mistake once again of confusing providence and ethics.

What is more, to use the text as though it somehow supported the argument that Scripture prohibits integration between the races but *not* between members of different nations of the same race is illogical and pure eisegesis. The Report here also ignores the whole point of the text: it is not a racial distinction that is being made but a distinction between Israel as a nation believing in Yahweh and the other nations as heathen nations who do not worship the true God.

Nor does Amos 9:7 supply any support at all for the Report's interpretation of Deut. 32:8 in opposition to racial integration—or for the idea that the races should be confined to 'homelands'. On the contrary, it refers once more to God's providence, not His command. It means merely that God has governed the history not only of the Israelites but also of the Philistines and the Syrians with sovereign grace; the Israelites therefore have no grounds for claiming God's favouritism and indulgence in the face of their sins.

One last point is worth making. The original Hebrew of Deut. 32:8 has something of the emphasis that the Old Testament so often places on the unity of mankind, because the Hebrew word for 'mankind' in line 2 is *Adam*. Even in their dispersion, then, even in being divided as nations each with its own god, all of mankind remains one family, the sons of Adam.

Acts 2:5-11

(5) Now there were staying in Jerusalem God-fearing Jews from every nation under heaven. (6) When they heard this sound, a crowd came together in bewilderment, because each one heard them speaking in his own language. (7) Utterly amazed, they asked: 'Are not these men who are speaking Galileans? (8) Then how is it that each of us hears them in his own native language? (9) Parthians, Medes and Elamites; residents of Mesopotamia, Judea and Cappadocia, Pontus and Asia, (10) Phrygia and Pamphylia, Egypt and the parts of Libya near Cyrene; visitors from Rome (11) (both Jews and converts to Judaism); Cretans and Arabs—we hear them declaring the wonders of God in our own tongues!'

The 1975 Report states, 'The great language miracle of Whit Sunday confirms that it is the will of God that each man should learn of the great deeds of God in his own language.'(45) It thus confirms the 'cultural identities, linguistic barriers and the psychological distinctiveness of each people (*volk*)'(46) Its effect is therefore to sanctify what God did in Gn. 1:28, 11:1-9 and Deut. 32:8. 'The natural diversity of man and peoples survives in the Church of Christ but is sanctified in Him.'(47) Thus the effect of Babel is carried over to, and is to be maintained in, the Church.

Certainly we must agree with the Report that the Scriptures should be translated and the Gospel preached to people in their own indigenous cultural forms, so far as these can be christianized or are not irreconcilable with the Gospel.(48) The Report, however, uses the story of Pentecost to buttress the idea of an excluding law that every person *must* thereafter hear the gospel in his own language, so that each language group must form its own separate, entirely autonomous Church and the transfer of members from one such Church to another may be hindered. To the extent that the Report does this we must reply both that the argument is illogical and that it quite perverts the meaning of Acts 2.

The Report altogether misses the point that after the 'language miracle' Peter preached to all those present from different countries in one language (presumably Aramaic), and that it was through this sermon that they were converted and brought into *one* Church, not separate, linguistically-divided Churches (Ac. 2:37–42).

The Report also quite misses the point that the miracle of Pentecost signifies precisely the reversal of what happened at Babel. It is the fulfilment of Zeph. 3 (if our interpretation of this passage was correct) and Isa. 66:15–23 (which actually appears to be a source for much of the account in Acts 2). The Lord, the King of Israel, has come into Israel's midst (Zeph. 3:14–17); and now He comes down with flames of fire like a mighty wind to gather men from 'all nations and tongues' to Jerusalem to see 'a Sign', and to 'change their speech to a pure speech', 'that all of them may call on the name of the Lord and serve him with one accord' (Isa. 66:15, 18–23; Zeph. 3:9f.). This pure speech is the one universal language of the Spirit, which makes itself understood in every language spoken by men, as a sign that through the reconciling work of Christ and the work of the Spirit the dividing effect of Babel is overcome. Though these different languages remain, the barrier of communication which they have set up between those who speak them is dramatically broken down.

Through the preaching of the Gospel, men from every country, speaking every language of the known world (Ac. 2:8–11), no matter how far they have been scattered (2:39), now themselves receive the gift of the same Spirit. This overcomes the dimension of mistrust, aversion and alienation which the language barrier has caused between them and thus overcomes their division from each other. And this is not merely a 'spiritual' unity but quite concretely one visible congregation 'in one place' (Ac. 2:1,44,47).

What Pentecost means, therefore, is that the gift of the Spirit at Jerusalem together with the proclamation of the Gospel reverses the centrifugal force of the curse of Babel. For the Spirit unites us into the *one* people of God, the one *body* of Christ (I Cor. 12). He does so quite visibly through the sacrament of baptism, across every barrier of language, culture or race (Ac. 2:41).

The Report very strangely assumes that Christ's work is so

limited in its effect that He does not overcome this curse, but instead actually sends His Spirit in order to reinforce it. This means that Christ's work contradicts itself, for He redeems us from the curse of the Law (Gal. 3:13), but re-establishes the curse of Babel. Scripture, however, teaches the opposite: in Christ the *blessing* upon Abram, which as we have already seen is the very counterpoint to the curse on the tower-builders, comes upon the Gentiles, so that by faith they receive the Spirit (Gal. 3:14). For Christ has redeemed us from every curse.

Acts 17:26

[God] made the entire human race [lit. *the whole race of men*] *from one man to dwell upon the whole face of the earth, having determined set seasons and the boundaries of their habitation* [i.e. *the area of land, bounded by the sea, on which they all could live*].

This text is also a very important one in the NGK argument for apartheid. This argument, however, depends on understanding and therefore translating the Greek text as follows: *[God] made every race (*or *nation) of men from one man to dwell upon the whole face of the earth, determining (*or *having determined) their ordained historical epochs and the borders (*grense*) of their territories.*

The popularity and importance of this text in the NGK is illustrated by the fact that from it as well as from Deut. 32:8 the title of the book *Grense* was derived. (This was an important book edited by the head of the Broederbond, written by NGK theologians and ministers, and published in 1961 to counter the critique of apartheid in Church and state in an earlier book, *Vertraagde Aksie*.)

The Report cites this text as supporting its interpretation of Gn. 1:28, i.e. the idea that in spite of the common origin of mankind 'diversity was implicit in the fact of creation'.(49) It also cites it as confirming its interpretation of Gn. 11 and Deut. 32:8 and Am. 9:7, i.e. the idea that 'God appointed specific times for the various nations as well as their homelands'.(50)

All this assumes that the second translation above is the correct one and ignores several decisive things about the Greek text. In fact, all the likelihood is that the first translation is the correct one. If this is so, the entire argument on the basis of this text collapses. The following points show how impossible the NGK's argument is.

1 The Report ignores what is probably the correct translation of the Greek word, *pan*. It is true that in Classical Greek and ordinarily also in the later, Hellenistic (or Koine) Greek of the New

Testament *pas* means 'every' when (as in this verse and also, for example, in Ac. 2:5, 10:35) no definite article precedes it, and means 'the whole' or 'the entire' only when a definite article does precede it. Occasional exceptions to this can, however, be found in Hellenistic Greek. Indeed in the very next phrase, in which it is quite clear that he does mean 'the whole', Luke writes the genitive form *pantos* without the article: 'upon the whole face of the earth'. (It is true that Greek idiom omits the article in certain prepositional phrases including 'in the face of' (51); but the insertion into this phrase of *pas* with the meaning 'the whole' strictly would require the article to be restored.) Such authorities as M. Dibelius in his pioneering *Studies in the Acts of the Apostles* (1956), F. Bruce in his new London Commentary (1954) and E. Haenchen in his, the most magisterial of all modern commentaries on Acts (16th ed. 1976) therefore come down in favour of the argument that *pas* must mean 'the whole' (or 'the entire') in *both* phrases here.(52)

2 Even if Dibelius, Bruce and Haenchen are wrong, the Report ignores that what Acts represents Paul as concerned to do here is to rebut the Athenians' proud claim that they were autochthonous (sprung from the soil of their native Attica) and thus essentially different in origin, nature and culture from the rest of mankind. It is against this point of view that he asserts that all men are descended from one man (or from the same stock) and are therefore essentially the same. Thus Paul's words expressly oppose the point of view of the Report, which approximates to that of the Athenians in asserting that racial differences are so basic.

3 The Report simply assumes without argument that the crucial phrase in this text should be translated 'determining (*or* having determined) their ordained historical epochs and the borders of their territories'. A careful examination of the Greek text, however, shows that this assumption is very probably wrong and that the alternative translation given above is very probably correct:

(a) The aorist and perfect tenses of the participles in this phrase in the Greek suggest action preceding that of the main verb.(53)

(b) The lack of any article before *prostetagmenous kairous* linking this to *auton*, and the parallel passage in Ac. 14:17 both clearly support the translation 'set (*or* ordered) seasons', rather than 'their ordained epochs'.

(c) The singular of the word *katoikias* obviously favours the singular in translation ('habitation'), especially because it stands in contrast to the plural word *kairous* ('times, seasons').

(d) The noun *katoikias* seems clearly to refer back to the preceding verb from the same root, *katoikein* ('to dwell'), which in either translation refers to the occupation or the habitation of the whole face of the earth.

Paul is referring to God's forming and preparation of mankind's home on the dry land of the earth and His setting of its limits against encroachment by the sea *before* mankind was created, rather than to a later 'determining' or fixing of the historical times of the rise and fall of nations and the borders of their separate territories (plural). In other words Paul is repeating the Old Testament ideas about creation in Gn. 1:9f.,14,28, 8:22-9:1, 9:7; Ps. 104:19–23,27 and especially to Ps. 74:17, rather than referring to Deut. 32:8—contrary to what the margin of the Afrikaans Bible (reference edition) indicates. On the other hand if the text is translated 'having determined . . . the borders of their territories', this would mean that God predetermined these borders before creation. Such an idea would still not derive from, or be supported by, Deut. 32:8. In fact even the Report's interpretation of Deut. 32:8 would strictly contradict it, because according to it Deut. 32:8 says that God set the borders of the nations only *after* creation.

Concerning the meaning of *kairous* Haenchen writes, 'The reader knows from 14:17 that the seasons of the year are meant'.(54) Dibelius and Bruce also agree with this argument.(55) But Gärtner in his book *The Areopagus Speech and Natural Revelation* has contended that the proper term for 'seasons' is *horai* and that *kairoi* by itself (without an accompanying qualifying adjective like 'fruitful' as in 14:17) cannot mean 'seasons'. Thus it must mean 'historical epochs', i.e. times of historical predominance, as in Ac. 1:7 (cf. the divinely ordained periods for the rise and fall of nations in Daniel). But this argument cannot stand. In Ac. 1:7 *kairos* appears to have its normal meaning of 'an appointed occasion or date', in distinction to *chronos*, the normal word for 'an extended period or epoch of time', which accompanies it there. (Cf. Mk. 13:32, I Thess. 5:1, Tit. 1:2f. NIV translates Ac. 1:7 and I Thess. 5:1 'times and/or dates'.) Moreover, while *hora* may well be the proper term for 'season' in Classical Greek and some later Greek writers, it is never used in that sense in the New Testament. On the contrary Haenchen quotes Eltester as 'correctly' objecting to Gärtner that whereas *horai* is 'the old word', which is still used by Atticists, 'in the Koine one speaks of *kairoi* as seasons of the year'.(56) A specific example against Gärtner's argument that *kairos* without an appropriate accompanying adjective cannot mean 'season' is in fact to be found in the Septuagint in one of the very texts that, we have argued, lies behind Ac. 17:26. Gn. 1:14 in the Septuagint reads, . . . *eis semeia kai eis kairous kai eis hemeras kai eis eniautous. Kairos* here has exactly the meaning we have argued for in this text. Neither Gärtner nor Haenchen have noticed this, but it clinches the argument.

4 Yet another point against the Report's interpretation of Ac. 17:26 is that their translation of this verse would fit into, and thus make sense in, the context only if it presupposed a valid post-lapsarian natural theology. It would mean that God, after Babel, arranged the historical epochs and boundaries of the nations so that in these men could see evidence of His existence. Consistently with this the Report shows evidence of leanings toward natural theology elsewhere (for instance in its mess of Egyptian pottage mentioned earlier). Such an interpretation, however, involves a point of view contrary to the rest of Scripture, including v. 23 in this very speech in Ac. 17; for v. 23 declares that the true God was unknown (*agnostos*) to the Athenians.

As John Calvin put it, the human mind, unaided by the Word of God, 'can in no way attain to God' through nature or in any other way.(57) 'It is useless to seek God unless Christ leads the way, for the majesty of God is higher than men's senses can reach. Nay more! A supposed knowledge of God outside Christ will be a deadly abyss.'(58)

5 The Report's interpretation of this text once more seeks to turn a statement about God's providence into a commandment for men, which as we have seen is such a fundamentally wrong way of thinking. Whichever of the two ways the text is translated, if the translation is taken seriously for what it actually says, it does not support but opposes the Report's use of it. For even if it were to mean that God has determined the historical epochs of the nations and fixed their national boundaries, this would be a statement about God's providence, which is not subject to man's presumptuous control. From every angle then the Report's interpretation reverses the actual meaning of this text.

SCRIPTURE TEXTS CONTRA APARTHEID

The above should prove that the Report's attempt to defend apartheid on the basis of Scripture altogether fails, and that the Scripture passages it uses for this in fact point in just the *opposite* direction. Moreover, by removing the grounds on which the Report seeks to build the defence of apartheid, we have left much more uncompromised what the Report itself says about other Scripture passages that urge the unity and integration of God's people. However, the Report either ignores or passes far too lightly over the many parts of Scripture that are centrally concerned with this issue, especially those parts of the New Testament that address the apartheid of the time when it was written. This was the apartheid between the Jews and the Gentiles. It was a strict apartheid, very similar to the one in our country and therefore has much to say by implication to us. The struggle of the Gospel against the apartheid of its time is too wide an issue for us to deal with exhaustively here, and so we shall only deal fairly briefly with some decisive passages.

Leviticus 19:33f.; Isaiah 56:3,6f.; Mark 11:17

One of the better sections in the 1975 Report is two pages on the Old Testament's attitude to the foreigner or alien.(59) The Old Testament lays down that *When an alien settles with you in your land, you shall not oppress him. He shall be treated as a native born among you, and you shall love him as a man like yourself, because you were aliens in Egypt.* (Lev. 19:33f.. Cf. Deut. 10:18f., 23:7; Mal. 3:5)

The Report itself recognizes that such foreigners must have included members of other races and that this did not exclude them from becoming part of the people of Yahweh.(60) Indeed the Old Testament specifically makes provision for them to be included in the rituals of Israel's faith like the Passover, if they are willing to be circumcised (Ex. 12:48f.).

In Isa. 56:3,6f., the prophet prohibits the exclusion of foreigners from the Temple; every member of another *volk* who has become a worshipper of the Lord shall be allowed to worship together with His people. No segregation is to be allowed, . . . *for my house will be called a house of prayer for all nations.*

The Report, however, fails to make any consistent application of this Old Testament principle to the Church. It fails to note that in the New Testament the same principle applies. Jesus cleanses the Temple, driving out the buyers and sellers and the money changers, precisely because they occupied the Court of the Gentiles, i.e. the area of the Temple grounds intended for the Gentiles (i.e. 'the nations') to use for worship. He quotes Isa. 56:7 to justify this drastic action against the prejudiced establishment of his day (Mk. 11:17).

Numbers 12

The Report very briefly acknowledges that according to this passage Moses, the greatest figure in the Old Testament, himself married an Ethiopian woman, who was thus 'of different racial origin'. It does not mention that he also married a Midianite (Ex. 2:16ff., Nu. 10:29) or a Kenite (Jud. 1:16, 4:11).

It is in fact not certain, as the Report assumes, that the woman mentioned in Nu. 12 was an Ethiopian in the sense of a black woman descended from the negroid people who inhabited the land south of Egypt. Nevertheless it is probable that the text does mean this. What the Report does not mention in this regard, however, is the terrible way in which God punished Miriam for criticizing this marriage, according to Numbers: she was struck with a dreadful leprosy that turned her own skin as white as snow (12:10). This punishment has all the more point, as profound irony, if it was to the woman's black skin that Miriam objected. It is also a warning about God's judgment of us if we share the same kind of prejudice against racially mixed marriages.

Mark 3:20–21, 31–35

These verses make up a whole, which Mark has split into two by inserting verses 22–30.

In verse 21 the Greek phrase *hoi par' autou* (literally 'those with him') should be translated 'his own people' or more precisely 'his family'.(61) The subject of the verb *elegon* ('they said') is then most naturally also his family (as in NIV), even though NEB, GNB and the new Afrikaans translation (1979) shy away from this by translating it 'people said'.

This text reports an occasion when Jesus and his natural family are at odds because of their want of sympathy for his aims and purposes (cf. Jn. 7:5). Jesus dramatically declares that the social ties of common obedience to God as defined by his ministry have a claim superior to the closest ties of blood. This is said with specific reference to the family, but in the Bible the ties of family are always regarded as closer than those of the *volk*. The same principle therefore applies *a fortiori* to the ties of *volk* and nation in relation to the ties of the community around Jesus that eventually became the Church.

What is important to notice is that Jesus is not speaking of any mere 'spiritual unity' here; he is speaking about whether he should go with his family or stay with his disciples, i.e. whether he should be with the one or the other in a quite concrete, physical way. He therefore does not resolve the clash between his loyalty to those to whom he is naturally related and his loyalty to those to whom he is spiritually related in anything like the way the 1975 Report does.

The Report exalts people's natural ties of blood and culture so that they predominate as normative and leave room for only a 'spiritual unity' and an occasional concrete expression of unity between Christians who do not share these natural ties. For Jesus, on the contrary, the ties of the community around him cut right across the closest natural ties, with a uniquely sovereign claim. This he makes clear again and again in his ministry (e.g. Mt. 8:21f.; Mk. 1:20, 10:28–31 cf. 1:30 and I Cor. 9:5; Lk. 14:26. cf. Ex. 32:29). The Gospels themselves in fact make it clear that this includes cutting across the natural ties of the *volk* (e.g. Mt. 3:9; Jn. 1:11–13, 8:39–47).

John 4:1–42 and Matthew 8:5–13

This story about Jesus and the Samaritan woman specifically draws attention to the fact that Jesus defied the convention of strict apartheid between Jews and Samaritans by associating with the Samaritan woman and asking her for a drink of water. Verse 9, though omitted by a few important manuscripts, is probably original to the text and not a later gloss. It should be translated 'For Jews do not use dishes Samaritans have used.'(62) This appears to refer to a regulation concerning ritual purity that was laid down in 65 or 66 AD and therefore to be anachronistic. Nevertheless, as we have seen, already in Jesus' own day the Jews held themselves apart from the Samaritans. According to Jn. 4 Jesus flouted this apartheid. In fact he went much further than merely asking for a drink out of the same vessel: he went to stay with the Samaritans in one of their homes (v. 40).

Similarly in Mt. 8 Jesus is quite willing to flout the Jewish rules about apartheid between Jews and Gentiles. (A pious Jew would not even allow the shadow of a Gentile to fall on him, because it would contaminate him.) He is ready to go into a Roman centurion's house to pray for his servant (v. 7). He commends the centurion's faith as superior to the Jews' (v. 10), and he predicts that such Gentiles will be gathered into the Kingdom while people of his own nation will be excluded (v. 11f.).

John 17:20–23

In this 'High-Priestly Prayer' Jesus prays that the Church may attain complete, perfect unity (v. 23). Because He needs to pray that the Church will attain it, this is no mere spiritual unity that Christians automatically share. It is nevertheless to be a unity actually as perfect as that between the Father and the Son within the one Godhead (v. 21f.). Indeed the unity of the Godhead is itself to be reproduced in them (v. 21–23). When Christians deny this unity by being divided from one another, therefore, they show that they are not perfectly united with the Father and the Son. On the other hand when they do show such unity, this is the supreme testimony to the Church's claim that Jesus is God's own emissary to the world.(63) 'Just as the Church's lack of unity is the greatest of stumbling-blocks to non-Christians, so will her unity be the chief argument for the divine character of Christ's mission.'(64)

The unity of which Jn. 17 speaks is of course based on faith in Christ in response to the Word of God (v. 20) and is in the first place a unity of mutual love. But such unity must be clearly and concretely visible to the world (v. 23). As the NGK Report itself concedes, this means 'it must be seen, heard and experienced'.(65) Such perfect, visible unity is obviously incompatible with the Report's defence of divided or segregated denominations or *Kerkverbande* which may not allow members to transfer from one to the other.(66) Indeed, because of Jesus' words, to argue the opposite is in a sense theological blasphemy, because it implies that the unity of the Godhead is only an occasional, imperfect unity.

Galatians 2:11–21, 3:28

This text reports how Peter as a Jew regularly shared the same table (for the *Agape* and Holy Communion) with the Gentile Christians in Antioch, until Jewish Christians from Jerusalem who stood for a stricter apartheid pressured him to withdraw and 'separate himself'. This separation Paul denounces as hypocrisy and a fundamental betrayal of the Gospel and of Christ himself, for it denies the Gospel that we are all justified by grace alone, and it implies that Christ 'died for nothing' (2:21). Later in the same epistle he categorically asserts, 'There is neither Jew nor Greek, slave nor free, male nor female, for you are all one in Christ Jesus', i.e. unlike in the Synagogue there is no room for any separating barrier of race, class or sex (Ga. 3:28, cf. Col. 3:11).

This text is particularly important because it was over the whole issue of the shared Table that apartheid began to be accepted into the NGK. Until 1829 the NGK was still faithful to Scripture and to John Calvin's interpretation of the texts in Scripture on the unity of the Church: until 1829 it clearly recognized that for Christians apartheid was contrary to the Word of God. For in that year its Synod declared that the administration of Holy Communion 'simultaneously to all members without distinction of colour or origin' was 'an unshakeable principle based on the infallible Word of God', and that 'therefore all Christian communities and each individual Christian are obliged to think and act accordingly'.

Already by this time, however, separate congregations for 'coloured' members were being formed, and some missionaries among the 'coloured' people were excluded from being called to white congregations. But even as late as 1857 the NGK Synod declared, 'The Synod regards it as desirable and Scriptural that wherever possible our members from among the heathen be received and incorporated in our existing congregations.' In the face of pressure from the white members of the Church, however, the same Synod also passed a resolution that for the first time officially permitted separate services and buildings for whites and 'coloureds' in the same parish. Even then it confessed that it made this as a concession to 'the weakness of some', i.e. on the expedient ground of yielding to the pressure of the prejudice of white members. Moreover, some outstanding churchmen like Andrew Murray strongly protested against the direction in which their Church thereby began to move.

In time such separation increasingly became the norm until, in contrast to the earlier stand, 'joint worship' between the races was actually actively discouraged, except 'under special circumstances' (as in the earlier NGK report of 1966).(67) In the process *ex post facto* attempts began to be made to justify the status quo of apartheid into which the NGK had drifted, and even to set forth apartheid as the answer to all South Africa's political problems.

Ephesians 2:11–22

This text emphasizes that, whereas before Christ came the Gentile nations were separated from the nation of Israel, now they are no longer 'excluded from citizenship in Israel', no longer 'foreigners to the covenants' made with the nation of Israel, no longer 'far away'. Now he who is 'our peace . . . has destroyed the barrier, the dividing wall of hostility'. Now he has fulfilled his purpose 'to create in himself one new man out of the two [races, i.e. Jew and Gentile], thus making peace, and in this one body to reconcile both of them to God through the cross, by which he put to death their hostility. . . . Consequently, you are no longer foreigners and aliens, but fellow-citizens with God's people and members of God's household.'

All this is directed against the apartheid between Jew and Gentile, and it by itself would destroy the Report's interpretation of Gn. 11. Some supporters of apartheid have resorted to the desperate expedient of arguing that this text refers only to the breaking down of the barriers between God and men, but it quite obviously refers also to the breaking down of the barriers between the Jewish and Gentile nations.

It is true of course that this text does not refer (explicitly) to blacks and whites, because it acknowledges only one racial distinction as really important: that between Jews and (all) Gentiles. It clearly does mean, however, to include all who are not Jews, however much they may classify themselves as different from one another, within the term 'Gentiles'. All these Gentiles have now been made one with the nation of Israel, so that all national and racial barriers now fall away in Christ.

Moreover all this is meant not only 'spiritually' but quite concretely and geographically. 'The barrier' which is 'the dividing wall of hostility' refers to the wall at the Temple in Jerusalem that separated the Court of the Jews from the Court of the Gentiles. This wall has been smashed down by the death of Christ, so that what divides all the Gentiles from all the Jews has in principle been done away with—and all the Christians on both sides have been united together to form 'one humanity'. So concretely and without any qualification does the text mean this, that the Greek actually says that they have been united together to form 'one new man' (*hena kainon anthropon*, v. 15). So drastically and triumphantly does it proclaim the obliteration of the *grense* as the effect of Christ's coming.

Thus in the New Testament in all the churches outside Palestine about whose membership we know anything, we find both Jews and Gentiles worshipping together and using the *lingua franca*, Greek, in which Paul, for instance, writes to them all. In fact in the church at Antioch one leading member was 'Simeon called Niger' (or 'the Black'), who may well have been an African (Ac. 13: 1). There was no place for racial segregation in the Church.

What is more, it is important to note that because Jewish and Gentile Christians became integrated like this, the Jewish Christians were eventually everywhere absorbed into the Gentile population. Except for new converts, no Jewish Christians remained after the second century. They all lost their 'separate identity'—and it was the uniting power of the Gospel that brought this about. The Gospel brought this about, however, only because the Jewish Christians allowed *it* rather than their distinctive religio-cultural identity to be their ultimate norm, and so did not struggle to preserve that identity as an absolute value.

The 1975 Report points out that the New Testament mentions Churches in the plural: the Churches of Galatia, of Asia, of Macedonia etc. It argues from this to justify separate *Kerkverbande* i.e. 'mother' and 'daughter' Churches, for the various population groups.(68) This argument, however, holds no water at all, because the analogy is quite false. These Churches in the New Testament are merely Churches in different geographical areas, not segregated Churches in the same place. Of course people who speak different languages and do not understand a common *lingua franca* well enough, or for cultural reasons prefer a very different way of worship, should be free to have their own services of worship. But that could not justify separate white and 'coloured' congregations in the same area when both speak the same language and share the same culture. Nor could it justify excluding blacks from holding their own services in churches built for white congregations and allowing them to meet only in church halls (or even in garages!). Nor could it justify dividing the black and white races into separate denominations, let alone rejecting any effective umbrella synod to unite them at the top. Nor could it justify any congregation's not immediately welcoming Christians of any other race to full membership on the purported ideological grounds that it is anxious to preserve the characteristic racial 'identity' of its members.

Philippians 3:1–11

In this famous passage Paul contrasts those who glory in things of the flesh and those who glory in Christ alone. He too could have glorified in things of the flesh, including being a member of the people of Israel, a Hebrew of the Hebrews (or, 'a pure-blooded Hebrew'). But all this he has decided to regard as so much *skubala* ('garbage' or 'excrement'), in order that he may gain Christ and the righteousness which comes through faith in him and not through one's nationality. Paul rejects his Jewish nationality as the ground of any confidence before God; for him, when the value one attaches to one's nationality stands athwart the Gospel and will of Christ in any way, its claims are to be rejected immediately.

Notes
Abbreviations used for versions of the Bible:
AV Authorized Version

GNB Good News Bible
NEB New English Bible
NIV New International Version
RSV Revised Standard Version
RV Revised Version

1 Cf. F. van Wyk (ed.), *Christian Principles in Multi-racial South Africa* (Johannesburg, 1954), p. 142ff. (I am referring particularly to the way they dealt with the question whether Scripture teaches that we are God's children by nature [creation] or by grace.)

2 Executive Council of the NGK (eds), *Human Relations and the South African Scene in the Light of Scripture* (Cape Town, 1976), p. 17, par. 9.1. Although I have consulted the Afrikaans version, particularly as the English translation is sometimes clumsy, all English quotations placed in inverted commas are from the English translation and all page references are to it as well. Paragraph numbers are included for ease of reference to the Afrikaans original. In a few cases where a quotation does not have its own footnote number, it is to be located by means of the number that follows next.

3 Ibid., p. 14, par. 9.

4 T. C. Vriezen, *An Outline of Old Testament Theology* (Oxford, 1962), p. 281.

5 W. Eichrodt, *Man in the Old Testament* (London, 1970), p. 33.

6 K. Barth, *Kirchliche Dogmatik*, III/4 (Zürich, 1957), p. 351.

7 G. von Rad, *Theologie des Alten Testaments* (München, 1969), Bd. I, p. 175.

8 C. Westermann, *Creation* (London, 1974), p. 49.

9 G. von Rad, *Das erste Buch Mose* (Göttingen, 1964), p. 47.

10 Committee on Current Affairs of the NGK, *Human Relations in South Africa* (Cape Town, 1967?), p. 3, par. 12. Cf. also Van Wyk, op. cit., p. 33.

11 Cf. Van Wyk, op. cit., p. 33f., W. B. de Villiers, (ed.), *Lunteren en die Rassekwessie* (Johannesburg, 1969), p. 26, and *Human Relations in SA*, p. 3f., par. 13.

12 *Human Relations and the SA Scene*, p. 16f., par. 9.1.

13 Ibid., p. 16f., par. 9.1; p. 21, par. 9.3.

14 Ibid., p. 16f., par. 9.1.

15 Ibid., pp. 16 and 17, par. 9.1.

16 Ibid., p. 17, par. 9.1.

17 Ibid., p. 18, par. 9.1.

18 Ibid., p. 19, par. 9.1.

19 In the following I am dependent on a few commentaries and also on Barth, op. cit., pp. 354–62.

20 H. Ringgren, *Israelite Religion* (London, 1974), p. 129.

21 W. Neil, *One Volume Bible Commentary* (London, 1962), p. 38.

22 Commentaries, including modern ones, often assume that behind the image of the tower in Gn. 11 stood the ziggurat Etemenanki in Babylon, which had a height of ninety-one and a half metres (e.g. G. von Rad, *Das erste*

Buch Mose, p. 125). E. A. Speiser, however, points out that Etemenanki was built only three or four centuries after the author of Gn. 11 (*Genesis, Anchor Bible* (Garden City, 1964), p. 75). Speiser himself proposes that the tower has a literary source: the account of minor gods building a high temple to Marduk in the Babylonian epic *Enuma elis*. This account, however, is so different that this proposal seems unlikely. Possibly an early predecessor of Etemenanki stood behind the story.

23 R. Niebuhr, *Faith and History* (New York, 1949), p. 76.

24 Neil, op. cit., p. 38.

25 On this paragraph see further G. von Rad, *Theologie des AT*, p. 177f., and *Das erste Buch Mose*, pp. 127-9.

26 F. A. van Jaarsveld, *The Afrikaner's Interpretation of South African History* (Cape Town, 1964), p. 21.

27 *Human Relations and the SA Scene*, p. 6f., par. 9.1.

28 Ibid., p. 17, par. 9.1.

29 L. L. Snyder, *The Idea of Racialism* (New York, 1962), p. 27f.

30 K. R. Popper, *The Open Society and its Enemies* (London, 1966), vol. II, p. 318, note 2.

31 Ibid., vol. I, p. 288, note 7.

32 *Human Relations and the SA Scene*, p. 43, par. 23; p. 44, par. 26.

33 *Human Relations in SA*, p. 4, par. 15.

34 *Human Relations and the SA Scene*, p. 23, par. 10.

35 Ibid.

36 Ibid.

37 Interestingly, in the Septuagint and Dead Sea Scrolls texts of Ex. 1:5 and in Ac. 7:14 the number is 75.

38 E.g. by H. Wheeler Robinson, in his commentary on Deuteronomy in W. F. Adney (gen. ed.), *Century Bible* (London, n.d.), vol. II, p. 222 (though Robinson actually prefers the Septuagint reading).

39 G. von Rad, *Das fünfte Buch Mose*, (Göttingen, 1964), p. 140, note 2.

40 Ibid.

41 R. Meyer, cited ibid., p. 140.

42 W. Gesenius, *Hebrew and Chaldee Lexicon to the Old Testament Scriptures* (London, 1857?), p. CLII.

43 Meyer, op. cit.

44 W. Gesenius, op. cit., p. DCLXXXVIII.

45 *Human Relations and the SA Scene*, p. 87, par. 60.

46 Ibid.

47 Ibid.

48 Ibid., p. 88f., par. 60.

49 Ibid., p. 17, par. 9.1.

50 Ibid., p. 31, par. 13.4.

51 F. Blass and A. Debrunner, *A Greek Grammar of the New Testament* (Chicago, 1961), par. 255; W. F. Moulton, A. S. Geden, H. K. Moulton (eds.), *A Concordance to the Greek Testament* (Edinburgh, 1970), p. 868f.

52 E. Haenchen, *The Acts of the Apostles* (Oxford, 1971), p. 523 note 3; M. Dibelius, *Studies in the Acts of the Apostles* (London, 1956), p. 28; F. F. Bruce, *The Book of Acts* (London, 1954), p. 358. Dibelius adduces as analagous examples of *pas* without the article Eph. 2:21 and an inscription (p. 28 note 4).

53 Ibid., par. 339, and, especially on this particular verse, J. H. Mouton, *A Grammar of New Testament Greek*, vol. I *Prolegomena* (Edinburgh, 1906), p. 133.

54 Haenchen, op. cit.

55 Dibelius, op. cit., p. 29; Bruce, op. cit., p. 358.

56 Ibid., p. 523, note 5.

57 J. Calvin, *Institutes of the Christian Religion*, I.vi.4. For Calvin's position on this issue see further I.i-vi, x, II.ii.18ff., vi.1, xvi.19, III.ii.16 and Calvin's Commentaries *ad* Ps. 19:2, 104:2; Jn. 6:46f.; Rom. 1:18 and 2:19.

58 J. Calvin, *Commentary on the Gospel according to St John* (Edinburgh, 1959), *ad* 6:46.

59 *Human Relations and the SA Scene*, p. 24f., par. 10.

60 Ibid., p. 25, par. 10.

61 Blass and Debrunner, op. cit., par. 237(2). NEB, NIV, GNB and the new Afrikaans translation (1979) all translate 'his family'. See V. Taylor *The Gospel According to St Mark* (London, 1952), p. 236.

62 See for instance C. K. Barrett, *The Gospel According to St John* (Philadelphia, 1978), p. 232. The definitive discussion of this matter is in D. Daube, *The New Testament and Rabbinic Judaism* (New York, 1973), pp. 373-82.

63 Barrett, op. cit., p. 512.

64 G. H. C. Macgregor, *The Gospel of John. Moffat NT Commentary* (London, 1928), p. 231.

65 *Human Relations and the SA Scene*, p. 49, p. 33.

66 Ibid., p. 46f., par. 29; p. 49, par. 33; p. 82f., par. 58; p. 47, par. 30.

67 *Human Relations in SA*, p. 29, par. 46.

68 *Human Relations and the SA Scene*, p. 50, par. 34; p. 82, par. 58. Cf. p. 46f., par. 29; p. 49, par. 33.

Appendix: Documentation

INTRODUCTION
The debate about apartheid and its rejection as un-Christian has a long history, to which the recent decisions by the SACC and the WARC, together with the subsequent responses by the Churches, has given new life. Ever since the policy was promulgated in 1948 many Churches in South Africa have voiced strong objections to it. It is, however, far beyond the scope of this book to publish anything like a significant proportion of the vast number of statements that have been made by them. We have therefore selected several historic statements, which, while they obviously reflect the age within which they were written, document this debate. They also provide the necessary background for understanding the WARC decision at Ottawa in 1982. We begin with a significant early statement made by the Catholic bishops in 1957 in which apartheid is rejected as being *fundamentally evil* and *intrinsically evil*.

During the course of the past thirty years, two events in particular have proved to be decisive for the Churches in their witness regarding aprtheid. The first was the Cottesloe Consultation held in December 1960; the second was the publication of *A Message to the People of South Africa* by the South African Council of Churches in 1968. Cottesloe marked a major turning-point in church relations in South Africa. What could have been a breakthrough in beginning the process of moving away from apartheid on the part of the Afrikaans Reformed Churches resulted in those Churches separating themselves from the wider ecumenical community in South Africa and becoming more confirmed than ever in their support for apartheid. The *Message to the People of South Africa*, which was subsequently endorsed either fully or in its shortened version by virtually all the member Churches of the SACC, represented the first major development since Cottesloe. Indeed, it was the next logical step for those Churches which had accepted the Cottesloe Statement but who believed it did not go far enough. Cottesloe allowed for some kind of policy of 'separate development'; the *Message* rejected apartheid totally as a *false gospel*. Whereas Cottesloe dealt mainly with issues of practical importance, the *Message* tackled the ideology head on and unequivocally rejected the theology underlying it.

We have included those documents which relate directly to the present debate on apartheid as a heresy. These include the decision by the World Lutheran Federation in 1978 which declared that a *status confessionis* exists in Southern Africa; the decision by the Alliance of Black Reformed Christians in South Africa (1981) to declare apartheid a heresy; the declaration by the WARC meeting in Ottawa to support and affirm that decision, and to suspend the membership of the NGK and NHK until such time as they stopped providing theological justification for the policy of apartheid; and those responses of the Churches in South Africa to that decision which were available to us at the time of publication, and which were officially adopted by their highest courts. (The SACC also declared apartheid a heresy at its national conference in 1982.)

One of the most significant aspects of the debate on apartheid as a heresy is the fact that much of the initiative for it has come from within the black Reformed church community, particularly members of the NG Sendingkerk. ABRECSA represents a new development within the church struggle for unity and justice in South Africa and for this reason it seemed appropriate that its aims and objectives should be more widely known. The Confession of Faith adopted by the NG Sendingkerk at its Synod in 1982 indicates that this Church has totally rejected the policy which in many respects gave it birth and has identified itself fully with the ecumenical community in South Africa in declaring apartheid to be a heresy and in committing itself to the struggle against racism in all its forms.

The translations of texts from Afrikaans are unofficial translations by the editors, except in the case of the Confession of Faith adopted by the NG Sendingkerk, which is the official translation.

1   *South African Catholic Bishops' Conference, 1957*
             STATEMENT ON APARTHEID
In 1952 the Catholic bishops of South Africa issued a statement on race relations which emphasized the evil of colour discrimination and the injustices which flow from it. This statement maintained that non-Europeans in South Africa had a strict right in justice to evolve towards full participation in the political, economic and

cultural life of the country. It pointed out, however, that this evolution could not take place unless the people concerned made their own vigorous contribution towards fitting themselves for the exercise of full citizenship.

Five years have gone by since this statement was issued. During that time there has been no change of direction in South Africa's racial policy. Rather, the old policy of segregation, responsible in large measure for the social pattern of the country, has under the name of apartheid received clearer definition and more precise application. Apartheid is officially held to be the only possible formula for South Africa's mixed society. Integration is considered unthinkable and partition into separate states impracticable.

The basic principle of apartheid is the preservation of what is called white civilization. This is identified with white supremacy, which means the enjoyment by white men only of full political, social, economic and cultural rights. Persons of other race must be satisfied with what the white man judges can be conceded to them without endangering his own privileged position. White supremacy is an absolute. It overrides justice. It transcends the teaching of Christ. It is a purpose dwarfing every other purpose, an end justifying any means.

Apartheid is sometimes described as separate development, a term which suggests that under apartheid different races are given the opportunity of pursuing their respective and distinctive social evolutions. It is argued that only in this manner will these races be doing the will of God, lending themselves to the fulfilment of His providential designs. The contention sounds plausible as long as we overlook an important qualification, namely, that separate development is subordinate to white supremacy. The white man makes himself the agent of God's will and the interpreter of His providence in assigning the range and determining the bounds of non-white development. One trembles at the blasphemy of thus attributing to God the offences against charity and justice that are apartheid's necessary accompaniment. . . .

From this fundamental evil of apartheid flow the innumerable offences against charity and justice that are its inevitable consequences, for men must be hurt and injustice must be done when the practice of discrimination is enthroned as the supreme principle of the welfare of the state, the ultimate law from which all other laws derive.

The condemnation of the principle of apartheid as something intrinsically evil does not imply that perfect equality can be established in South Africa by a stroke of the pen. There is nothing more obvious than the existence of profound differences between sections of our population which make immediate total integration impossible. People cannot share fully in the same political and economic institutions until culturally they have a great deal in common. All social change must be gradual if it is not to be disastrous. Nor is it unjust for a state to make provision in its laws and administration for the differences that do exist. A state must promote the well-being of all its citizens. If some require special protection it must be accorded. It would be unreasonable, therefore, to condemn indiscriminately all South Africa's differential legislation. It would be unfair to disparage the services provided for less advanced sections of the population and the noble and dedicated labours of many public officials on their behalf.

Many who suffer under the sting of apartheid find it hard to accept counsels of moderation. Embittered by insult and frustration, they distrust any policy that involves a gradual change. Revolution not evolution is their slogan. They can see redress only in the sweeping away of every difference and the immediate extension of full civil rights to all. They do not stop to contemplate the confusion that will ensue, the collapse of all public order, the complete dissolution of society and perhaps their own rapid destruction in the holocaust. This is particularly true of those who find atheistic communism the inspiration of their present striving and their hope for the future.

A gradual change it must be: gradual, for no other kind of change is compatible with the maintenance of order, without which there is no society, no government, no justice, no common good. But a change must come for otherwise our country faces a disastrous future. That change could be initiated immediately if the ingenuity and energy now expended on apartheid were devoted to making South Africa a happy country for all its citizens. The time is short. The need is urgent. Those penalized by apartheid must be given concrete evidence of the change before it is too late. This involves the elaboration of a sensible and just policy enabling any person, irrespective of race, to qualify for the enjoyment of full civil rights. To achieve this will undoubtedly take statesmanship of a higher order for the difficulties are not to be minimized. It is no easy matter to dispel fears and prejudices and introduce measures so contrary to the main trends and customs of the past. . . .

To our beloved Catholic people of white race, we have a special word to say. The practice of segregation, though officially not recognized in our churches, characterizes nevertheless many of our church societies, our schools, seminaries, convents, hospitals and the social life of our people. In the light of Christ's teaching this cannot be tolerated for ever. The time has come to pursue more vigorously the change of heart and practice that the law of Christ demands. We are hypocrites if we condemn apartheid in South African society and condone it in our own institutions.

This does not mean that we can easily disregard all differences of mentality, condition, language and social custom. The Church does not enforce human associations that, because of these differences, can produce no good. She understands that the spiritual welfare of her children cannot be fostered in a social atmosphere wholly alien and uncongenial. But the Christian duty remains of seeking to unite rather than separate, to dissolve differences rather than perpetuate them. A different colour can be no reason for separation when culture, custom, social condition and, above all, a common faith and common love of Christ impel towards unity. . . .

To all white South Africans we direct an earnest plea to consider carefully what apartheid means: its evil and anti-Christian character, the injustice that flows from it, the resentment and bitterness it arouses, the harvest of disaster that it must produce in the country we all love so much. We cannot fail to express our admiration for the splendid work done in many quarters to lessen prejudice, promote understanding and unity and help South Africa along that path of harmony and co-operation which is the only one dictated by wisdom and justice. On the other hand we deeply regret that it is still thought necessary to add to the volume of restrictive and oppressive legislation in order to reduce contact between various groups to an inhuman and unnatural minimum.

2   *The Cottesloe Consultation Statement, 1961*

I

We have met as delegates from the member churches in South Africa of the World Council of Churches, together with representatives of the World Council itself, to seek under the guidance of the Holy Spirit to understand the complex problems of human relationships in this country, and to consult with one another on our common task and responsibility in the light of the Word of God. Our worship, Bible study, discussion and personal contacts have led us to a heightened appreciation of one another's convictions and actions. Our next task will be to report to our several Churches, realizing that the ultimate significance of our meeting will consist in the witness and decisions of the Churches themselves in consequence of these consultations.

The general theme of our seven days together has been the Christian attitude towards race relations. We are united in rejecting all unjust discrimination. Nevertheless, widely divergent convictions have been expressed on the basic issues of apartheid. They range on the one hand from the judgment that it is unacceptable in principle, contrary to the Christian calling and unworkable in practice, to the conviction on the other hand that a policy of differentiation can be defended from the Christian point of view, that it provides the only realistic solution to the problems of race relations and is therefore in the best interests of the various population groups.

Although proceeding from these divergent views, we are nevertheless able to make the following affirmations concerning human need and justice, as they affect relations among the races of this country. In the nature of the case the agreements here recorded do not—and we do not pretend that they do—represent in full the convictions of the member Churches.

The Church of Jesus Christ, by its nature and calling, is deeply concerned with the welfare of all people, both as individuals and as members of social groups. It is called to minister to human need in whatever circumstances and forms it appears, and to insist that all be done with justice. In its social witness the Church must take cognizance of all attitudes, forces, policies and laws which affect the life of a people; but the Church must proclaim that the final criterion of all social and political action is the principles of Scripture regarding the realization of all men of a life worthy of their God-given vocation.

We make bold therefore to address this appeal to our Churches and to all Christians, calling on them to consider every point where they may unite their ministry on behalf of human beings in the spirit of equity.

II

1 We recognize that all racial groups who permanently inhabit our country are a part of our total population, and we regard them as indigenous. Members of all these groups have an equal right to make their contribution towards the enrichment of the life of their country and to share in the ensuing responsibilities, rewards and privileges.

2 The present tension in South Africa is the result of a long historical development and all groups bear responsibility for it. This must also be seen in relation to events in other parts of the world. The South African scene is radically affected by the decline of the power of the West and by the desire for self-determination among the peoples of the African continent.

3 The Church has a duty to bear witness to the hope which is in Christianity both to white South Africans in their uncertainty and to non-white South Africans in their frustration.

4 In a period of rapid social change the Church has a special responsibility for fearless witness within society.

5 The Church as the body of Christ is a unity and within this unity the natural diversity among men is not annulled but sanctified.

6 No one who believes in Jesus Christ may be excluded from any Church on the grounds of his colour or race. The spiritual unity among all men who are in Christ must find visible expression in acts of common worship and witness, and in fellowship and consultation on matters of common concern.

7 We regard with deep concern the revival in many areas of African society of heathen tribal customs incompatible with Christian beliefs and practice. We believe this reaction is partly the result of a deep sense of frustration and a loss of faith in Western civilization.

8 The whole Church must participate in the tremendous missionary task which has to be done in South Africa, and which demands a common strategy.

9 Our discussions have revealed that there is not sufficient consultation and communication between the various racial groups which make up our population. There is a special need that a more effective consultation between the Government and leaders accepted by the non-white people of South Africa should be devised. The segregation of racial groups carried through without effective consultation and involving discrimination leads to hardship for members of the groups affected.

10 There are no Scriptural grounds for the prohibition of mixed marriages. The well-being of the community and pastoral responsibility require, however, that due consideration should be given to certain factors which may make such marriages inadvisable.

11 We call attention once again to the disintegrating effects of migrant labour on African life. No stable society is possible unless the cardinal importance of family life is recognized, and, from the Christian standpoint, it is imperative that the integrity of the family be safeguarded.

12 It is now widely recognized that the wages received by the vast majority of the non-white people oblige them to exist well below the generally accepted minimum standard for healthy living. Concerted action is required to remedy this grave situation.

13 The present system of job reservation must give way to a more equitable system of labour which safeguards the interests of all concerned.

14 Opportunities must be provided for the inhabitants of the Bantu races to live in conformity with human dignity.

15 It is our conviction that the right to own land wherever he is domiciled, and to partake in the government of his country, is part of the dignity of the adult man, and for this reason a policy which permanently denies to non-white people the right of collaboration in the government of the country of which they are citizens cannot be justified.

16 (a) It is our conviction that there can be no objection in principle to the direct representation of coloured people in Parliament. (b) We express the hope that consideration will be given to the application of this principle in the foreseeable future.

17 In so far as nationalism grows out of a desire for self-realization, Christians should understand and respect it. The danger of nationalism is, however, that it may seek to fulfil its aim at the expense of the interests of others and that it can make the nation an absolute value which takes the place of God. The role of the Church must therefore be to help to direct national movements towards just and worthy ends.

III

Judicial Commission on the Langa and Sharpeville Incidents

The Consultation expresses its appreciation for the prompt institution of enquiries into the recent disturbances and requests the Government to publish the findings as soon as possible.

Justice in Trial

It has been noted that during the recent disturbances a great number of people were arrested and detained for several months without being brought to trial. While we agree that abnormal circumstances may arise in any country necessitating a departure from the usual procedure, we would stress the fact that it belongs to the Christian conception of law, justice and freedom that in normal circumstances men should not be punished except after fair trial before open courts for previously defined offences. Any departure from this fundamental principle should be confined to the narrowest limits and only resorted to in the most exceptional circumstances.

Position of Asians in South Africa

We assure the Indian and other Asian elements in the population that they have not been forgotten in our thoughts, discussions and prayers. As Christians we assure them that we are convinced that the same measures of justice claimed here for other population groups also apply to them.

Freedom of Worship

Bearing in mind the urgent need for the pastoral care of nonwhite people living on their employer's premises, or otherwise unable without great difficulty to reach churches in the recognized townships or locations, the Consultation urges that the State should allow the provision of adequate and convenient facilities for nonwhite people to worship in urban areas.

The Consultation also urges European congregations to co-operate by making their own buildings available for this purpose whenever practicable.

Freedom to Preach the Gospel

The Church has the duty and the right to proclaim the Gospel to whomever it will, in whatever the circumstances, and wherever possible, consistent with the general principles governing the right of public meetings in democratic countries. We therefore regard as unacceptable any special legislation which would limit the fulfilment of this task.

Relationship of Churches

The Consultation urges that it be laid upon the conscience of us all that whenever an occasion arises that a Church feels bound to criticize another Church or church leader it should take the initiative in seeking prior consultation before making any public statement. We believe that in this way reconciliation will be more readily effected and that Christianity will not be brought into disrepute before the world.

Mutual Information

The Consultation requests that means be found for the regular exchange of all official publications between the member Churches for the increase of mutual understanding and information. Furthermore Churches are requested to provide full information to other Churches of their procedures in approaching the Government. It is suggested that in approaches to the Government, delegations, combined if possible, multiracial where appropriate, should act on behalf of the Churches.

Co-operation in Future

Any body which may be formed for co-operation in the future is requested to give its attention to the following:

(a) A constructive Christian approach to separatist movements;

(b) The education of the Bantu;

(c) The training of non-white leaders for positions of responsibility in all spheres of life;

(d) African literacy and the provision of Christian literature;

(e) The concept of responsible Christian society in all areas in South Africa, including the Reserves;

(f) The impact of Islam on Southern Africa.

Residential Areas

The Consultation urges, with due appreciation of what has already been done in the provision of homes for non-white people, that there should be a greater security of tenure, and that residential areas be planned with an eye to the economic and cultural level of the inhabitants.

Migrant Labour

The Consultation urges the appointment of a representative commission to examine the migrant labour system, for the Church is painfully aware of the harmful effects of this system on the family life of the Bantu. The Church sees it as its special responsibility to advocate a normal family life for the Bantu who spend considerable periods of time, or live permanently, in white areas.

We give thanks to Almighty God for bringing us together for fellowship and prayer and consultation. We resolve to continue in this fellowship, and we have therefore made specific plans to enable us to join in common witness in our country.

We acknowledge before God the feebleness of our often divided witness to our Lord Jesus Christ and our lack of compassion for one another.

We therefore dedicate ourselves afresh to the ministry of reconciliation in Christ.

3 *South African Council of Churches, 1968*
A MESSAGE TO THE PEOPLE OF SOUTH AFRICA

In the name of Jesus Christ

We are under an obligation to confess anew our commitment to the universal faith of Christians, the eternal Gospel of salvation, and security in Christ alone.

What the Christian Gospel says

The Gospel of Jesus Christ

—is the good news that in Christ God has broken down the walls of division between God and man, and therefore also between man and man;

—declares that Christ is the truth who sets men free from all false hopes of grasping freedom for themselves, and that Christ liberates them from a pursuit of false securities;

—declares that, in the crucifixion of Jesus, sin has been forgiven, and that God has met and mastered the forces that threaten to isolate man and destroy him;

—declares that, in the resurrection of Jesus, God showed himself as the conqueror and destroyer of the most potent of all forms of separation, namely death, and he proved the power of his love to overthrow the evil powers of fear, envy and pride which cause hostility between men;

—declares that, by this work of Christ, men are being reconciled to God and to each other, and that excluding barriers of ancestry, race, nationality, language and culture have no rightful place in the inclusive brotherhood of Christian disciples;

—declares that God is the master of this world, that his is the mind and purpose that shapes history, and that it is to him alone, and not to any subsection of humanity, that we owe our primary obedience and commitment;

—declares that we live in the expectation of a new heaven and a new earth in which righteousness dwells; that the Kingdom of God is present already in Christ and through the Holy Spirit; and that it therefore now demands our obedience to his commandments and our faith in his promises.

Our Concern

This, in summary, is the Gospel of salvation in Jesus Christ. It offers hope and security for the whole life of man; it is to be understood not only in a mystical and ethical sense for the salvation of the individual person, and not only in a sacramental and ecclesiastical sense within the framework of the Church. The Gospel of Christ is to be understood in a cultural, social (and therefore political), cosmic and universal sense, as the salvation of the world and of human existence in its entirety. Further, the Gospel of Christ is not only the object of our hopes; it should be experienced as a reality in the present.

For this reason, Christians are called to witness to the significance of the Gospel in the particular circumstances of time and place in which they find themselves. We, in this country, and at this time, are in a situation where a policy of racial separation is being deliberately effected with increasing rigidity. The effects of this are to be seen in a widening range of aspects of life—in political, economic, social, educational and religious life; indeed, there are few areas even of the private life of the individual which are untouched by the effects of the doctrine of racial separation. In consequence, this doctrine is being seen by many not merely as a temporary political policy but as a necessary and permanent expression of the will of God, and as the genuine form of Christian obedience for this country. But this doctrine, together with the hardships which are deriving from its implementation, forms a programme which is truly hostile to Christianity and can serve only to keep people away from the real knowledge of Christ.

There are alarming signs that this doctrine of separation has become, for many, a false faith, a novel Gospel which offers happiness and peace for the community and for the individual. It holds out to men a security built not on Christ but on the theory of separation and the preservation of their racial identity. It presents separate development of our race-groups as a way for the people of South Africa to save themselves. Such a claim inevitably conflicts with the Christian Gospel, which offers salvation, both social and individual, through faith in Christ alone.

This false offer of salvation is being made in this country in the name of Christianity. Therefore, we believe that the Church must enable all our people to distinguish between this false, novel Gospel and the true eternal Gospel of Jesus Christ. We believe that it is the Church's duty to enable our people to discriminate more carefully between what may be demanded of them as subjects or citizens of the State of South Africa and what is demanded of them as disciples of Jesus Christ.

The Gospel's claim

The Christian Gospel declares that there is no other name than that of Christ whereby men must be saved. Thus salvation in Christ exposes the falsity of hope of salvation through any other means.

The first Christians, both Jews and Gentiles, discovered that God was creating a new community in which differences of race, nation, culture, language and tradition no longer had power to separate man from man. We are under an obligation to assert this claim and to live by it. We are under an obligation to assert that the most significant features of a man are not the details of his genetic inheritance, nor the facts of his ancestry. The most significant features of a man are the characteristics which enable him to be a disciple of Christ—his ability to respond to love, to make choices, to work as a servant of his fellowmen; these are the gifts of the grace of God at work in the individual person; and to insist that racial characteristics are more important than these is to reject our own humanity as well as the humanity of the other man.

But, in South Africa, everyone is expected to believe that a man's racial identity is the most important thing about him. Until a man's racial identity is established, virtually no decisions can be taken; but, once it is established, it can be stated where he can live, whom he can marry, what work he can do, what education he can get, whose hospitality he can accept, where he can get medical treatment, where he can be buried—and the answer to multitudes of other questions can be supplied once this vital fact is established. Thus, we are being taught that our racial identity is the final and all-important determining factor in the lives of men. As a result of this faith in racial identity, a tragic insecurity and helplessness afflicts those whose racial classification is in doubt. Without racial identity, it appears, we can do nothing: he who has racial identity has life; he who has not racial identity has not life. This amounts to a denial of the central statements of the Gospel. It is opposed to the Christian understanding of the nature of man and community. It, in practice, severely restricts the ability of Christian brothers to serve and know each other, and even to give each other simple hospitality. It arbitrarily limits the ability of a person to obey the Gospel's command to love his neighbour as himself.

Attempts have been made to support racial separation from Scripture. For instance, it is said to have the authority of an order of creation, which was divinely confirmed by the confusion of tongues at the Tower of Babel and emphasized again at Pentecost. The fact is, however, that the event of Pentecost asserts and demonstrates the power of the Holy Spirit to draw men into one community of disciples in spite of differences of languages and culture and it is thus the way by which the disunity of Babel is healed.

The Bible's teaching about creation has nothing to say about the distinctions between races and nations. God made man—the whole human race—in his image. God gave to man—the whole human race—dominion over the rest of creation. Where differences between people are used as badges or signs of opposing groups, this is due to human sin. Any scheme which is proposed for the rectifying of our disorders must take account of this essentially sinful element in the divisions between men and between groups of men. Any scheme which is claimed to be Christian must also take account of the reconciliation already made for us in Christ. The policy of separate development does not take proper account of these truths. It promises peace and harmony between the peoples of our country not by a faithful and obedient pursuit of the reconciliation wrought by Christ, but through separation, which, being precisely the opposite course, is a demonstration of unbelief and distrust in the power of the Gospel. Any demonstration of the reality of reconciliation would endanger this policy; therefore the advocates of this policy inevitably find themselves opposed to the Church if it seeks to live according to the Gospel and if it shows that God's grace has overcome our hostilities. A thorough policy of racial separation must ultimately require that the Church should cease to be the Church.

Everywhere, sin corrupts God's creation; particularly, it exploits differences to generate hostility. The policy of separate development is based on the domination of one group over all others; it depends on the maintenance of white supremacy; thus it is rooted in and dependent on a policy of sin. The Christian Gospel declares that God has acted to overthrow the policy of sin. God is bringing us from a living death to a new life; and one of the signs that this has happened is that we love the brethren. But, according to the Christian Gospel, our 'brethren' are not merely the members of our own race-group, nor are they the people with whom we may choose to associate. Our brother is the person whom God gives to us. To dissociate from our brother on the grounds of natural distinction is to despise God's gift and to reject Christ.

The Gospel of Jesus Christ declares that God is love. This is not an easy doctrine. It is not 'sentimental humanism'. It is far easier to believe in a god who is less than love and who does not require a discipleship of love. But if God is love, separation is ultimately the opposite force to God. The will to be separate is the most complete refusal of the truth. The life of separation is the most plain denial of life. The Christian Gospel declares that separation is the supreme threat and danger, but that in Christ it has been overcome. According to the Christian Gospel, we find our identity in association with Christ and with each other. Apartheid is a view of life and a view of man which insists that we find our identity in dissociation and in distinction from each other. A policy of separate development which is based on this concept therefore involves a rejection of the central beliefs of the Christian Gospel. It calls good evil. It rejects as undesirable the good reconciliation and fellowship which God is giving to us by his Son. It seeks to limit the limitlessness of God's grace by which all men may be accepted in Jesus Christ. It seeks to confine the operation of God's grace within the barriers of human distinctions. It reinforces divisions which the Holy Spirit is calling the People of God to overcome. This policy is, therefore, a form of resistance to the Holy Spirit.

Our task

People should be able to see the Gospel of Christ expressed in the life of the Church. They should be able to see in the Church an inclusive fellowship and a freedom of association in the Christian brotherhood. They should be able to see the power of God at work in the Church changing hostility into love of the brethren. We are indeed thankful for these signs of God's grace where they are to be seen in the life of the Church. But, even in the life of the Church, there is conformity to the practices of racial separation; and the measure of this confomity is the measure of the Church's deviation from the purpose of Christ.

Our task is to work for the expression of God's reconciliation here and now. We are not required to wait for a distant 'heaven' where all problems will have been solved. What Christ has done, he has done already. We can accept his work or reject it: we can hide from it or seek to live by it. But we cannot postpone it, for it is already achieved. And we cannot destroy it, for it is the work of the eternal God.

We must obey God rather than men

The Gospel of Jesus Christ declares that Christ is our master, and that to him all authority is given. Christians betray their calling if they give their highest loyalty, which is due to Christ, to one group or tradition, especially where that group is demanding self-expression at the expense of other groups. Christ is the master and critic of all of us and of all our groups. He is the judge of the Church also. If the Church fails to witness for the true Gospel of Jesus Christ it will find itself witnessing for a false Gospel. If we seek to reconcile Christianity with the so-called 'South African way of life' (or any other way of life), we shall find that we have allowed an idol to take the place of Christ. Where the Church thus abandons its obedience to Christ, it ceases to be the Church; it breaks the links between itself and the Kingdom of God. We confess, therefore, that we are under an obligation to live in accordance with the Christian understanding of man and of community, even if this be contrary to some of the customs and laws of this country.

Many of our people believe that their primary loyalty must be to their group or tradition or political doctrine, and that this is how their faithfulness will be judged. But this is not how God judges us. In fact, this kind of belief is a direct threat to the true salvation of many people, for it comes as an attractive substitute for the claims of Jesus. It encourages a loyalty expressed in self-assertion: it offers a way of salvation with no cross. But God judges us, not by our faithfulness to a sectional group, but by our willingness to be made new in the community of Christ. We believe that we are under an obligation to state that our country and Church are under God's judgment, and that Christ is inevitably a threat to much that is called 'the South African way of life'. We must ask ourselves what features of our social order will have to pass away if the lordship of Christ is to be fully acknowledged and if the peace of God is to be revealed as the destroyer of our fear.

But we believe that Christ is Lord, and that South Africa is part of his world. We believe that his Kingdom and its righteousness have power to cast out all that opposes his purposes and keeps men in darkness. We believe that the word of God is not bound, and that it will move with power in these days, whether men hear or whether they refuse to hear. And so we wish to put to every Christian person in this country the question which we ourselves are bound to face each day, to whom, or to what, are you truly giving your first loyalty, your primary commitment? Is it to a sub-section of mankind, an ethnic group, a human tradition, a political idea; or to Christ?

May God enable us to be faithful to the Gospel of Jesus Christ, and to be committed to Christ alone!

4 *Presbyterian Church of Southern Africa, 1973*

DECLARATION OF FAITH

We believe in God the Father, who created all the world, who will unite all things in Christ and who desires all men to live together as brothers in one family.

We believe in God the Son, who became man, died, and rose in triumph, reconciling all the world to God, breaking down every wall that divides men, every barrier of religion, race, culture or class, to create one united humanity. He is the one Lord who has authority over all. He summons both the individual and society, both the Church and the State, to reconciliation, unity, justice and freedom.

We believe in God the Spirit, who is the pledge of God's coming Kingdom, who gives us power to proclaim God's judgment, and forgiveness of men and nations, to love and serve all men, to struggle for justice and peace, and to summon all the world to recognize God's reign here and now.

5 *Lutheran World Federation, 1977*

SOUTHERN AFRICA: CONFESSIONAL INTEGRITY

At the Sixth Assembly of the Lutheran World Federation at Dar-es-Salaam in June 1977 the following statement was issued:

The Lutheran Churches are confessional Churches. Their unity and mutual recognition are based upon the acknowledgment of the Word of God and therefore of the fundamental Lutheran confessional writings, particularly the Augsburg Confession, as normative.

Confessional subscription is more than a formal acknowledgment of doctrine. Churches which have signed the confessions of the Church thereby commit themselves to show through their daily witness and service that the Gospel has empowered them to live as the people of God. They also commit themselves to accept in their worship and at the table of the Lord the brothers and sisters who belong to other Churches that accept the same confessions. Confessional subscription should lead to concrete manifestations in unity in worship and in working together at the common task of the Church.

Under normal circumstances Christians may have different opinions in political questions. However, political and social systems may become so perverted and oppressive that it is consistent with the confession to reject them and to work for changes. We especially appeal to our white member Churches in Southern Africa to recognize that the situation in Southern Africa constitutes a *status confessionis*. This means that, on the basis of faith and in order to manifest the unity of the Church, Churches would publicly and unequivocally reject the existing apartheid system.

6 *Alliance of Black Reformed Christians in Southern Africa, 1981*
ABRECSA CHARTER

1. Definition

A broad movement of Black Reformed Christians based on Church affiliation and open to individual members to join. We understand black to mean a condition and an attitude and not merely the pigmentation of one's skin. We recognize that in South Africa the oppressors who enjoy social privileges, wield political power and possess economic advantages are white and that the oppressed who are socially underprivileged, politically powerless and economically exploited are black. At the same time we also recognize that there are blacks whose attitude and condition is such that they have clearly opted to be on the side of the oppressor and that there are whites whose attitude and condition is such that they have clearly opted to be on the side of the oppressed.

Membership is subject to acceptance of the Theological Basis, the Declaration and the Commitment.

1.1 *Theological Basis*

(a) The Word of God is the supreme authority and guiding principle revealing all that we need to know about God's will for the whole existence of human beings. It is this Word that gives life and offers liberation that is total and complete.

(b) Christ is Lord of all life even in those situations where his Lordship is not readily recognized. It is our task in life not only to recognize the Lordship of Christ but also to proclaim it.

(c) We as Christians are responsible for the world in which we live, and to reform it is an integral part of our discipleship and worship of God.

(d) God institutes the authority of the State for the just and legitimate government of the world. Therefore we obey government only in so far as its laws and instructions are not in conflict with the Word of God. Obedience to earthly authorities is only obedience *in God*.

(e) The unity of the Church must be visibly manifest in the one people of God. The indivisibility of the body of Christ demands that the barriers of race, culture, ethnicity, language and sex be transcended.

1.2 *Declaration*

We, as members of ABRECSA, unequivocally declare that apartheid is a sin, and that the moral and theological justification of it is a travesty of the Gospel, a betrayal of the Reformed tradition, and a heresy.

1.3 *Commitment*

We, as members of ABRECSA, commit ourselves to implementing and fulfilling the aims of ABRECSA as set out in the Charter to the best of our abilities.

2. Motivation

There are important and imperative reasons why an Alliance of Black Reformed Christians in Southern Africa should be formed:

2.1. The Black Reformed Churches in Southern Africa are by tradition 'mission Churches', struggling to find their own authentic identity, autonomy and independence, and also to give expression to their own theological understanding of their faith in the South African context.

2.2. Being 'mission Churches', they have been divided into separate denominations by the 'mother' missionary societies even though they share the same confessional base, and these divisions are not of their making.

2.3 As heirs of the Reformed tradition they are faced with a crisis because the system of apartheid has been and is still justified theologically mainly by people of that very tradition. Yet the people of these Churches, representing the victims of apartheid, reject that system as evil and contrary to the Word of God. The question that this poses is whether they are also rejecting their confessional heritage from which so much support for the system stems.

2.4 To answer the above questions it has become absolutely necessary for Black Reformed Christians to come together and struggle with the question: 'What does it mean to be Black and Reformed in Southern Africa today?'

2.5 It is also important for Black Reformed Christians to make a more positive and specifically Southern African contribution to the witness of the World Alliance of Reformed Churches in the ecumenical field. An initial opportunity is available to them in preparing for the WARC Assembly to be held in Ottawa, Canada, in 1982.

3. Aims

To bring together Black Reformed Christians from the different Churches:

The NG Kerk in Afrika

The NG Sending Kerk

The Reformed Church in Africa

The Evangelical Presbyterian Church in South Africa

The Presbyterian Church of Africa

The Presbyterian Church of Southern Africa

The Reformed Presbyterian Church of Southern Africa

The United Congregational Church of Southern Africa

and other existing Black Reformed Churches.

3.1 To promote the unity of these Churches in organization, in action and in witness.

3.2 To strengthen the prophetic witness of these Churches by challenging both their leadership and their membership to live out the Gospel in the context of the struggle for a just society in South Africa.

3.3 To promote the understanding of involvement in the struggle for liberation as an act of obedience and theological necessity.

3.4 To provide supplementary and alternative theological understanding by action/reflection models of theologizing.

3.5 To create an ecumenical network with other Reformed Christians who share the same commitment and vision and thereby to form groups of solidarity. This is important not only with regard to South Africa, but also to those minority groups struggling in Western Churches.

3.6 To create a network of understanding and support for those blacks in Reformed Churches elsewhere who find themselves in minority positions.

3.7 To create possibilities for co-ordination of efforts in Reformed circles across Southern Africa and the world to support each other in our different struggles but especially concerning the struggle in South Africa.

3.8 To be better able to give content to the awareness of ecumenical bodies and/or Churches who concern themselves with the South African situation.

7 *Alliance of Black Reformed Christians in Southern Africa, 1981*
BLACK AND REFORMED

1. For the first time in 300 years Black Reformed Christians in South Africa have gathered to discuss the meaning of being Black

and Reformed. As black people in South Africa today we are oppressed, powerless and voiceless in the country of our birth. Dis-
possessed of our land, we are displaced people confined to thirteen
per cent of the country and robbed of our citizenship. Blackness
means being dehumanized and suffering under a myriad of unjust
laws.

2. The Reformed tradition in South Africa is seen as responsible
for political oppression, economic exploitation, unbridled capitalism, social discrimination and the total disregard for human dignity.
By the same token, being Reformed is equated with total, uncritical acceptance of the status quo, sinful silence in the face of human
suffering and manipulation of the Word of God in order to justify
oppression. Being Reformed is to exhibit the pig-headedness and in-
transigence of our present rulers with its counterpart in the uncon-
ditional submission on the part of the oppressed.

3. This represents our dilemma in being Black and Reformed.
We ask ourselves the question: 'Is it a burden to be cast off or a
challenge towards the renewal of the Church and of our society?'

4. We reject the interpretation of the Reformed tradition which
is equated with oppression, racism and the justification of tyranny.
In this interpretation we observe the following:

4.1 The Word of God subjected and made subservient to the
claims of cultural and racist ideology.

4.2 The Lordship of Christ confined to a narrow 'spiritual' realm
and the rest of life surrendered to the power of false gods.

4.3 The life of the Christian compartmentalized and his responsibility to be involved in the world for the sake of the Kingdom of
God denied.

4.4 The demand of paying uncritical allegiance to the State,
which is regarded as divinely instituted.

4.5 The heresy that the unity of the Church is a mystical one,
where ethnicity and culture in fact become a mark of the Church.

5. We, however, in the Spirit of the true Reformed tradition reaffirm that:

5.1 The Word of God is the supreme authority and guiding principle revealing all that we need to know about God's will for the
whole existence of human beings. It is this Word that gives life and
offers liberation that is total and complete.

5.2 Christ is Lord of all life even in those situations where his
Lordship is not readily recognized. It is our task in life not only to
recognize the Lordship of Christ but also to proclaim it.

5.3 We as Christians are responsible for the world in which we live, and to reform it is an integral part of our discipleship and worship of God.

5.4 God institutes the authority of the just and legitimate government of the world. Therefore we obey government only in so far as its laws and instructions are not in conflict with the Word of God. Obedience to earthly authorities is only obedience *in God*.

5.5 The unity of the Church must be visibly manifest in the one people of God. The indivisibility of the body of Christ demands that the barriers of race, culture, ethnicity, language and sex be transcended.

6. In the light of our rejection of the false interpretation of the Reformed tradition, and in relation to our situation as blacks, we commit ourselves to come to a truer understanding of the Reformed tradition and accept the challenge to articulate our faith in terms which are authentic and relevant.

7. We begin doing so by declaring unequivocally that apartheid is a sin and that the moral and theological justification of it is a travesty of the Gospel, a betrayal of the Reformed tradition, and a heresy.

8. In this struggle, which we share with all our people, we take courage and comfort in life and in death from the assurance, given to us by the Belgic Confession, that 'the faithful and elect shall be crowned with glory and honour; and the Son of God will confess their names before God and his Father. . . . All tears shall be wiped from their eyes; *and their cause which is now condemned by many judges and magistrates as heretical and impious will then be known to be the cause of the Son of God. . . .*'

9. This is our tradition. This we will fight for.

Dialogue with the NGK

1. We, assembled at Hammanskraal at the ABRECSA Conference from 26–30 October, wish to make it clear that we are not against dialogue with the white Dutch Reformed Churches. However we cannot engage in dialogue with the white Dutch Reformed Churches as long as

(a) they continue not only to talk from within the framework of their acceptance of apartheid, but also to give it a moral and theological justification;

(b) they continue to use the instruments of power at their disposal to manipulate such discussions to suit their own ends;

(c) they continue to refuse to declare apartheid sinful and to confess their complicity in the suffering and oppression of our people.

2. All this became clear at the meeting of the Dutch Reformed and other Protestant Churches held on 27 August 1981 in Pretoria. The agenda of that meeting reflected the three points made above.

(a) The basis for the discussions was no different from the prop-agandistic framework provided by the government; namely to discuss 'the *total mustering* of forces of unbelief against Christ and his Church—liberalism, modernism, marxism, revolution, black theology'.

(b) The meeting was seemingly used by the Dutch Reformed Church to 'prove' to the Federation of Swiss Protestant Churches that the Dutch Reformed Church is engaged with other Churches in discussion about the fundamental issues in our society. In actual fact that agenda proved that this was *not* the case.

(c) The absence of what are for blacks the real issues—racism, apartheid, exploitation, oppression and the distortion of the Gospel—is evidence enough of the white Dutch Reformed Church's refusal to declare the present system in South Africa unjust and contrary to the Gospel.

3. White Churches here and overseas who still believe that they can enter into discussion with the white Dutch Reformed Churches should realize that meaningful dialogue can only take place if and when the conditions required and alluded to above are met. Furthermore, we are convinced that it is only from within the black Reformed Churches that the challenge to the white Dutch Reformed Churches on the real issues that affect the lives of the oppressed people in this land can come. But for the moment, we have come to the realization that, in the present situation, silence and the refusal to speak with the white Dutch Reformed Churches on their terms is the most effective means of communication.

Overseas Churches should accept that in this situation they must be guided by our judgment, and that their complicity in the South African situation makes them part of the problem rather than part of the solution. We would appeal to them to see their task as providing prayerful and active support for the efforts of those of us who resist apartheid and who seek a true humanity for all our people.

Black Christians have always been and remain ready to extend the hand of true friendship, reconciliation and forgiveness to white people in this land. But we are also painfully aware that white Christians, particularly in the white Dutch Reformed Churches, are more eager to accept the white hand of friendship extended to them from distant lands, whilst rejecting the black hand outstretched to them from within.

Appendix

The WARC and its role in South Africa

1. Conference acknowledged with gratitude the Statemu...
issued by the WARC (either in General Council or through its Executive) in 1964, 1970 and 1976, concerning the whole vexed question of apartheid in South Africa. It noted that the Statements were a clear declaration of the WARC's own position on racism, and a challenge to those of its members who seek to justify apartheid theologically or morally. However Conference believes that the present situation is now very different from what it was a decade ago. Statements or Declarations are no longer an adequate response to apartheid. What is now required is a programme of action based on the rejection of apartheid on the theological grounds contained in the previous statements. To that end Conference expressed the strong hope that the General Council of Ottawa would create a desk in the offices of WARC to deal specifically with these issues, to evolve a programme of action, to engage the participation of member Churches and to liaise with the Programme to Combat Racism of the World Council of Churches.

2. Conference also felt that the WARC should urge its members to scrutinize very closely all the arguments used by the Dutch Reformed Churches in South Africa to justify apartheid. Whenever and wherever these arguments take on a theological or moral dimension contradicting the Gospel truths and betraying the Reformed tradition, the WARC and its members should not hesitate to dissociate themselves from such false interpretations.

3. Conference felt that the WARC should challenge its member Churches, particularly those from the Western World, to examine themselves and their own complicity with apartheid. It is a known fact that the Western nations, through their strong economic links with South Africa, offer tremendous support for the continuation of the present regime. The Churches in these countries ought to challenge their own authorities, secular and ecclesiastical, to examine the oppressive role which economic power plays, even when used to help the liberation of the oppressed and exploited.

4. Conference felt very strongly that the members of the WARC should help support South African exiles in their own countries. It did not feel competent to prescribe what type of help should be given, but stressed that many exiles lack material support, educational and training opportunities as well as pastoral care. The Churches in those countries where South African exiles are to be found can play a significant role in meeting these needs.

5. Conference appealed to the WARC and its member Churches

to understand that the initiative for change in South Africa had now passed into black hands. Although the whites were still in the seat of power, politically and economically, they could no longer initiate any change of direction and expect blacks to acquiesce. Blacks were no longer prepared to be passive participants of white-initiated programmes, even of the best intentioned whites. With regard more specifically to the Churches of the Reformed tradition, the same attitude had become increasingly manifest. The blacks in these Churches were determined to work out their own programmes for unity and the witness of the Church in South Africa. All they sought was the understanding and support of their fellow Christians in the WARC.

8   *United Congregational Church of Southern Africa, 1982*
RESOLUTION ON APARTHEID
Assembly endorses the resolution of ABRECSA taken at the Conference at Hammanskraal from 26–30 October 1981, namely, 'We are not against dialogue with the white Dutch Reformed Churches. However, we cannot engage in dialogue with the white Dutch Reformed Churches as long as:

   (a) they continue not only to talk from within the frame-work of their acceptance of "apartheid", but also to give it a moral and theological justification;

   (b) they continue to use the instruments of power at their disposal to manipulate such discussions to suit their own ends;

   (c) they continue to refuse to declare "apartheid" as sinful and to confess their complicity in the suffering and oppression of our people.'

9   *World Alliance of Reformed Churches, 1982*
RACISM AND SOUTH AFRICA

*Statement adopted by the General Council in Ottawa
on 25 August 1982*

I

God in Jesus Christ has affirmed human dignity. Through his life, death and resurrection he has reconciled people to God and to themselves. He has broken down the wall of partition and enmity and has become our peace. He is the Lord of his Church who has brought us together in the one Lord, one faith, one baptism, one God who is the father of us all (Eph. 4:5,6).

The Gospel of Jesus Christ demands, therefore, a community of believers which transcends all barriers of race—a community in which the love for Christ and for one another has overcome the divisions of race and colour.

The Gospel confronts racism, which is in its very essence a form of idolatry. Racism fosters a false sense of supremacy, it denies the common humanity of believers, and it denies Christ's reconciling, humanizing work. It systematizes oppression, domination and injustice. As such the struggle against racism, wherever it is found, in overt and covert forms, is a responsibility laid upon the Church by the Gospel of Jesus Christ in every country and society.

At the present time, without denying the universality of racist sin, we must call special attention to South Africa. Apartheid (or 'separate development') in South Africa today poses a unique challenge to the Church, especially the Churches in the Reformed tradition. The white Afrikaans Reformed Churches of South Africa through the years have worked out in considerable detail both the policy itself and the theological and moral justification for the system. Apartheid ('separate development') is therefore a pseudo-religious ideology as well as a political policy. It depends to a large extent on this moral and theological justification. The division of Reformed Churches in South Africa on the basis of race and colour is being defended as a faithful interpretation of the will of God and of the Reformed understanding of the Church in the world. This leads to the division of Christians at the table of the Lord as a matter of practice and policy, which has been continually affirmed save for exceptional circumstances under special permission by the white Afrikaans Reformed Churches. This situation brings a particular challenge to the WARC.

This is not the first time that the Alliance has dealt with this issue. In 1964 the General Council, meeting in Frankfurt, declared that racism is nothing less than a betrayal of the Gospel: 'The unity in Christ of members, not only of different confessions and denominations, but of different nations and races, points to the fullness of the unity of all in God's coming kingdom. Therefore the exclusion of any person on grounds of race, colour or nationality from any congregation and part of the life of the Church contradicts the very nature of the Church. In such a case, the Gospel is actually obscured from the world and the witness of the Churches made ineffective.' In 1970, the General Council held in Nairobi confirmed this stance: 'The Church must recognize racism for the idolatry it is. . . . The Church that by doctrine and/or practice affirms segregation of peoples (e.g. racial segregation) as a law for its life cannot be regarded as an authentic member of the body of Christ.' This strong language by the WARC was not heeded by the Nederduitse Gereformeerde Kerk and the Nederduitsch Hervormde Kerk, who were mentioned by name, and it was not given any follow-up by the WARC itself.

The General Council of the WARC meeting in Ottawa 1982 declares: The promises of God for his world and for his Church are in direct contradiction to apartheid ideals and practices. These promises, clearly proclaimed by the prophets and fulfilled in Christ, are peace, justice and liberation. They contain good news for the poor and deliverance for the oppressed, but also God's judgment on the denial of rights and the destruction of humanity and community.

We feel duty-bound by the Gospel to raise our voice and stand by the oppressed. 'None of the brethren can be injured, despised, rejected, abused, or in any way offended by us, without at the same time injuring, despising, and abusing Christ by the wrongs we do. . . . We cannot love Christ without loving him in the brethren.' (Calvin)

In certain situations the confession of a Church needs to draw a clear line between truth and error. In faithful allegiance to Jesus Christ it may have to reject the claims of an unjust or oppressive government and denounce Christians who aid and abet the oppressor. We believe that this is the situation in South Africa today.

The Churches which have accepted Reformed confessions of faith have therefore committed themselves to live as the people of God and to show in their daily life and service what this means. This commitment requires concrete manifestation of community among races, of common witness to injustice and equality in society, and of unity at the table of the Lord. The Nederduitse Gereformeerde Kerk and the Nederduitsch Hervormde Kerk, in not only accepting, but actively justifying the apartheid system by misusing the Gospel and the Reformed confession, contradict in doctrine and in action the promise which they profess to believe.

Therefore, the General Council declares that this situation constitutes a *status confessionis* for our Churches, which means that we regard this as an issue on which it is not possible to differ without seriously jeopardizing the integrity of our common confession as Reformed Churches.

We declare with black Reformed Christians of South Africa that apartheid ('separate development') is a sin, and that the moral and theological justification of it is a travesty of the Gospel and, in its persistent disobedience to the Word of God, a theological heresy.

II

1. The General Council of the WARC affirms earlier statements on the issue of racism and apartheid ('separate development') made in 1964 and 1970, and reiterates its firm conviction that apartheid ('separate development') is sinful and incompatible with the Gospel on the grounds that:

(a) it is based on a fundamental irreconcilability of human beings, thus rendering ineffective the reconciling and uniting power of our Lord Jesus Christ;

(b) in its application through racist structures it has led to exclusive privileges for the white section of the population at the expense of the blacks;

(c) it has created a situation of injustice and oppression, large-scale deportation causing havoc to family life, and suffering to millions.

Apartheid ('separate development') ought thus to be recognized as incurring the anger and sorrow of the God in whose image all human beings are created.

2. The General Council expresses its profound disappointment that, despite earlier appeals by the WARC General Councils, and despite continued dialogue between several Reformed Churches and the white Dutch Reformed Churches over twenty years, the Nederduitse Gereformeerde Kerk (in the Republic of South Africa) and the Nederduitsch Hervormde Kerk van Afrika have still not found the courage to realize that apartheid ('separate development') contradicts the very nature of the Church and obscures the Gospel from the world; the Council therefore pleads afresh with these Churches to respond to the promises and demands of the Gospel.

3. The General Council has a special responsibility to continue to denounce the sin of racism in South Africa as expressed in apartheid ('separate development'). It is institutionalized in the laws, policies and structures of the nation; it has resulted in horrendous injustice, in the suffering, exploitation and degradation of millions of black Africans for whom Christ died; and it has been given moral and theological justification by the white Dutch Reformed Churches in South Africa who are members of the WARC and with whom we share a common theological heritage in the Reformed tradition.

4. Therefore, the General Council, reluctantly and painfully, is compelled to suspend the Nederduitse Gereformeerde Kerk (in the Republic of South Africa) and the Nederduitsch Hervormde Kerk

van Afrika from the privileges of membership in the WARC (i.e. sending delegates to General Councils and holding membership in departmental committees and commissions), until such time as the WARC Executive Committee has determined that these two Churches in their utterances and practice have given evidence of a change of heart. They will be warmly welcomed once more only when the following changes have taken place:

(a) Black Christians are no longer excluded from church services, especially from Holy Communion;

(b) Concrete support in word and deed is given to those who suffer under the system of apartheid ('separate development');

(c) Unequivocal synod resolutions are made which reject apartheid and commit the Church to dismantling this system in both Church and politics.

The General Council asks the Executive Committee of the WARC to keep this whole issue regularly under review.

III

Even as we say these things, we, the delegates at the General Council, confess that we are not without guilt in regard to racism. Racism is a reality everywhere and its existence calls for repentance and concerted action. And so, certain questions emerge for our Churches:

(a) How do we combat racism in our own societies and our own Churches?

(b) How do we come to understand our complicity in the racist structures of South Africa through the economic involvement of especially Western European and North American countries and Churches?

(c) How do we remain sensitive to the insidious way in which racism and social injustice are so often excused in the name of economic interest and national security?

(d) How can we give concrete manifestation to our concern for and solidarity with the victims of racism in South Africa and elsewhere in their struggle for justice, peace, reconciliation and human liberation?

(e) Churches should endeavour to develop relationships with black Reformed Churches in South Africa and with Churches and Christians (black and white) who are engaged in this struggle.

(f) In expressing solidarity with those who struggle for justice in this situation, we also ask the Churches to struggle with the painful and difficult questions of how to witness to the reconciling grace of God for those whom we see as oppressive and in error.

10   *Nederduitsch Hervormde Kerk, 1982*
STATEMENT ON THE WARC DECISION

At a meeting held on 17 September 1982, a commission of the General Assembly of the Nederduitsch Hervormde Kerk received a report from its representatives on the meeting of the WARC which was held in Ottawa from 16–27 August 1982. The report dealt both with the proceedings and with the specific decisions of this meeting of the World Alliance. In the light of this report the commission has responded to the implications of the decisions of the World Alliance with regard both to the future position of the Nederduitsch Hervormde Kerk as a member of the World Alliance and to the motives and tendencies which led to this decision.

From the report which we have received and from the documents of the meeting at our disposal it is clear to us that the World Alliance has, by and large, departed from its Reformed basis in favour of a theology which:

1. Has not dealt earnestly with the objective reality and existence of the Triune God independent of this world and above time.

2. Politicizes and socializes the person and work of Jesus Christ in a biased manner.

3. Assails the authority of Holy Scripture as the only source from which one can come to know God and as the only norm for faith and life, and superficially manipulates it by means of association and speculation in order to provide grounds for a theology which has little to do with the God who reveals himself in the Holy Scriptures.

4. Denies the totality and the radicality of sin by a naïve exemption of 'those who are sinned against' as being less defiled, and as limited to categories which are made to synchronize easily with the political views out of which the theology arises.

5. Neglects the call to faith in Jesus Christ as the only Saviour in favour of a summons to solidarity with a so-called liberation struggle.

This shift in the theological point of departure of the World Alliance, which has come about not suddenly but indeed gradually, and was already clear in the pronouncements of the Nairobi meeting in 1970, has now taken on further concrete form in the decision by which the Alliance has degraded the Nederduitsch Hervormde Kerk to second-class membership. By this decision the World Alliance of Reformed Churches wants to prescribe to us how to arrange the life and practice of our Church and what our attitude ought to be towards socio-political problems in our land while, at the same time, it holds before us by implication a political policy which is said to be good and right.

We reject this claim by the Alliance:

1. To deprive us of our obligation and privilege to organize our Church life in a manner which is constantly tested against the demands of Holy Scripture, and to strive for the best practical way in which to fulfil our apostolic calling to be the Church of Jesus Christ giving due consideration to our experience within the unique South African ethnic situation [*volkere-situasie*].

2. To prescribe for us a political choice whereby we become a partner of those forces which, with disregard to the truth, with misuse of theology, and with reckless promotion of revolution, promote the objectives of godless communist imperialism. We claim the privilege as a Church of Jesus Christ to make our own choice concerning what we regard to be responsible politics within our situation with full responsibility towards God and with a good conscience in relation to him.

3. To make a dogmatic pronouncement, with arrogant hypocrisy, concerning the political policy and circumstances in South Africa in response to misrepresentations, malicious exaggeration, and the calculated suppression of specific information.

The Nederduitsch Hervormde Kerk continues to maintain that its regulations concerning membership do not constitute a doctrine, but must be seen as a practical regulation concerning the peaceful furtherance of the Gospel. We are further convinced that a political policy of separate development and equal opportunities is not in conflict with Holy Scripture. The irrefutable fact is that this policy has greatly improved the quality of life and brought more freedom to our peoples than in many countries of the Third World, not to mention Marxist countries. Our question to the world still stands: where is a land with a similar ethnic composition which can serve as a model for our situation? As long as the World Alliance sings in the same choir as international politics with its questionable motives, we cannot treat its judgment seriously. We do not feel challenged at the level of conscience by such a condemnation.

The Nederduitsch Hervormde Kerk cannot comply with the requirements set by the World Alliance and it, therefore, has no choice but to withdraw. This Church will continue to determine its course in response to an earnest investigation of Holy Scripture and in consideration of its experience gained through the ages, both with regard to its own internal policies and also with regard to South African politics. We cannot take an apologetic attitude toward an ecumenical body that allows itself to be misused in this way. Over against such a position, and before Almighty God and the Father of our Lord Jesus Christ, we stand continually in deep repentance for our sins and we endeavour day by day to improve and change. The Gospel itself continues to bring about change and we wish to offer no resistance to this, but we must offer resistance to a false Gospel which offers people little more than political power as an ultimate destination, and in so doing has already brought nameless misery to millions of people in the world.

We thus hereby inform the World Alliance of Reformed Churches and everyone who may be concerned with this decision that we have terminated our membership of the Alliance.

In making this decision we do not wish to indicate that we intend to live without any ecumenical relationships. We have, however, repeatedly found that the World Alliance of Reformed Churches is not a useful instrument for genuine ecumenical contact. Concerning the future, we are still prepared to engage in dialogue concerning our communal task and calling with Christians and fellow believers both in our own country and throughout the world.

11   *Nederduitse Gereformeerde Sendingkerk, 1982*
        A STATEMENT ON APARTHEID
        AND A CONFESSION OF FAITH

Reconciliation and Apartheid

Proposition

The political and ecclesiastical order of South Africa is an order within which irreconcilabilty has been elevated to a fundamental social principle within which, in spite of supposed good intentions, the greed and prejudice of the powerful and the privileged are entrenched at the cost of those who are powerless and without privileges.

Responsibility

Apartheid is a system within which people are separated from one another, *and kept apart from one another.*

The possibility that these groups *can* be brought together and that peaceful co-existence *can* replace tension and conflict is ruled out as a matter of principle. Therefore, ethnic groups, to the extent that this is possible, must be compelled, by law if necessary, to remain separate from one another, because the bringing of these groups of people together will necessarily result in conflict and the mutual threatening of one another.

The use of the phrase 'separate development' in an attempt to replace the hated word 'apartheid' in essence results in no change to the basic point of departure: the development of each group must still take place apart from that of other groups, because the development of one group is regarded as a threat to that of the other. Similarly, communal development is regarded as a threat to individual development.

In the light of this unchanged point of departure, it is not surprising that when we are requested to give more attention to the positive aspects of apartheid, this repeatedly breaks down in the face of reality, which is that the white section of the population always benefits most from such development.

The choice of the term 'irreconcilability' in the decision of the Synod of 1978 was intentional. The Synod translates its witness into its own language, that of the Church and theology. *Irreconcilability* always stands in contradiction to *reconciliation*; the main artery of the Christian Gospel is also the main artery of the existence and the proclamation of the Church.

The visible effect of reconciliation between God and man is the existence of the Church as a *reconciling community of people*, a unified community. The message of reconciliation is entrusted to this Church. The invitation is extended to the world and to all people who inhabit it to reconcile themselves to God and to one another. In Christ, the Church says, there is new hope, there are new possibilities for the world. Sinfulness and hatred, enmity and separation need not be the last word, but rather reconciliation and peace. Christ has made this possible.

The Church will always bear witness to the fact that no order of communal living which fundamentally affirms the irreconcilability of people and groups of people can be regarded as acceptable. Such a point of departure binds people to their past history of enmity and hate—it invalidates the Gospel.

We do not simply present one or more Bible texts. It is always easy to use biblical texts to one's own end, even to the extent that it was possible for many years for it to be said that apartheid is Scriptural, and, indeed, on the ground of only two texts: the story of the Tower of Babel (Genesis 11:1-9 and Acts 17:26).

No! The touchstone for apartheid is the essential biblical message of reconciliation. If it fails here, a few disparate biblical texts cannot save it. In fact, the traditional exposition of these texts then needs to be fundamentally questioned.

The Decision of the 1978 Synod with regard to Apartheid

In addition to the theological proposition regarding irreconcilability, the Synod went further to say that the system which necessarily results from such a policy must inevitably lead and has led to an increasing polarization between people. It does more than merely keep them apart from one another. It moves them further apart from one another. It polarizes and creates conflict. In turn, this conflict is then used as an alibi to maintain this separation at all costs. So everyone is drawn into this vicious circle—which can only be broken by changing the point of departure.

The Demand of Justice and Self-concern

The decision of the Synod goes further to demonstrate that, in practice, it can be shown undeniably that 'within the system one section of the population, the whites, is privileged, and that as a result of this the Gospel demand of justice for all has not been satisfied'. In a system within which concepts such as the 'own' (*eie*) and the 'separateness' (*afsonderlike*) receive so much attention, people are indeed going to concern themselves essentially with their 'own'. The result is that the powerful and privileged are not willing to share their power and privilege, but rather are tempted to acquire still more for themselves. In conclusion the Synod shows that through the system of apartheid 'it is not only the humanity of the underprivileged sections of the population that is affected but also the humanity of everybody involved within this system'.

Racism and Apartheid

Racism is an ideology of racial domination which includes a belief in the inherent, cultural and biological inferiority of certain races and racial groups. It is also a political and an economic system that determines the unequal treatment of these groups at the level of law, structures and institutions. Racism does not merely concern the attitude of people, it is also structural. It does not merely concern the *feeling* of inferiority in relation to another person or group, but the *system* of political, social and economic domination. In a racist situation certain groups of people are excluded because of their race from participation in the political decision-making process, from participation in the economic decision-making processes, and as a result, they are discriminated against both economically and socially. This exclusion is, however, not merely on the basis of race and colour, it is exclusively aimed at the domination of the other. Where this racism is regimentally imposed in Church and communal structures it denies the community of believers the possibility of being human and it denies the reconciling and the humanizing work of Christ.

In South Africa apartheid in the Church and in society leans to a significant extent on the theological and moral justification of the system. Apartheid is therefore a pseudo-religious ideology as well as a political policy. It allows itself to be validated within the realms of both Church and state, and in so doing it influences and structurally controls the entire South African society.

Article 9 of the Apostles' Creed

The specific character of the pseudo-religious ideology of apartheid makes it practically impossible for the confession 'I believe in one, holy, catholic Church, the community of the saints' to determine the structures of the Church. In reality, the secular Gospel of apartheid structures the way in which the Church is realized and the way in which Church unity is manifest within the Dutch Reformed Churches in South Africa.

Resolutions

Because the secular Gospel of apartheid threatens in the deepest possible way the witness of reconciliation in Jesus Christ and the unity of the Church of Jesus Christ in its very essence, the NG Mission Church in South Africa declares that this constitutes a *status confessionis* for the Church of Jesus Christ. (A *status confessionis* means that we regard this matter as a concern about which it is impossible to differ without it affecting the integrity of our communal confession as Reformed Churches.)

We declare that apartheid (separate development) is a sin, that the moral and theological justification of it makes a mockery of the Gospel, and that its consistent disobedience to the Word of God is a theological heresy.

The decision of Ottawa and the decisions with regard to racism and therefore apartheid (separate development) cannot be regarded as an alternative to the decision of the Synod of 1978, but rather as a consequence.

According to the conviction of the Synod the NGK believes in the ideology of apartheid, which is in direct conflict with the evangelical message of reconciliation and the visible unity of the Church.

Therefore the 1978 decision of the Mission Church (as argued on the level of principle at the beginning of this statement) makes it clear that we can do no other than with the deepest regret accuse the NGK of theological heresy and idolatry. This is done in the light of her theologically formulated standpoint and its implementation in practice.

The NG Mission Church makes this statement in deep humility and self-examination so that we may keep ourselves 'from being disqualified after having called others to the contest' (I Cor. 9:27).

A Confession of Faith

1. We believe in the triune God, Father, Son and Holy Spirit, who gathers, protects and cares for his Church by his Word and his Spirit, as he has done since the beginning of the world and will do to the end.

2. We believe in one holy, universal Christian Church, the communion of saints called from the entire human family. We believe:

—that Christ's work of reconciliation is made manifest in the Church as the community of believers who have been reconciled with God and with one another;

—that unity is, therefore, both a gift and an obligation for the Church of Jesus Christ; that through the working of God's Holy Spirit it is a binding force, yet simultaneously a reality which must be earnestly pursued and sought: one which the people of God must continually be built up to attain;

—that this unity must become visible so that the world may believe; that separation, enmity and hatred between people and groups is sin which Christ has already conquered, and that accordingly anything which threatens this unity has no place in the Church and must be resisted;

—that this unity of the people of God must be made manifest and active in a variety of ways, in that we: experience, practise and pursue community with one another; are obligated to give ourselves willingly and joyfully to be of benefit and a source of blessing to one another; share one faith, have one calling, are of one soul and one mind; have one God and Father, are filled with one Spirit, are baptized with one baptism, eat of one bread and drink of one cup, confess one Name, are obedient to one Lord, work for one cause, and share one hope; together come to know the height and the breadth and the depth of the love of Christ; together are built up to the stature of Christ, to the new humanity; together know and bear one another's burdens, thereby fulfilling the law of Christ; need one another and upbuild one another, admonishing and comforting one another; that we suffer with one another for the sake of righteousness; pray together; together serve God in this world; and together fight against all which may threaten or hinder this unity;

—that this unity may be made manifest only in freedom and not under constraint; that the variety of spiritual gifts, opportunities, backgrounds, convictions, as well as the various languages and cultures, are, by virtue of the reconciliation in Christ, opportunities for mutual service and enrichment within the one visible people of God;

—that true faith in Jesus Christ is the only condition for membership of this Church.

Therefore we reject any doctrine:

—which absolutizes either natural diversity or the sinful separation of people in such a way that this absolutization hinders or breaks the visible and active unity of the Church, or even leads to the establishment of a separate Church;

—which professes that this spiritual unity is truly being maintained in the bond of peace whilst believers of the same confession are in effect alienated from one another for the sake of diversity and in despair of reconciliation;

—which denies that a refusal earnestly to pursue this visible unity as a priceless gift is a sin;

—which explicitly or implicitly maintains that descent or any other human or social factor should be a consideration in determining membership of the Church.

3. We believe:

—that God has entrusted to his Church the message of reconciliation in and through Jesus Christ; that the Church is called to be the salt of the earth and the light of the world; that the Church is called blessed because it is a peacemaker; that the Church is witness both by word and deed to the new heaven and the new earth in which righteousness dwells;

—that God by his lifegiving Word and Spirit has conquered the powers of sin and death, and therefore also of irreconciliation and hatred, bitterness and enmity; that God, by his lifegiving Word and Spirit will enable his people to live in a new obedience which can open new possibilities of life for society and the world;

—that the credibility of this message is seriously affected and its beneficial work obstructed when it is proclaimed in a land which professes to be Christian, but in which the enforced separation of people on a racial basis promotes and perpetuates alienation, hatred and enmity;

—that any teaching which attempts to legitimate such forced separation by appeal to the Gospel, and is not prepared to venture on the road of obedience and reconciliation, but rather, out of prejudice, fear, selfishness and unbelief, denies in advance the reconciling power of the Gospel, must be considered ideology and false doctrine.

Therefore, we reject any doctrine which, in such a situation, sanctions in the name of the Gospel or of the will of God the forced separation of people on the grounds of race and colour and thereby in advance obstructs and weakens the ministry and experience of reconciliation in Christ.

4. We believe:

—that God has revealed himself as the One who wishes to bring about justice and true peace among men; that in a world full of injustice and enmity he is in a special way the God of the destitute, the poor and the wronged and that he calls his Church to follow him in this; that he brings justice to the oppressed

and gives bread to the hungry; that he frees the prisoner and restores sight to the blind; that he supports the downtrodden, protects the stranger, helps orphans and widows and blocks the path of the ungodly; that for him pure and undefiled religion is to visit the orphans and widows in their suffering; that he wishes to teach his people to do what is good and to seek the right; that the Church must therefore stand by people in any form of suffering and need, which means, among other things, that the Church shall witness against and strive against any form of injustice, so that 'justice may roll down like waters, and righteousness like an ever-flowing stream';
–that the Church as God's possession must stand where he stands, namely against injustice and with the wronged; that in following Christ the Church must witness against all the powerful and privileged who selfishly seek their own interests and thus control and harm others.

Therefore we reject any ideology which would legitimate forms of injustice and any doctrine which is unwilling to resist such an ideology in the name of the Gospel.

5. We believe that, in obedience to Jesus Christ, its only Head, the Church is called to confess and to do all this, even though authorities and laws forbid them, and even though punishment and suffering be the consequence.
Jesus is Lord.
To the one and only God, Father, Son and Holy Spirit, be the honour and the glory for ever and ever.

The Relationship between the NG Mission Church and the NGK in terms of the Status Confessionis

1. The Synod resolves that its decision regarding the *status confessionis* be officially handed to the NGK at its General Synod sitting in Pretoria and that it also be sent to the different regional synods.

2. The NG Mission Church regrets that its relationship with the NGK is seriously threatened. The Synod is of the opinion that the road of reconciliation can only be walked if the NGK confesses its guilt regarding the moral and theological grounding of apartheid, and concretely demonstrates her repentance by working out what the consequences of this confession of guilt mean in both Church and state. In so doing the NG Mission Church does not deny its own guilt in the situation and declares itself ready to walk in love and forgiveness with the NGK in seeking to develop and not to break the relationship with that Church. We ask the NGK to work urgently together with us to make this possible. The NG Mission Church's most sincere prayer is that the NGK will walk this way of conversion and will not allow the bond between us to be broken.

3. The Synod resolves that the NG Mission Church will with

pastoral compassion fulfil her role as prophet and priest toward the NGK in South Africa. With all the weight and the channels at her disposal she will zealously endeavour to lead the NGK to the point where this Church will acknowledge her share and guilt in the realization and establishment of the pseudo-religious ideology of apartheid and a political policy which has deprived and continues to deprive people of their humanity, and has resulted and continues to result in numerous acts of sorrow and suffering for countless people in this country.

4. The synod resolves that the NG Mission Church should call on the NGK to hear the words of II Chronicles 7:13 and 14. The Lord says: 'Whenever I hold back the rain or send locusts to eat up the crops or send an epidemic on my people, if they pray to me and repent and turn away from the evil they have been doing, then I will hear them in heaven, forgive their sins, and make their land prosperous again.'

Therefore in deep compassion and humility we bow before the Lord with our own guilt and complicity in the unreconciled relationship between believers in our family and we confess that we have withheld this truth from you in many different ways. We do not condemn you, so that we ourselves may not be condemned.

We owe you nothing other than love because therein alone is the fulfilment of the law. See Romans 14:8, 'Be under obligation to no one—the only obligation you have is to love one another. Whoever does this has obeyed the law.' Also I John 4:7, 'Dear friends, let us love one another, because love comes from God. Whoever loves is a child of God and knows God.'

We address you as our sister in this language, because the Gospel of love which you preach to us continues to be our guide and source of comfort.

Sola Scriptura!

12   *Methodist Church of Southern Africa, 1982*
RESOLUTION ON APARTHEID
Conference affirms that apartheid is a negation of

1. the dignity with which God has endowed man in creating him in his own image;

2. the work of Jesus Christ through his coming into the world to live, die and rise for mankind, thus freeing it from bondage for fullness of life;

3. the reconciliation effected by Christ between man and God, and man and man.

Apartheid is not simply a socio-political policy, but a sinful c̶
tradition of the Gospel which cannot be justified on biblical or
theological grounds and is, therefore, an ideology which the Methodist Church rejects as heresy.

Conference appeals to the Nederduits Gereformeerde Kerk, the
Hervormde Kerk and the Gereformeerde Kerk in Christian love,
likewise, to reject an ideology which is continuing to cause untold
suffering to the majority of South Africans, and to bring discredit
to the Church of Christ.

Conference refers the full statement on this subject, adopted by
the National Conference of the SACC, to the Justice and Reconciliation and the Ecumenical Affairs Committees for consideration
and report to the Conference of 1983 with recommendations as to
further action.

13   *Nederduitse Gereformeerde Kerk, 1982*
            RESOLUTION ON THE WARC DECISION

Die Kerkbode (27 October 1982) summed up the debate concerning the WARC membership of the NGK by indicating that the
Synod considered three basic responses: 'To maintain membership
for ecumenical reasons; to immediately terminate membership; not
to terminate membership at this time, because this would be to play
into the hands of those seeking to isolate the NGK. The last-men-
tioned option has become the official position of the Church after
a two-thirds majority could not be obtained in support of the summary termination of relations which was being asked for.' The
resolution which was ultimately adopted reads as follows:

The Synod notes with regret the course of events and the decisions of the
WARC which mean that:

—a one-sided picture of the NGK has been presented to the member churches
in Ottawa;

—a shocking judgment by the WARC concerning the NGK has been executed
in a manner and on grounds which were not made allowance for in the
constitution of the WARC (at the time when the NGK became a member),
and in this way the membership of the NGK has been terminated;

—certain conditions are imposed on the NGK, which must be complied with
before it can again be accepted as a full member;

—these decisions of the WARC are undoubtedly taken from a standpoint of
liberation theology, which according to the NGK is undoubtedly in certain
essential respects in conflict with the Bible and Reformed theology.

The NGK is placed in an extremely difficult position, and is left with no
alternative but to resolve as follows:

—that the NGK does not willingly accept the termination of its membership, and

—that the NGK, under these circumstances, for practical purposes regards itself as no longer being a full member of the WARC.

It was also decided that this Church would no longer accept its financial responsibilities to the WARC, and the moderature will communicate these decisions officially to the WARC.

Die Kerkbode seems to have captured the mood of the Synod in quoting the moderator, Ds Kobus Potgieter, as saying immediately prior to the vote that the question amounted to whether they 'resign now, or a little later'.

The Synod also issued the following statement:

Racism is a sin
Because the New Testament affirms the principle of equality (Report 31.1) and the actual differentiation (Report 13.4, 13.7 and 23) of all people and nations, each with its own right of existence (Report 9), as well as the unity of the entire human family (Report 8 and 31.2), and because the commandment to love one's neighbour, which also manifests itself in justice (Report 13.9), is the ethical norm for ordering human relations (Report 13.8), the general Synod rejects all racism as unscriptural and as sin (cf. The Heidelberg Catechism, Sunday 40), because it regards and treats some nations as superior and others as inferior. The Synod gives further expression to its conviction that race-consciousness and the love of one's own nation is not sinful, but when race and/or nation become absolutized, we are dealing with racism and that is sinful. ['Report' is the NGK publication *Human Relations and the South African Scene in the Light of Scripture.*]

14 *Church of the Province of South Africa (Anglican), 1982*
RESOLUTION ON APARTHEID
Whereas Apartheid by exalting a biological attribute to a universal principle thereby denies that what gives persons infinite value is the fact that they are created in God's image;

whereas Apartheid further denies a central teaching of the Christian faith, namely that God was in Christ reconciling the world to himself since it teaches the irreconcilability of certain races;

whereas it further has involved an unacceptable cost in human suffering;

this Synod resolves that Apartheid is totally un-Christian, evil and a heresy.

The Synod further resolves respectfully to ask the Metropolitan to appeal to the white Dutch Reformed Church to denounce apartheid as unscriptural and then to enter into dialogue with the SACC Churches.